The Fiction of Joseph Conrad

ANGLO-AMERIKANISCHE STUDIEN
ANGLO-AMERICAN STUDIES

Herausgegeben von Rüdiger Ahrens und Kevin Cope

Band 12

PETER LANG
Frankfurt am Main · Berlin · Bern · New York · Paris · Wien

Nic Panagopoulos

The Fiction of Joseph Conrad

The Influence of Schopenhauer and Nietzsche

PETER LANG
Europäischer Verlag der Wissenschaften

Die Deutsche Bibliothek - CIP-Einheitsaufnahme

Panagopoulos, Nic:

The fiction of Joseph Conrad : the influence of Schopenhauer and Nietzsche / Nic Panagopoulos. - Frankfurt am Main ; Berlin ; Bern ; New York ; Paris ; Wien : Lang, 1998
(Anglo-american studies ; Bd. 12)
Zugl.: London, Univ., Diss., 1994
ISBN 3-631-33759-0

ISSN 0177-6959
ISBN 3-631-33759-0
US-ISBN 0-8204-3623-2

Printed in Germany 1 2 4 5 6 7

for Lini

Contents

Acknowledgements

First and foremost I would like to thank Dr. Robert Hampson of the English Department at Royal Holloway College, University of London, for his many hours revising, editing and proof-reading the various drafts of this work when it was a postgraduate thesis. His expertise, encouragement and understanding have been invaluable and a constant source of inspiration to me.

Of course, I must thank my family for their support, both financial and moral, and in particular my brother Chris who literally saved this project while still in its infancy. Were it not for his timely intervention at a very critical moment, many years of hard work (and some of the best of my life!) may all have been in vain. Heart-felt acknowledgements must also go out to Ms Astrid Baumgarten who was often the only person I could talk to about the many problems I encountered writing it.

Last but not least, I would like to express my deepest affection and gratitude to Danny Scheinmann who dragged me across the finishing line of my Doctoral dissertation when I could go no further. He was sent by providence.

This book was published with the kind help of the John F. Kostopoulos Foundation of the Pisteos Bank of Greece.

Abbreviations of Philosophical Works

(AOM): *Assorted Opinions and Maxims*

(BGE): *Beyond Good and Evil*

(BT): *The Birth of Tragedy and the Geneology of Morals*

(D): *Daybreak*

(GS): *The Gay Science*

(HA): *Human, All Too Human*

(WWR): *The World as Will and Representation*

Introduction

Arthur Schopenhauer's *The World as Will and Representation* was a hugely influential work. Although it was published as early as 1818, it only received public attention after the writer's death in 1860, and became well-known in England from 1880 onwards. In it Schopenhauer investigated the inner nature of man, what later on in the century came to be called the 'unconscious'.[1] Schopenhauer termed this hidden essence "the will" and meant by it "an irrational blind, insatiable force without conscious purpose or direction which is the very source of man's conduct".[2] The unconscious was anthropomorphized as the *döppelganger* in contemporary literature of the time and was represented in such works as Stevenson's *Dr Jekyl and Mr Hyde* which stressed the duality of man's nature, embracing within it the opposite poles of good and evil.

Schopenhauer can also be said to have analyzed the pessimism that characterizes modern thought. This pessimism is closely linked to his theory of the will because, as Thomas Mann points out, will is "unrest, a striving for *something* - it is want, craving, avidity, demand" and "a world of will is nothing but a world of suffering".[3] Schopenhauer's pessimism was also derived from the Transcendentalist idea that there is no order or structure in the world other than that which the mind projects onto it. This led him to believe not only that life had no essential meaning or purpose in itself but that human beings were born into a world of unpredictability and uncertainty. As Cedric Watts points out, the late nineteenth century was a time when "the vistas of thought were particularly depressing since so many of the advances of science and technology" seemed "to blight man's faith in God and a benevolent universe."[4] At the same time Schopenhauer stressed the enormous egoism lying at the heart of man's nature and the fact that every man was entirely preoccupied with his own pleasures and pains. His philosophy took empiricism to the extent of solipsism. "It is a philosophy", writes Linda Hall, "which suggests that all

---

1 As Alex Comfort has pointed out, Freud who is accredited with the discovery of the unconscious attributes this honour to poets and philosophers before him and to Schopenhauer in particular. *Darwin and the Naked Lady*, p30.

2 Linda M. Hall, *The Theme of the Outcast*, p10.

3 *The Living Thoughts of Schopenhauer*, p8.

4 Cedric Watts, *A Preface to Conrad*, p78.

men are imprisoned in the self", that "the condition of man is to be locked in subjectivity, cut off from communion with his fellows".[5]

The turn of the century was a time of confusion and bewilderment, of disillusion and malaise. John Lester argues that the transition from materialistic determinism to a world of change involved "the urgent and pained necessity of a 'transvaluation of values' to keep man's imaginative life alive under conditions which seemed unliveable".[6] Nietzsche, like Schopenhauer, was a philosopher very much in fashion. Bernard Bergonzi regards Nietzsche as "the dominant intellectual figure of the *fin de siecle*" since his work "embodies all its various strands".[7] Michael Hamburger suggests that Nietzsche's impact on England, though never as strong and immediate as his influence on the rest of Europe, was if not an earthquake, a tremor in the atmosphere.[8] The first few volumes of Nietzsche's works in translation appeared in England in 1896 and from that time his name and ideas were very much in the air. G. B. Shaw reviewed one of the volumes in *Saturday Review* (1896) and Havelock Ellis wrote on Nietzsche in the first of two issues of *The Savoy* in the same year. By the end of the century upwards of sixty articles and book reviews on Nietzsche had appeared in England and America, not to mention several books either entirely or partially devoted to him, such as Havelock Ellis's influential *Affirmations: Nietzsche, Casanova and Zola* (1898) and Max Nordau's *Degeneration* (1895).

As T. H. Gibbons points out, "Nietzsche's optimistically 'existentialist' challenge to current forms of scientific determinism appears to have constituted a basic attraction for the period", and his later works "had found admirers in England not only for their advocacy of the Superman, but for their hostility to liberalism, Romanticism, 'decadence', and asceticism."[9] Nietzsche's most influential ideas were the superman, the transvaluation of values and the master and slave moralities. He can also be said to have brought about a deepening concern with psychology in the contemporary English novel. In an article published by Edward Garnett in *Outlook*, July 8 1899, the author outlines the theory of the superman as follows:

---

[5] *The Theme of the Outcast*, p15.

[6] John Lester, *Journey Through Despair, 1880-1914: Transformation in British Literary Culture*.

[7] Bernard Bergonzi, *The Early H.G. Wells*, p9.

[8] Michael Hamburger, *From Prophecy to Exorcism: The Premises of Modern German Literature*, p28.

[9] T. H. Gibbons, *Literary Criticism and the Intellectual Milieu*, pp11-12.

> Nietzsche's ideal of a stern, hard, noble nature, with an instinct for beauty, for fineness of life, is evoked from his innate hostility to all the cheapness, compromise, and cowardness of average human nature that is conquered by life, moulded by despicable circumstances, stunted and warped, crushed even beneath itself through its lack of power.[10]

The article goes on to say that Nietzsche regarded Christianity, democracy and scientific materialism as means by which those crushed and enslaved by life try to assert power over the natural aristocrats, those who would master life. "There are two moralities in society", he writes, "the morality of the conquerors, the aristocrats, that which is a free, joyous, ascending triumph in life, and the morality of the slaves, that which is a sick, ascetic, resigned, religious distrust of life and a reliance on a life-to-come".[11] Even if Nietzsche's books were not widely read, his ideas formed a central part of the contemporary *zeitgeist* so that he became recognized as the representative of certain tendencies and movements such as the anti-positivist movement and the subjective trend in philosophy.

There have been no full-length studies exclusively dealing with Conrad's relationship to Nietzsche and Schopenhauer. Although various critics have pointed out that Conrad may have been influenced by Schopenhauer, no one has gone to the trouble of systematically tracing the parallels between their works. William Bonney devotes the first chapter of his book, *Thorns and Arabesques*,[12] to Conrad and Schopenhauer but he deals more with the Oriental influences in Schopenhauer's *The World as Will and Idea*[13] and the way they may have trickled through into Conrad's work than to Schopenhauer's own philosophy and its bearing on Conrad's oeuvre. He writes that "a familiarity with the primary sources of Oriental philosophy cannot be claimed with any certainty for Conrad, but he did read Schopenhauer, and Schopenhauer assimilated a great deal of this material in *The World as Will and Idea*".[14] Nevertheless, Bonney does make the important point that an "understanding of this work is necessary for

10 This article was reissued in *Friday Nights*, The Travellers Library Series.

11 Ibid., p16.

12 William Bonney, "Eastern Logic under my Western Eyes: Conrad, Schopenhauer and the Orient", pp3-30.

13 Different critics use different translations of this work which gloss *Vorstellung* as either 'idea' or 'representation'. I use the translation by E. F. J Payne, *The World as Will and Representation, Vol. I & II.*

14 Ibid., p9.

any comprehensive response to Conrad's fiction"[15] and this assessment is borne out by the present study.

In the introduction to her doctoral dissertation, *Joseph Conrad: The Theme of the Outcast*, Linda M. Hall has written a useful analysis of Schopenhauer's influence on the ideas and literature of the late nineteenth century and discusses certain important parallels between Schopenhauer's and Conrad's central concerns such as the relationship between instinct and reason and the idea of negation and withdrawal. As regards *Victory*, for example, she concludes that although the novel is finally "anti-Schopenhauerian" in that it "rejects negation and is affirmative", it is "imbued with the spirit of the German philosopher".[16]

Lee M. Whitehead has written two very important essays on the subject of Conrad 's philosophy. In "Conrad's 'Pessimism' Re-examined"[17] he argues that the vision of life presented in Conrad's tales changes from a pessimism very like Schopenhauer's in the works before *The Nigger of the Narcissus* to a tragic vision very like Nietzsche's in *The Birth of Tragedy* in the major works of his middle period. Whitehead's conclusion in this essay comes very close to that expounded in the present study: he claims that "art had for Conrad as much as it had for Nietzsche a 'healing power' capable of turning our nausea into wonder and our despair into affirmation."[18] In his second essay, "The Active Voice and the Passive Eye: *Heart of Darkness* and Nietzsche's *The Birth of Tragedy*"[19] Lee M. Whitehead argues that "Conrad's affinities are not to the author of *The Will to Power*, but to early Nietzsche who thought that this suffering world could be redeemed by art" and this also accords with my own findings. He goes on to suggest that Marlow's function in *Heart of Darkness* is "very similar to that attributed by Friedrich Nietzsche [...] to the Greek tragic chorus" and that "he is the means of mediation, formulation, and understanding between Kurtz and his listeners".[20]

In *Conrad's Existentialism* Otto Bohlmann makes some pertinent comparisons between Conrad's and Nietzsche's ideas but he does not pursue this topic in any depth since he is concerned with a wide range of

---

15 Ibid., p9.

16 *The Theme of the Outcast*, p13. Two other works which compare Conrad's and Schopenhauer's ideas in passing are Ian Watt's *Conrad in the Nineteenth Century*, and Tony Tanner's essay "Joseph Conrad and the Last Gentleman", *Critical Quarterly*, Vol. 28, nos. 1 & 2, pp109-142.

17 *Conradiana*, *Vol.* 2, No. 3, Spring 1969-70, pp25-38.

18 "Conrad's 'Pessimism' Re-examined", p37.

19 *Conradiana* 7 (1975) pp121-35.

20 "The Active Voice and the Passive Eye", p121.

existentialist writers including Heidegger, Jaspers, Kierkegaard, Sartre, Freud, and Camus. Edward W. Said,[21] on the other hand attempts to give a comprehensive answer to the question of Conrad's relationship to Nietzsche and argues that "turning up circumstantial evidence of actual borrowings" from Nietzsche and Conrad is not "the most interesting or useful way of considering the two writers together."[22] He prefers to read them in terms of a common tradition which he terms "the radical attitude towards language". The essay goes on to discuss three important ways in which Conrad and Nietzsche can be compared: (a) their common view of language as "perspective, interpretation, poverty and excess", (b) their sense of "intellectual adventure" and their discovery of the "inevitable antithesis" to be found everywhere in human existence, and (c) their tendency to view the world as "repeatable force".[23]

Another important essay dealing specifically with Conrad and Nietzsche is George Butte's "What Silenus Knew: Conrad's Uneasy Debt to Nietzsche".[24] This critic claims that Conrad's responses to Nietzsche were contradictory, and included "unwilling sympathy and hostility, imitation and parody" as Conrad seems to argue with Nietzsche about the best response to knowing the worst of our condition".[25] The main thesis of the essay is that Conrad's use of the Silenus legend in *The Secret Agent* must derive from Nietzsche's *The Birth of Tragedy* since "that is the one book in which Conrad could reasonably have come across this rare version of the Silenus motif."[26] Although *The Birth of Tragedy* didn't appear in English until 1909, this critic argues that Conrad could have read the book in French, the French translation of which was published in 1901. The essay briefly touches upon a central structuring principle in my own work, the antithesis between Dionysos and Apollo. Butte argues that whereas in *The Birth of Tragedy* these two forces are seen to combine, producing tragedy, in *The Secret Agent*, "no mysterious union of contrary, interdependent forces occurs."[27]

There is very little historical evidence regarding Conrad's known reading of Schopenhauer and Nietzsche. We are limited to John Galsworthy's statement that "of philosophy he had read a good deal", and

---

[21] In Norman Sherry, (ed.) "Conrad and Nietzsche", in *Joseph Conrad: A Commemoration*, Papers from the 1974 International Conference on Conrad.

[22] Ibid., p66.

[23] Ibid., pp68-74.

[24] *Comparative Literature*, 41 (1989) pp155-169.

[25] Ibid., p155.

[26] Ibid., p157.

[27] Ibid., p165.

that "Schopenhauer used to bring him satisfaction".[28] As to which works of Schopenhauer he was familiar with, we cannot be certain although his reference to the "inscrutable Maya" in a letter to a reviewer of *The Nigger of the 'Narcissus'*[29] suggests that he had read *The World as Will and Representation* in which the Vedic philosophies are expounded. That Conrad knew about Nietzsche's main ideas is equally beyond doubt but not that he had actually read any of his works first hand.[30] Between 1899 and 1919 Conrad refers to him in several letters and in one published essay. None of these references are flattering and most are quite hostile. Writing to Helen Sanderson, he refers to the "mad individualism of Niet[z]sche"[31] and in "The Crime of Partition" he associates Nietzsche with the morality of "Germanic Tribes".[32] After reading Garnett's article on Nietzsche in the *Outlook* of 8 July 1899, he writes "I had letters about your Nietzsche from all sorts of people. You have stirred some brains! I don't think there's anything wrong with *your* wits."[33] In another letter to Ford Madox Ford (written in reference to *The Inheritors*), Conrad remarks scathingly "That's what Niet[z]sche's philosophy leads to - here's your overman".[34] But, as the editors of *The Collected Letters* note, *The Daily Chronicle* review (11 July) had already seen a connection between the 'Fourth Dimensionists' of *The Inheritors* and the *Übermensch* so this reference is no proof that Conrad had read about the idea of the "overman" first hand.

In this work I try to show how a knowledge of Schopenhauer's and Nietzsche's philosophical ideas can help illuminate the central concerns of Conrad 's fiction. By examining five of Conrad's major works, *Lord Jim, Heart of Darkness, The Secret Agent, Under Western Eyes* and *Victory,* I suggest that the novelist was often grappling with the same problems as these two philosophers and that his work can be seen as a response to certain key concerns of the idealistic movement in the history of ideas. Although I sometimes argue that Conrad was working with specific works in mind such as *The World as Will and Representation* or *The Birth of Tragedy,* I am not primarily concerned with tracing instances of borrowing in

---

28 John Galsworthy, *Reminiscences of Conrad,* p52.

29 *The Collected Letters of Joseph Conrad, Vol. I,* 9/12/1897, p421.

30 In *Under Western Eyes,* however, Conrad writes that Razumov was caught between "drunkennes" and "dream-intoxication" which suggests that he had read *The Birth of Tragedy* in which these precise terms are used to describe Dionysos and Apollo.

31 *The Collected Letters of Joseph Conrad, Vol. II,* 22/7/99, p188.

32 *Notes on Life and Letters,* p125.

33 *The Collected Letters of Joseph Conrad, Vol. II,* 26/10/99, p209.

34 Ibid., 23/7/1901, p334.

Conrad's work, but with shedding light on the philosophical presuppositions which underlie them.

Conrad shared with Schopenhauer the basic assumption that the world of the senses is devoid of substance or meaning save that which the individual projects onto it in the act of perception. All knowledge and intention is thus reduced to the level of illusion in the world-view of both writers and a world-weary pessimism attends their awareness of universal solipsism and the essential groundlessness of being. At the same time, the metaphysical force which lies behind all phenomena - in Schopenhauer this is termed "the will" while in Conrad it is "the darkness" - is seen to be neither subject to reason nor morality. Thus, the dawning of self-knowledge with the apprehension of this blind, amoral force at the heart of nature is viewed by both writers as a process which inevitably repels man from life, leading to a desire for annihilation. But, whereas in Schopenhauer this is viewed as desirable, we see in Conrad's fiction an unremitting struggle to redeem and re-affirm existence coupled with a deep scepticism as to the possibilities of doing so.

In his desire to escape Schopenhauer's Buddhistic negation of the will, Conrad approaches Nietzsche's position. Like Nietzsche, Conrad lamented the loss of myth as a result of the Socratic tendency in modern science, but courageously faced the consequences of the "death of God" in western culture and the idea that man had to become his own artist and the sole creator of values in the world. Whereas in Nietzsche the new 'man-artist', or *Übermensch,* recognizes no limits to his will to power over nature and other men, Conrad posits the continuing need for humility and solidarity to curb the destructive excesses of natural egoism which would make our inheritance "too arid to be worth having", as he put it. Conrad also shares with Nietzsche a rejection of the moral outlook on life in favour of a strategy of transcendence in which existence is justified and justifiable only as an aesthetic phenomenon. Although only a temporary bulwark against the inevitable and nauseating growth of empirical knowledge, art is regarded by Conrad as the last stronghold of those "saving illusions" which can alone redeem life and make it worth living. Thus, Conrad's work can be to be poised between a Schopenhauerian pessimism very close to that expounded in *The World as Will and Representation* and a life-affirmation similar to that found in Nietzsche's *The Birth of Tragedy*.

Chapter one, "Art and the 'Veil of Maya'" looks at the way *Lord Jim* is informed by the Eastern idea that life is comparable to a dream and presents itself as a "continuous deception". Jim's history is viewed first from a Schopenhauerian perspective which stresses the destructive effects of illusion on the individual and then through the prism of Nietzsche's theory that illusion is the "only possible mode of redemption". I argue that Jim's following the dream of his romantic ideal to the fantasy realm of Patusan is comparable to the artist's life-affirming recreation of the world in his imagination, and accords with Nietzsche's belief that only as an aesthetic phenomenon can existence be endured. The chapter ends on a Schopenhauerian note, suggesting that life is unworthy of attachment and can afford man no lasting satisfaction.

Chapter two, "Will and Wilderness" looks at *Heart of Darkness* in the light of Schopenhauer's theory of the will to live and Nietzsche's theory of the will to power. It also shows how the scientific quest for knowledge is ultimately self-defeating in that it discovers, not any objective and fixed laws, but the limits of reason and a complete absence of meaning and order in the world. Again we see Conrad adopting Nietzsche's position that, in order to live, man requires to deceive himself. The final part of the chapter compares two possible avenues open to modern man in a world deprived of God: Nietzsche's "superman" and Schopenhauer's compassionate man. Through the characters of Kurtz and Marlow, Conrad shows how the former position leads to self-destruction while the latter offers civilization some hope of survival.

Chapter three, "Linguistic Explosions and the 'Death of God'" takes an existentialist perspective on *The Secret Agent* and examines the full implications of the loss of religious faith in western culture brought on by the rise of empiricism. I argue that Conrad's aim in the novel is very close to that of Nietzsche's philosophy: to explode the myths which have traditionally supported modern social structures by exposing the decay and corruption which those structures serve to conceal. Conrad's relentless irony in the novel can be seen as a sort of linguistic terrorism designed to make room for new values and new artistic approaches. This chapter also looks at Winnie as an existential heroine and shows that Conrad clearly understood existentialist notions of morality, identity and personal freedom even if his characters are unable to rise to the challenges of a brave yet terrible new world.

In my fourth chapter, "Reason and Feeling", I argue that *Under Western Eyes* illustrates Schopenhauer's theory that objectivity is beyond the reach of the intellect and that what an individual perceives is determined by their psychological needs. Reason is thus viewed by the novel as limited and subservient to feeling and instinct whereas illusion, as in Nietzsche's work, is regarded as salutary as long as it can be maintained. Although I argue that Conrad shows a knowledge of Nietzsche's theory of tragedy in terms of the balance between Dionysos and Apollo, the philosophical content of this novel is not finally as important as the psychological insights it provides. The chapter ends with a discussion of *Under Western Eyes* as tragic in the traditional sense.

Chapter five, "The Functional and the Ornamental", shows how *Victory* echoes the critique of empiricism found in idealistic philosophy and reflects both the pervasiveness of the scientific discourse and its inability to offer more than surface descriptions of an imponderable and mysterious world. It shows how art through metaphors and comparisons points to an essential unity behind phenomena which science fails to establish using rational positivism alone. This chapter goes on to examine *Victory* through the extended metaphor of coal and diamonds and suggests that this metaphor can be seen as a model for the many different types of relationship, both abstract and human, found in the novel. I conclude that the novel rejects Schopenhauer's prescription of detachment as an escape from the snares of the world while incorporating his fundamental ontology as regards the will and representation. Conrad's personal attitude to life is finally seen to be more Nietzschean as it advocates affirmation rather than denial of the will to live.

1

Lord Jim: Art and the "Veil of Maya"

Life as the dream

Lord Jim is based on the Schopenhauerian principle that "life presents itself as a continuous deception in small matters as well as in great"(WWR II 573).[35] The protagonist is both victim and perpetrator of a "gigantic deception"(100) that envelopes all the characters in a way reminiscent of the Hindu goddess Maya whose veil "covers the eyes of mortals and causes them to see a world which one cannot say that it is, or it is not; for it is like a dream"(WWR I 7).[36] Whether human deception is salutary or destructive, redeems life or renders it unliveable, makes for a tragic or merely a pitiful existence, the novel reserves judgement. For, like the moral appraisal of Jim's jump, it is one of those "disputes impossible of decision if one had to be fair to all the phantoms in possession"(111) and Conrad is not prepared to take a "definite part" in it.[37] On the one hand, Jim's case appears to support Schopenhauer's argument that "sooner or later, every error must do harm, and this harm is all the greater, the greater the error"(WWR II 68), while at the same time illustrating the opposite theory, proposed by Nietzsche, that "illusion is the only possible mode of redemption"(BT 10).

The dream is a metaphor and leitmotif of considerable importance in *Lord Jim*. In Stein's famous speech, it is used to assert the inherently romantic[38] quality of human perception for a "man that is born falls into a

---

[35] All quotations from the novel refer to the Penguin Classics *Lord Jim*, ed. Cedric Watts and Robert Hampson, with an introduction by Cedric Watts, 1987.

[36] According to Ian Watt, "By the dream Conrad means nothing more or less than man's necessity to justify himself by the "idea", to idealise himself and his actions into moral significance of some order."(*Conrad in the Nineteenth Century*, p326) As I argue in the present study, by the dream Conrad also means the subjective errors, self-deceptions and illusions naturally arising from the "veil of Maya".

[37] "In concluding inconclusively", writes Leon Seltzer, "the book faithfully reflects on the imagination that created it - an imagination that insisted on its inability to clear away the eternal mists of life."(*The Vision of Melville and Conrad*, p50)

[38] As H.M. Daleski points out, "the term 'romantic' seems virtually to be synonymous with 'human', for it is 'man' who denies the base reality of mud and tries to live according to his dream-image of himself."(*Joseph Conrad: The Way of Dispossession*, p96).

dream as easily as a man falling into the sea."(200) Jim, who is used as the model for the romantic sensibility in the novel, is motivated throughout his career by "dreams"(58) of "valorous deeds" and "imaginary achievements" which nevertheless represent for him "the best parts of life, its secret truth, its hidden reality."[39] Yet, even for the rationalistic Marlow, trying to deliver Jim's story is like trying to describe a dream; hence those narratorial vacillations and difficulties of transmission which critics of the novel are so fond of discussing.[40] Conrad was all too aware that "we live as we dream - alone"(HD 57), so that an individual's reality is as unique and personal as their dreams. "Nothing so easy as recounting a dream", he wrote to Henry James, "but it is impossible to penetrate the soul of those who listen with its bitterness and its sweetness. One does not communicate the poignant reality of illusions!"[41] Moreover, the dream is often the only term which can convey certain experiences in the novel that defy both realistic description and rationalistic explanation. Marlow's attempt to shoot the "spectre"(276) of fear during his interview with Jewel is called an "enterprise for a dream" and the whole experience is said to leave behind "the detailed and amazing impression of a dream"(278). Jim will finally be driven away from Jewel "by a dream"(301), by some accursed thing he had heard or seen in his sleep"(300). "And yet", asks Marlow, "is not mankind itself, pushing on its blind way, driven by a dream of its greatness and its power [...] And what is the pursuit of truth, after all"(301).

For Conrad as for Schopenhauer, the terms `life' and `dream' were interchangeable[42] because, being perceived always in the sphere of

---

[39] Nietzsche claimed that "of the two halves of life - the waking and the dreaming - the former is generally considered not only the more important but the only one which is truly lived." (*The Birth of Tragedy, & The Genealogy of Morals*, p32). Daniel W. Ross has pointed out that "the dream is the only means of penetrating a deeper truth than the surface of reality reveals." ("*Lord Jim* and the Saving Illusion", *Conradiana Vol.* 20, No. 1, 1988: 45-69) p45.

[40] Douglas Hewitt has (notoriously) claimed that Conrad "does not present [Marlow's muddled speeches] that we see them as deliberate, part of the portrayal of a man who is bewildered. They come rather from [Conrad's] own uncertainty as to the effect at which he is aiming. There is very clearly a conflict in his own mind."(*Joseph Conrad: A Reassessment*, p37-38) John A. Palmer, on the other hand, takes a far more fruitful perspective on the problem of Marlow's narratives: "There is a great deal of evidence," he writes, "especially in *Lord Jim*, that the inconclusive, enigmatic quality of the Marlow stories [...] is wholly intentional on Conrad's part: and that far from betraying his inability to come concretely to grips with his subject, it represents his way of dramatizing a high epistemological point *much like that of the religious mystic when he maintains the ineffability of experience.*"(my italics) *Joseph Conrad's Fiction*, p42.

[41] *The Collected Letters of Joseph Conrad, Vol. I*, 30/11/1897, p414.

[42] As Schopenhauer argued, "the world must be recognized, from one aspect at least, as akin to a dream, indeed as capable of being put in the same class as a dream. For the same brain

individual consciousness rather than in any objective realm, our waking and sleeping realities remain perpetually in doubt. Hence Marlow's insistence on the difficulties of seeing Jim except through mist or fog[43] - a difficulty which Marlow experiences even when viewing his own person and which could account for the mysterious bond he feels between himself and this elusive, young dreamer: "it seemed to me the less I understood the more I was bound to him in the name of that doubt which is the inseparable part of our knowledge. I did not understand so much more about myself."(206) Marlow's `bond of doubt' which is said to unite us all was also felt by Conrad towards his fellow men, and in the Author's Note he describes his conscious motivation for depicting Jim's character in terms of human sympathy and solidarity: "I saw his form pass by - appealing - significant - under a cloud - perfectly silent. [...] It was for me, with all the sympathy of which I was capable, to seek fit words for his meaning. He was 'one of us'."(44) Jim can be said to be one of us both *because* he is "under a cloud" - that is difficult to understand - and *in spite of* being "under a cloud" - that is out of favour with his fellows.

This would explain why Jim feels so strongly the need of "confessing, explaining [...] living"(216) before Marlow when his self-confidence has been undermined by the Patna incident. For Marlow to receive Jim's confidences and entertain his illusions at a time when all men doubt him is for Jim's reality to be re-affirmed: "You are an awfully good sort to listen like this", says Jim to Marlow, "You don't know what it is for a fellow in my position to be believed"(137). In fact Marlow doesn't know whether to believe Jim or not but he knows that Jim, in being "one of us", deserves a compassionate hearing and this gives Jim the impression of being "believed".

---

function that conjures up during sleep a perfectly objective, perceptible, and indeed palpable world must have just as large a share in the presentation of the objective world of wakefulness. Though different as regards their mater, the two worlds are nevertheless obviously moulded from one form. This form is the intellect, the brain function."(WWR II 4).

[43] Various interpretations have been put forward for this important leitmotif in *Lord Jim*. Albert Guerard has summarised some of these as follows: "*Fog, mist, cloud* and *veil* form a cluster with *moonlight* and with *dream*, to dramatize certain essential distinctions: between the conscious mind and the unconscious, illusion and reality, the "ego-ideal" and the self's destiny as revealed by its actions." (*Conrad the Novelist*, p162) As I argue in the present work, all of these can be further reduced to Schopenhauer's central antithesis between the "phenomenon" and "the thing in itself". Wilfred S. Dowden has claimed that "it is only [Jim's] own misconception of his destiny on earth which places him in an atmosphere of opaqueness."(*Joseph Conrad: The Imaged Style*, p58) but this is clearly not the case. As Marlow suggests in the quoted passage, Jim's "opaqueness" is an integral part of his human identity and also produced by our lack of perspicacity.

Schopenhauer argued that "existence and perceptibility are convertible terms"(WWR I 4) and there is also literal sense in which Jim can be said to exist as a result of being perceived by Marlow: "after all", says Marlow, "it is only through me that he exists for you. I've led him out by the hand; I have paraded him before you. Were my commonplace fears unjust?"(208) Judging from this last question, Marlow too feels the need to be confirmed in his opinions, to be `perceived' by his audience, and if we trace this solipsistic paradigm to its source, it may afford us a better understanding of the impulses behind Conrad's own story-telling.[44]

The theme of the strength of shared convictions is established by the novel's epigram which runs: "It is certain that my conviction gains infinitely the moment another soul will believe in it"(Novalis). Conrad's ontological doubts are eased merely by the reader perceiving the novel he has written and "what is a novel", he asks, "if not a conviction of our fellow men's existence strong enough to take upon itself a form of imagined life clearer than reality?" One's impressions of an empirical world may be illusory and have no more objective warrant than one's dreams but when these `illusions' are communicated, shared, reproduced in another consciousness their reality is instantly enhanced and may sometimes surpass that of mere surface appearances. As Nietzsche wrote, somewhat facetiously, "One is always in the wrong but with two truth begins - One alone cannot prove himself right; but two are already beyond refutation." (GS 207) In other words, we may "live as we dream", but our dreams are mutually sustaining.

Egoism and the "*principium individuationis*"

During his `unofficial inquiry' into the Patna affair, Marlow discovers that loneliness is "a hard and absolute condition of existence"(175) yet, at the same time, "we exist only in so far as we hang together"(207). This is a fact of life which Jim, in his youthful self-centredness, is quite unaware of. For Schopenhauer a crucial part of life's deception arises from the "*principium individuationis*" according to which, a man "regards his person as absolutely different from every other and separated from it by a wide gulf,

[44] As Peter J. Glassman points out, "Just as Marlow recovers from his fear that he has no character by producing a linguistic or a narrative self, so Conrad, by telling Marlow's tale, by attaching himself to Marlow as Marlow attaches himself to Jim, may be though at last to have produced and secured a serviceable personality of his own."(*Language and Being*, p272)

a knowledge to which he adheres with all his might since it alone suits and supports his egoism"(WWR II 365).[45] Jim is one of five sons but he quite literally falls into "the dream of individuation", to use Schopenhauer's terms, "as easily [and literally] as a man falls into the sea"(200): he goes off to join the ranks of the merchant marine.

On the officer training ship Jim's station was in the fore-top, and "from there he looked down with the contempt of a man destined to shine in the midst of dangers"(43), yet these dangers are no more clearly visualised than "the hazy splendour of the sea in the distance" because both are part of Jim's dream of life. When Jim does not occupy this privileged position, having to share instead the lower deck amidst a "babel of two hundred voices", he would "forget himself", that is, forget his sense of uniqueness and experience himself as just one of two hundred would-be seamen. But he escapes from this `self-forgetting' by fleeing into his dream of heroism once more - "the sea-life of light literature" - in which he always plays he role of the "hero".

Although Jim fails to distinguish himself during an incident in which two men are rescued by a cutter from his training vessel while he stands paralysed by fear, his egoism refuses to accept a negative verdict regarding his "avidity for adventure"(50) and "many sided courage" and he rationalises away his failure in a way which once again separates him creditably from his fellow trainee-officers:[46] "He had enlarged his knowledge more than those who had done the work. When all men flinched, then - he felt sure - he alone would know how to deal with the spurious menace of wind and seas."(49) In other words, Jim stubbornly adheres to those illusions which sustain his self-importance while disputing those which in any way undermine it and in this respect can be said to reflect a tendency which Schopenhauer regarded as natural in human beings. As he remarks:

> What opposes the heart is not admitted by the head. All through life we cling to many errors, and take care never to examine their ground, merely from a fear of which we ourselves are unconscious, of possibly making the discovery

---

[45] The implication in Schopenhauer which is explicit in the *Vedas* is that, perceived correctly, all of humanity is really one being. J. I. M. Stewart is thus making an important point when he remarks that "Jim is one of us because we are all one."(*Joseph Conrad*, p109).

[46] "Conrad's vulnerable heroes", observes Thomas Moser, "are all egoists. Their deepest impulses and longings are directed not toward a dutiful place in the ranks but toward self-aggrandizement."(*Joseph Conrad: Achievement and Decline*, p31).

> that we have so long and so often believed and maintained what is false (WWR II 218).

Indeed, Schopenhauer's words seems to encapsulate Jim's whole career, for he clings to his false self-image until the very end. Even after Patusan has been effectively destroyed as a direct result of his misjudgement of Gentleman Brown and Doramin has taken revenge on him for the death of Dain Waris, Jim's "sublimated idealised selfishness"(173) is still very much in evidence and, in a final characteristic gesture, "the white man sent right and left at all those faces a proud and unflinching glance. Then [...] he fell forward dead."(351)

Jim does indeed make a name for himself in the merchant marine but not quite in the way he had anticipated. Despite taking a berth on the Patna for essentially the same escapist reasons as the rest of her indolent crew, he regards them as not belonging to "the heroic world of adventure"(61) in which he, in his imagination at least, features so largely: "The quality of these men did not matter; he rubbed shoulders with them but they could not touch him; he shared the air they breathed, but he was different". That this difference between Jim and his fellow crew-members is illusory and, like the difference between the right and wrong of the Patna affair, does not amount to a "hair's breadth"(139) or "the thickness of a sheet of paper"(138), is clearly borne out by the accident at sea which unites them all in ignominy. Yet, during the Malabar interview, Jim is anxious that Marlow "should not confound him with his partners [...] in crime [...] He was not of them: he was altogether of another sort."(101)

Relating the scene in which the crew desperately try to release a life-boat for their own safety, Jim stresses that "there was nothing in common between him and these men". "It is more than probable", speculates Marlow, "he thought himself cut off from them by a space that could not be traversed, by an obstacle that could not be overcome [...] He was as far as he could get from them - the whole breadth of the ship"(119). But the "breadth of a ship", especially one "lean like a greyhound"(53), is not so great and, when the crew finally succeed in freeing the life-boat, this space that "couldn't be traversed", this obstacle that "couldn't be overcome" is done so quite easily because the next thing Jim knows is that he has jumped and landed "in the same boat"(134) as his cowardly ship-mates. The man who would set himself apart as "an example of devotion to duty"(47) and "as unflinching as a hero in a book", suffers the worst kind of public disgrace and becomes associated instead with a group of notorious scoundrels.

Jim is not the only character in the novel who, finding the "*principium individuationis*" flattering to his ego, allows himself to be deceived by it. The skipper of the Patna, "a sort of renegade New South Wales German"(53) refuses to identify with any nation or group except where he feels it might be to his personal advantage: he was "very anxious to curse publicly his native country", but when he loses his English seaman's certificate for neglect of duty, he announces: "You Englishmen are all rogues [...] a man like me don't want your verfluchte certificate. [...] I vill an American citizen begome."(73-4) Indeed, the more a character attempts to deny his kinship with his fellow men, the more the narrative subverts the attempt: Jim's denial of kinship with the Patna crew ends with him "in the same boat" while the captain's denial of kinship with the pilgrims ("dese cattle") ends with him as a "frightened bullock"(54).[47]

The second engineer also looks down on the pilgrims and revels in the incidental distinction of being white - a collective illusion of some force in the novel. He refers to the pilgrims as "the vermin"(61) yet it is he, along with his fellow white crew-members who, in deserting an apparently sinking ship, play the role of rats. The awnings which cover the deck of the ship and isolate "the five whites on board"(55) from the "human cargo" can be seen as one of the many images employed by the novel to signify the "veil of Maya". When this veil which supports men's egoism threatens to be lifted by "the approach of death"(120) before which all men , regardless of colour, are "equal"(56), the officers are desperate to restore it once more by distancing themselves physically from the unconscious mass of sleeping bodies on their ship symbolising undifferentiated humanity. "You silly fool!", says the chief to Jim, "do you think you'll get the ghost of a show when that lot of brutes is in the water?"(119) Yet, by completely disregarding their moral and professional duties and abandoning ship, it is the officers who behave like instinctive "brutes" and not their relatively civilised charges who have taken the dangerous journey "at the call of an idea"(53) and remain obliviously calm throughout the apparent emergency.

Even the consistently compassionate Marlow is not without his moments of egoistic disavowal. While Jim is relating to him his increasingly desperate attempts to avoid identifying with the rest of the crew - "I made up my mind to keep my mouth shut"(121); "I tried to be deaf"(135) - Marlow is experiencing a similar resistance with regard to Jim:

---

47 The "liability to be despicably less than human", writes H.M. Daleski, is part of the human condition", yet the "threat to civilised resides in a man's denial of his humanity."(p84-85).

"I held my peace [...] It behoved me to make no sound lest by a gesture or a word I should be drawn into a fatal admission about myself which would have some bearing on the case"(121). Marlow's judicious desire to maintain strict impartiality in his `unofficial inquiry' may be more intellectually defensible than Jim's reasons for withholding his solidarity from his fellow ship-mates but what Marlow cannot deny is that, given the same conditions as those prevailing on the Patna, he too would have jumped. As Jim claims: "Leap! By heavens! you would take one spring from where you sit and land in that clump of bushes yonder"; to which Marlow inwardly replies, "I would have landed short by several feet and that's the only thing I am fairly certain of."(122)

As Gentleman Brown suggests to Jim in a way which obtains the latter's subconscious identification, when "it came to saving one's life in the dark, one didn't care who else went - three, thirty, three hundred people"(329) and, according to Schopenhauer, this egoistic paradigm would hold good for all men.[48] We can see just how much Conrad's and Schopenhauer's philosophies converge at times by comparing Brown's utterance above with the following passage taken from *The World as Will and Representation*:

> every individual, completely vanishing and reduced to nothing in a boundless world, nevertheless makes himself the centre of the world and considers his own existence and well-being before everything else [...] he is ready for this to sacrifice everything else; he is ready to annihilate the world, in order to maintain his own self, that drop in the ocean, a little longer. This disposition is *egoism* which is essential to everything in nature. (WWR I 332)

Ironically, even Brown's motives for revealing this 'natural law' to Jim are essentially egoistic and Jim lets brown off the hook because he too is "thinking of himself"(92) and would like to be forgiven his own past transgressions.

Another character who stubbornly clings to the illusions produced by the "*principium undividuationis*", regarding himself unique and separate from all other beings, is Captain Brierly. In many respects Brierly is the mirror-image of Jim but whereas the former is keenly aware of the

[48] As Thomas Moser has pointed out, "one of the central convictions of Conrad the psychologist [is] that egoism is the motive force of most men's actions."(p31).

responsibilities inherent in the code of seamanship, the latter is interested solely in the opportunities for adventure which the life of the sea affords. The result is that Brierly has successfully realised those heroic dreams which in the pre-Patusan Jim remain "abstract"(45) desires: Brierly "had saved lives at sea, had rescued ships in distress [...] and was the owner of an inscribed gold chronometer and of silver-mounted binoculars testifying to the excellence of [his] seaman-ship and indomitable pluck"(85). The facile use of superlatives at the end of this description as well as the trite reference to his tokens of success undercuts Brierly's achievements, suggesting they are as deceptive and devoid of substance as every other flattering illusion in the realm of Maya. The key to both men's character is not so much ambition as egoism and what Marlow calls a "complacent [...] self-satisfaction"(86) which holds a powerful charm for him because it reflects his own latent self-love. As regards Brierly, Marlow says: "I found I could bear my share of good-natured and contemptuous pity for the sake of something indefinite and attractive in the man [...] I envied him"(85-6) and concerning the nature of Jim's appeal, he confesses: "he had reached the secret sensibility of my egoism"(155).

When Brierly has to sit in judgement on Jim, he too, like Marlow before Jim or Jim before Brown, cannot help identifying with the 'outlaw' so that the surface distinctions between noble/ignoble, dutiful/non-dutiful, lawful/unlawful which have sustained Brierly's impeccable career are irrevocably and fatally undermined. The "*principium individuationis*" which had hitherto supported Brierly's enormous egoism ("neither you nor I [...] had ever thought so much of ourselves", p91) is instantly seen through and what he perceives is that all men, given the right circumstances are potential deserters. As the French Lieutenant points out, "One talks, [...] but at the end of the reckoning one is no cleverer than the next man - and no more brave."(159) Just as Jim is shocked and embarrassed by the sight of the officers acting like "knockabout clowns in a farce" at "the approach of death or dishonour"(120), Brierly confesses to feeling "like a fool all the time"(91) he is acting as nautical assessor in the Patna case. This is because besides judging Jim, he is also "holding silent inquiry into his own case"(86) and "thinking of himself"(92). Jim also conceives of his experience with the crew of the Patna as a trial but one in which he, rather than they, is the accused: "Was there ever any one so shamefully tried?"(120), he asks Marlow. Again we see a character's idea of individuation being subverted by a perception of kinship.

Appropriately enough, both men express their subconscious identification[49] with those whom they are judging - and by association with humanity in general whom they are wont to look down on - by the same symbolic act: jumping from a great height. Brierly's jump could be interpteted as a mystical suicide in the eastern tradition according to which the individual, having seen through the veil of deception, willingly embraces personal 'annihilation' in the hope of attaining reintegration into the primal unity. Yet the considerable irony which Conrad introduces into the description of this jump suggests not only that Brierly has no faith in any existence after death but that his motives for suicide, being cowardly, are still very much of this world: "He jumped overboard at sea barely a week after the end of the inquiry [...] as though on that exact spot in the midst of waters he had suddenly perceived the gates of the other world flung open wide for his reception."(86) These "gates of the other world" which are said to open for an instant to swallow the unfortunate captain serve as another image for the "veil of Maya" which has been lifted from Brierly's blemishless life with disastrous effect. Yet, his disillusionment has not taken place in this ironic "exact spot in the midst of waters" but a week earlier in the court of inquiry where, looking at Jim in the witness-box, Brierly had began to suspect that there may not be any real difference between opposites at all and "courage may be merely a kind of cowardness [...] of softness"(92). After such a realisation, any spot on land or water would have served Brierly's purpose.

Yet even in this supreme act of self-effacement, as in Jim's surrendering himself to the wrath of Doramin after Dain Waris' death, we can see the workings of egoism and that brand of self-deception which the novel regards as essential to life: "Who can tell what flattering view [Brierly] had induced himself to take of his own suicide?"(90), asks Marlow and the same question can equally be asked of Jim at the end of the novel. Brierly commits suicide at the height of his career to avoid even the semblance of failing the code and in order to sustain even unto death "that belief in his own splendour"(90) which had set him apart from his fellow men throughout his life. For what he has found most "shocking" about the Patna case is not so much its implications about the strength or validity of the seaman's code *in extremis*, but the fact that "there [Jim] sits while all these confounded natives, serangs, lascars, quartermasters, are giving evidence that's enough to burn a man to ashes with shame"(92). The

[49] Albert Guerard has claimed that "*Lord Jim* is perhaps the first major novel solidly built on a true intuitive understanding of sympathetic identification as a psychic process, and as a process which may operate both consciously and less than consciously."(p147).

shame derives from the perception of the white man as essentially no different from the mass of humanity represented by "natives, serangs, lascars, quartermasters": the narrative suggests that, as a means of differentiating humanity, neither race nor class have any real value.

In clinging to one's sense of uniqueness, one is tempted to deny the same right to others for one can only claim to be different in relation to someone else. Thus, when Marlow refuses to bribe Jim into disappearing so that the code of seamanship may escape scrutiny and Brierly's embarrassment may be curtailed, Brierly made a gesture with his arm that seemed to deprive [Marlow] of [his] individuality, to push [him] into the crowd"(92). This egoistic gesture is echoed by Jim when he claims that, following the Patna incident, the rest of the crew "went away [...] not one of them would face it...They!' He moved his hand slightly to imply disdain"(156). But whether Jim really is facing it by subjecting himself to the official inquiry is highly debatable. Marlow, for one, remains undecided on this point: "It might have been flight and it might have been a mode of combat"(187), he concludes inconclusively. In any case, an interesting pattern emerges in which the crew of the Patna look down on the pilgrims for not being white, Jim looks down on the crew for not being heroic, Marlow is aggrieved against Jim for "robbing their common life of the last spark of its glamour"(139), and Brierly looks down on everyone else for not being "*the* fortunate man of the earth, not Montague Brierly in command of the Ossa"(86) - and all with equal justification.

"Ontological security and insecurity" - lowering and lifting the veil

If Brierly's world of "indomitable pluck" and "excellence of seamanship"(85) is based on the reliability of surface appearances, Jim's paradoxical example as cowardly deserter who refuses to flee the judicial process fatally undermines that world by introducing what R. D. Laing would term "ontological insecurity"[50] into the captain's mind. "Such an affair destroys one's confidence"(93), confesses Brierly, while Marlow calls it "one of those trifles that awaken ideas - start into life some thought with which a man unused to such companionship finds it impossible to

---

[50] See R. D. Laing, *The Divided Self* and *Self and Others*. A. D. Nuttall also employs this term in *A Common Sky*, which is referred to in Cedric Watts' *A Preface to Conrad*, p85. Furthermore, the term has a central position in R. G. Hampson, *Joseph Conrad: Betrayal and Identity* (Basingstoke: Macmillan, 1992).

live"(86). As Schopenhauer argued, besides flattering their egoism, the "*principium individuationis*" deceives individuals into desiring the continuation of their being by producing in them with a false sense of security regarding their environment. This idea was later taken up by Nietzsche in his first book, *The Birth of Tragedy* which expands on many of the central ideas found in Schopenhauer's work: "Nature often uses illusions", writes Nietzsche, "in order to achieve its secret purposes. The true goal is covered over by a phantasm, we stretch out our hands to the latter, while nature, aided by our deception, attains the former."(BT 31)

Every major character in *Lord Jim* is deceived by life in this way, beginning with Jim who can be said to represent the man caught in the "veil of Maya" and completely taken in by the phenomenal world. From the fore-top of his training vessel he enjoys looking down at the peaceful, work-a-day world below, secure in the solidity of that which helps him define his adventurous, escapist identity[51]: "He could see the big ships departing, the broad-beamed ferries constantly on the move, the little boats floating far below his feet, with the hazy splendour of the sea in the distance, and the hope of a stirring life in the world of adventure"(47). Jim's life on the fore-top is indeed a secure and hopeful dream but it will be replaced by a fear-inspired nightmare during his first experience of danger at sea, setting up a pattern of "ontological security" followed by "ontological insecurity" which will recur throughout the novel.[52] The rain which, during this incident, slanted in sheets that flicked and subsided"(48) allowing Jim "threatening glimpses of the tumbling tide", serves as another veil metaphor and, at the height of the emergency, this veil appears to be completely lifted: "The next gust seemed to blow all this away." The result is that, like Brierly in the court of inquiry, Jim's hitherto familiar world is turned upside down and opposites merge menacingly: "The air was full of flying water." In a nightmare vision, Jim turns the storm into an awe-inspiring adversary whose appearance alone has the power to paralyse him, like some fearful Medusa's head: "there was a fierce purpose in the gale, a furious earnestness in the screech of the wind, in the brutal tumult of the earth and sky, that seemed directed at him, and made him hold his breath in awe. He stood still."(48) Although Jim is not alone, the gale seems "directed at him because his reality is as self-

---

51 "On the training ship, at his station in the fore-top", writes Royal Roussel, "Jim abandons himself to his imaginary life, but this activity is inextricably in*Vol.*ved with his impression of a secure and stable world which frames it."(*The Metaphysics of Darkness*, p81).

52 Hampson argues that the illusion of security in dream and the apprehension of insecurity in reality are *both* symptoms of 'ontological insecurity' in Laing's sense of the term.

generated as a dream and, in his own eyes, he always appears at the centre of things, always the "hero in a book"(47).

The impression which Jim has with the lifting of this veil is that nature, instead of constituting an agent of Providence, benevolently assisting individuals in the realisation of their goals, is a potentially hostile force ready to amorally destroy her creatures at a moments notice. Echoing this new view of nature which nineteenth-century biological science projected, Schopenhauer notes: "it is not for the individual that nature cares, but only the species [...] therefore nature is always ready to let the individual fall, and the individual is accordingly not only exposed to destruction in a thousand different ways from the most insignificant accidents, but is even destined towards this and is led towards it by nature herself."(WWR I 276) Yet, as soon as the emergency is over on Jim's training vessel, he is ready to deceive himself once more regarding the security of his earthly existence so that the "tumult and menace of wind and sea now appeared very contemptible"(49) to him.

The second time Jim experiences the feeling of "ontological insecurity" is during his first voyage as chief mate of a merchant ship and this feeling will again be linked to a momentary glimpse behind the veil allowing him a privileged insight into the workings of nature: "he had a glimpse of the earnestness in the anger of the sea. That truth is not so often made apparent as people might think", remarks the narrator, "and it is only now and then that there appears on the face of facts a sinister violence of intention"(50). During this storm Jim is disabled by a falling spar and has to be taken below deck but there his fear "grows shadowy; and imagination, the enemy of men, the father of all terrors, unstimulated, sinks to rest in the dulness of exhausted emotion."(50) Jim's feelings of anxiety persist longer on this occasion and "the unintelligent brutality of an existence liable to the agony of such sensations filled him with a despairing desire to escape at any cost. Then fine weather returned and he thought no more about it." It is clear that the visual impression of his nature has great power over Jim's state of mind so that the return of fine weather after his harrowing experience is sufficient to restore in him the will to live. But, after every lifting of the veil, Jim is psychologically scarred and loses some of his youthful "elasticity of spirits"(99): hence his symbolic lameness[53] which results from this accident and persists even unto Patusan.

---

[53] C. B. Cox has offered a comparable interpretation of this image: "the imaginative man is necessarily lamed by his peculiar quality of vision", he writes, "Sensitivity to the realities of the

Convalescing back on shore, Jim abandons himself to the physical appeal of his environment: "a gentle breeze entering through the windows, always flung wide open, brought into the bare room the softness of the sky, the languor of the earth, the bewitching breath of the Eastern waters. There were perfumes in it, suggestions of infinite repose, the gift of endless dreams."(51-52) After his recovery, rather than going home as he had originally intended, Jim takes a berth on the Patna[54] - an event which signals his reconciliation to life and the restoration of his "ontological security". The "veil of Maya" is also firmly in place for the eight hundred pilgrims on their way to Mecca who unwisely entrust the Patna with their lives and their salvation. Despite being "eaten up with rust worse than a condemned water-tank"(53), she is "painted outside and white-washed inside" to conceal her un-seaworthy condition.[55]

Serving on the Patna, an "easy billet"(52) of the kind that lazy seamen dream of, Jim has every opportunity to indulge in his heroic reveries and abandon himself to the contemplation of a peaceful nature - two activities which, as we have already seen, go hand in hand: "a marvellous stillness pervaded the world, and the stars together with the serenity of their rays seemed to shed upon the earth the assurance of everlasting peace."(55) Until Jim sets up his 'ideal republic' in Patusan, this is the last time he will be able to enjoy any measure of "ontological security" and, on the bridge of the Patna, he is like an infant slumbering in the arms of a nature whose appearance recalls "the certitude of fostering love upon the placid tenderness of a mother's face."(56) The waking and sleeping states have fused totally and "the line dividing [Jim's] meditation from a surreptitious doze on his feet" is said to be "thinner than a thread on a spider's web."(61) . But, as Schopenhauer claimed, "If we were to bring to the sight of everyone the terrible sufferings and afflictions to which his life is constantly exposed," wrote Schopenhauer, "he would be seized with horror"(WWR I 325) and this is precisely the "horror" which the crew of the Patna experience when their ship carrying eight hundred sleeping

---

Post-Darwinian world make man unfit for action, and this is symbolically represented by physical disability."(*Joseph Conrad: The Modern Imagination*, p31).

[54] Both the Patna which is named after an Indian city on the Ganges and the view from Jim's hospital window, have a distinctly eastern flavour in keeping with the mystical roots of Schopenhauer's philosophy. Peter Caracciolo has pointed out that the Patna is "a city sacred to Buddhism". 'Buddhist Teaching Stories and their Influence on Conrad, Wells, and Kipling: The Reception of the *Jataka* and Allied genres in Victorian Culture', *The Conradian, Vol.* 11, no. 1. (May 1986, pp24-34). p30.

[55] This symbol of hypocrisy links the Patna with the "whited sepulchre" of Brussels in *Heart of Darkness*.

pilgrims, steams over a submerged wreck in the middle of the night. "What had happened?", asks the narrator, "Had the earth been checked in her course? [...] suddenly the calm sea, the sky without a cloud appeared formidably insecure in their immobility, as if poised on the brow of yawning destruction."(62)

The Patna can be said to represent the earth for she is "old as the hills"(53) and moves so imperceptibly in her course "as though she had been a crowded planet speeding through the dark spaces of ether behind the swarm of suns."(59) In keeping with the theme of Maya, everyone on this "planet" is intoxicated in some form - either asleep or drunk or both. Jim's heroic dreams make his soul "drunk with the divine philtre of an unbounded confidence in itself"(58); the skipper is "only half awake" and still in his sleeping jacket; the second engineer is drunk and "demonstrating in the air the shape and extent of his courage"(62); the chief engineer is "sleeping sweetly like a little child, with a bottle of prime brandy under his pillow"(60); the pilgrims are fast asleep and, both literally and metaphorically, dreaming the dream of faith and salvation. Yet, in the engine room below the reader is given a glimpse into the violent and chaotic physical forces which are keeping this ship moving, this "planet" turning, and which are only kept hidden from view by the deck of the ship acting as a thin veil: "short metallic clangs bursting out suddenly in the depths of the ship, the harsh scrape of a shovel, the violent slam of a furnace door, exploded brutally, as if the men handling the mysterious things below had their breasts full of fierce anger"(57). The revelation which takes place comes from beneath the ship and brings into sudden focus the powerlessness and vulnerability of the human order when set against the might of nature: "A faint noise as of thunder, of thunder infinitely remote, less than a sound, hardly more than a vibration, passed slowly and the ship quivered in response, as if the thunder had growled deep in the water."(62) Just as the ship is said to quiver in response to this "thunder" in the water, the crew is described "swaying strangely in the common torment of fear"(119). Like the workers in the engine room whose "breasts full of anger"(57) reflect the fierceness of the furnaces they are handling, the men above deck are taking their cue from the ship they are supposed to be commanding which is itself echoing the "growl" in the water. "Everything is entirely in nature," wrote Schopenhauer, "and she is entirely in everything [...] Against the mighty voice of nature, reflection can do little."(WWR I 281-2) Thus, although Jim doesn't mean to desert the Patna along with his ship-mates, his rational self, suggests Conrad, can no more oppose the impulses of his instinctive self than a ship can refuse to be moved by sea it is sailing on.

As a result of the accident Jim is rudely awakened from his heroic reveries to the reality of human cowardice and from his illusions of security to the knowledge of life's precariousness. Throughout the emergency Jim is powerless to act because he is "too busy watching the threatening slant of the ship, the suspended menace discovered in the midst of the most perfect security - fascinated by the sword hanging by a hair over his imaginative head."(114) This "sword hanging from a hair" refers to the story of Damocles and Dionysius which Conrad also alludes to in *The Mirror of the Sea*: "A flavour in the mouth of the real abiding danger that lurks in all the forms of human existence. It is an acquisition too, that feeling. A man may be the better for it but he will not be the same [...] the feast shall not henceforth have the same flavour."(69) On the Patna, Jim's newly acquired knowledge of the "danger which lurks in all the forms of human existence" merely paralyses his will to act: "his first impulse was to shout and straightaway make all those people leap out of sleep into terror; but such an overwhelming sense of his helplessness came over him that he was not able to produce a sound."(105) Later, on Patusan, it is the "true perception of his extreme peril"(229) which makes Jim drop the Rajah's clock marking the start of his new career.

The novel stresses that it is the quality of Jim's imagination which, more than anything else, sets him apart from his fellow men and which is responsible for showing him the proverbial sword hanging over his head. For it is not that his imagination is of a particularly wayward or unreliable kind - quite the contrary; for moments at a time it seems to penetrate the "veil of Maya" to the timeless, universal truths beyond: "each time he closed his eyes a flash of thought showed him that crowd of bodies laid out for death, as plain as daylight."(121) The pilgrims may not be destined to die as a result of this particular accident but the "ontological insecurity" which Jim experiences during the emergency is capable of impressing upon him with irresistible force the inescapable fact of human mortality and helplessness before death. He was "a gifted poor devil with the faculty of a swift and forestalling vision", says Marlow, "The sights it showed him had turned him into cold stone from the soles of his feet to the nape of his neck"(114). Again we see the Medusa effect which lifting the veil can have on whoever is unfortunate enough to possess penetrating vision.

The irony is that Jim is both deceived and undeceived at the same time because, although life is undoubtedly precarious in a general sense, in this particular instance it proves remarkably resilient, and the ships hull emerges as tough as "the spirit of some men we meet now and then, worn to a shadow and breasting the weight of life."(115) At the climax of the emergency, when the crew in the boat are ignoring eight hundred living people and "yelling after one dead man to come down and be saved"(124), Jim has convinced himself that the ship is finally about to sink and jumps: "She was going down, down, head first under me...' He raised his hand deliberately to his face and made picking motions with his fingers as though he had been bothered with cobwebs"(124). As Jim is recounting these crucial moments before his jump, the cobweb image is again conjured up but, whereas it was previously associated with "ontological security", here it is associated with the opposite feeling.[56] The theme of entrapment intimated by Jim's earlier outburst is now made explicit: "It maddened me to see myself caught like this. I was angry, as though I had been trapped. I was trapped!"(118) Yet, it is not so much the external world which has "betrayed"(113) Jim as his own senses through which he perceives that world.

Every appearance during the emergency appears in hindsight to have been without substance - from Jim's heroic exterior to the danger which the ship was in, to the bullying of the crew when they discover that Jim rather than George has jumped with them into the boat: "it was all threats, all a terribly effective feint, a sham from beginning to end, planned by the enormous disdain of the Dark Powers"(132). The collision itself which severely damages the bulkhead is so deceptively gentle and of such short duration that it seems "as though the ship had steamed across a narrow belt of vibrating water and humming air."(62) What has undeniable reality in *Lord Jim,* is the effect which impressions have on the consciousness perceiving them for, as Schopenhauer wrote, "*Consciousness* alone is immediately given"(WWR I 5). Thus the effect of the collision on the crew, regardless of its cause, is strong enough to scatter "their self-command like chaff before the wind"(120) and even kill the "donkeyman"(160) who collapses on deck at the height of the panic. "May I be shot", exclaims Jim, "if he hadn't been fooled into killing himself. Fooled - neither more or less. [...] Ah! If he had only kept still; if he had only told them to go to the devil when they came to rush him out of his bunk because the ship was

[56] The image of a spider's web referred to above serves as an ominous reminder that all appearances are part of the "veil of Maya" and, as such, are designed to entrap the individual in an existence which is essentially precarious and full of woe. As Jacques Berthoud writes: "The timing of [the] catastrophe is designed to suggest that the security it interrupts is as much an intoxication as the panic it provokes."(*The Major Phase*, p74).

sinking"(122) This suggests that Jim would have done better to trust in the unseen as the pilgrims do than to follow the example of his doubting shipmates who have faith only in what their unreliable senses tell them.

Jim's feeling of "ontological insecurity" reaches its peak when he has landed in the boat with the rest of the crew and the lights of the Patna can no longer be seen: "There was no going back. It was as if he had jumped into a well - into an everlasting deep hole..."(125) By jumping off the Patna Jim can be said to have abandoned the world of reassuring surface appearances and collective illusions and landed into an ontological wilderness. This predicament suggests the extreme solipsism of modern man: "You couldn't distinguish the sea from the sky; there was nothing to see and nothing to hear. Not a glimmer, not a shape, not a sound."(127) Just like his crime which exiles Jim from the white community of the sea to the dark Malayan forests, this glimpse into nature's "heart of darkness" will forever deny Jim the security of the phenomenal world which, from the fore-top of his training vessel, used to sustain his high self-esteem. As Marlow claims, "He had tumbled from a height he could never scale again"(125), which can be read as an allusion to the fall of man: for in having acquired knowledge of the precariousness of life and happiness, Jim cannot henceforth rejoin the innocent part of creation symbolised by the faithful, trusting pilgrims sleeping aboard the ship. This analogy is reinforced by origin of the phrase "one of us" which comes from Genesis 3:22 and originally denoted "the acquisition by Adam of moral knowledge and experience".[57]

Conrad weaves a plethora of mythical,[58] psychological, and philosophical ideas into this single incident but it is clear that his primary intention in reworking the Patna affair into the basis for *Lord Jim* was to present his readers with a multi-layered metaphor for human disillusionment and the loss of innocence[59]: "When your ship fails you, your whole world seems to fail you; the world that made you, restrained you, took care of you [...] Of course, as with belief, thought, love, hate, conviction, or even the visual aspect of material things, there are as many ship-wrecks as there are men."(132) The irony is that instead of the ship

---

[57] See note 3 of the Penguin Classics *Lord Jim*, p354.

[58] One critic notes that "After the jump, Jim enters hell itself: 'the sea hissed like twenty thousand kettles' [...] as though the serpents of Paradise Lost [...] who gather round Satan, the fallen Lucifer, are here gathering round Jim, the fallen Adam." (see John Batchelor's *Lord Jim*, p99).

[59] As Albert Guerard has pointed out, "nearly everyone has jumped off some Patna and most of us have been compelled to live on, desperately or quietly engaged in reconciling what we are with what we would like to be."(p127).

failing Jim, he has failed the ship and the ship-wreck is more metaphorical than real. Even the apocalyptic aftermath of the desertion is only a figment of Jim's imagination, his own personal "end of the world"(125), so that the stress is always on solipsism and inescapable subjectivity: "His saved life was over for want of ground under his feet, for want of sights for his eyes, for want of voices in his ears. Annihilation - hey! And all the time it was only a clouded sky [...] Only a night: only a silence."(127) At one point, the Patna's mast-head light seems to drop "like a lighted match you throw down"(128) giving the impression that the ship has finally sunk, but what has in fact happened is that the wind has swung her around, obscuring the main lights on board. The fact that the lights are obscured because of the position of the viewer again stresses the unavoidable subjectivity of a world conceived as Maya.

When objective facts about the incident emerge during the official inquiry, they only pertain to the "superficial how"(84) of the affair rather than the "fundamental why" which can only be conjectured about since Jim's examination is "as instructive the tapping with a hammer on an iron box, were the object to find out what's inside." These facts can afford Jim no relief for they merely confirm that appearances are infinitely deceptive and the human intellect powerless to apprehend the truth until it is too late: "As to what sensations [Jim] experienced when he got [ashore] and heard the unforeseen conclusion of the tale in which he had played such a pitiful part [...] it is difficult to imagine", says Marlow in his un-presupposing manner, "I wonder whether he felt the ground cut from under his feet?"(122) Marlow certainly feels the ground cut from under his feet" when he considers that "he would have trusted the deck to that youngster on the strength of a single glance [..] and it wouldn't have been safe. There are depths of horror in that thought"(76), he confesses.

With hindsight, it appears that both Jim's dream visions inspiring "ontological security" and his nightmare visions inspiring "ontological insecurity" have been deceptive so that he can never be said to have perceived the essential truth. As Schopenhauer claimed, "a perfect understanding of the [..] inner nature [...] of the world, extending to the ultimate ground and meeting every requirement is impossible."(WWR II 642). Or, as Conrad put it "There is joy and sorrow. There is sunshine and darkness, and all are within the same smile of the inscrutable Maya."[60] This is in keeping with the idea reiterated in much of his non-fictive

60 *The Collected Letters of Joseph Conrad, Vol. I*, 9/12/1897, p421.

writing that "the world, whether seen in a convex mirror or a concave mirror is always but a vain and fleeting appearance."[61]

Facts and misconceptions

There might be "depths of horror"(76) in the thought that one cannot tell truth from appearances but there is mercy too: the Patna *doesn't* sink, the pilgrims are *not* destined to die a watery death and Jim's "saved life"(127) is *not* quite "over" following his desertion of duty. Indeed, for Conrad, illusions constitute the only defence which human beings possess against the "darkness" - the "outward and inward terrors"(75) of life. As the example of the pilgrims on the Patna and the Malay crewmen suggests, there is greater security in remaining ignorant[62] and trusting than in perceiving the inherent deceptiveness of the phenomenal world and becoming disillusioned as a result. For some men ignorance is indeed bliss:"The ship of iron, the men with white faces, all the sights, all the sounds, everything on board to that ignorant and trusting multitude was strange alike, and as trustworthy as it would forever remain incomprehensible." (106)

Before they abandon ship, the white crew members are desperate to avoid the fact of physical death but having deserted the Patna and betrayed the seaman's code they are plunged into a moral and ontological wilderness signifying the extinction of all civilizing illusions[63]: "After the ship's lights had gone out anything might have happened in that boat [...] and the world no wiser. We were like men walled up quick in a roomy grave", recalls Jim, "No fear, no law, no sound, no eyes"(132). In the process of saving their lives, they have given the lie to those illusions which, in *Lord Jim*, redeem life and make it worth living. This nihilistic state in which the crew find themselves on the boat is likened by Jim to a living death and is regarded by the novel as considerably worse than

---

61 *The Collected Letters of Joseph Conrad, Vol. II,* to R. B. Cunninhame Graham, 31/1/1898, p30.

62 "Given the bleakness of the vistas opened by scientific discovery, it is not surprising", writes Cedric Watts, "that many writers entertained the idea (paradoxically, since they *were* writers) that ignorance might after all be bliss."(p54).

63 As Cedric Watts has claimed, "Conrad conveys to us directly or subliminally, a wide array of his fears: the fear that decency might be fighting a doomed rearguard-action against barbarism, the fear that human rationality is opposed by a crude irrationality in the universe, and the fear that an infinity of bleak extinction awaits mankind as a race just as surely as it awaits man as a mortal individual."(p88).

actual death; hence the distinction between the "donkeyman" who is merely fooled into killing himself by the disaster and Jim who, in losing his dreams of adventure, "the best parts of life, its secret truth, its hidden reality"(58) suffers a fate "worse than death"(160). Similarly, the sentence of the court of inquiry which deprives Jim of his honour while sparing his life is viewed by Marlow as "infinitely worse than a beheading"(159) it being "unrelieved by the hope of rest and safety following the fall of the axe"(159).

As Nietzsche points out, "The falseness of a judgement is not necessarily an objection to a judgement [...] The question is to what extent it is life-advancing, life-preserving [...] to renounce false judgements would be to renounce life, would be to deny life."(BGE 4) Nietzsche's claim offers an illuminating context for Jim's strange behaviour throughout the novel which is characterized by a constant flight eastwards towards the rising sun and, symbolically, the Apollonian realm of illusion. Naturally, this flight from fact becomes particularly urgent and desperate following Jim's disgrace on the Patna: "His incognito, which had as many holes as a sieve, was not meant to hide a personality but a fact. When the fact broke through the incognito he would leave suddenly the seaport where he happened to be at the time and go to another - generally farther east."(46) Although Jim is not as "unflinching as a hero in a book"(47), he refuses to surrender this false judgement" about himself despite all the evidence to the contrary because it provides him with the necessary self-esteem to face life. The "dogged self-assertion"(45) which he displays as a water-clerk is indeed "a necessity" as is his "spotlessly neat", "immaculate white" appearance for these serve to conceal, as much from "himself as from anybody else", the fact of his sullied reputation and "the acute consciousness of lost honour"(44). As Conrad writes in the Author's Note, such a consciousness "may be wrong, or it may be right, or it may be condemned as artificial" but the important thing to note is that a sense of personal honour is an essential part of Jim's ego-ideal and has subjective value as such, regardless of its objective warrant.

When facts catch up with Jim during the official inquiry rendering his heroic illusions untenable, he is compared to a "creature that, finding itself imprisoned within an enclosure of high stakes dashes round and round, distracted in the night, trying to find a weak spot, a crevice, a place to scale, some opening through which it may squeeze itself and escape."(65) Jim contemplates suicide as the only means of escape from an ignominious existence: "He had found that to meditate about because he thought he had saved his life, while all its glamour had gone with the ship in the night."(138) Ironically enough, what is consoling Jim and keeping him alive when all else is gone is the prospect of death which, in the abstract at least, appears more attractive than the fact of an existence deprived of honour and the possibility of ever acquiring it. Later, Stein will offer Jim Patusan as another avenue of escape, but whether this is essentially different from the suicide which he himself contemplates is debateable for it too is presented as a sort of "grave". As Nietzsche pointed out, "we are in prison, we can only *dream* ourselves free not make ourselves free"(AOM 33).[64]

The Birth of Tragedy and the vital fiction

In Nietzsche's *The Birth of Tragedy*, the state beyond words, images and illusions of every kind is personified by the Greek god Dionysos who also represents for Nietzsche "the desire to tear asunder the veil of Maya, to sink back into the original oneness of nature"(BT 27). His opposite number is Apollo, the god of art, who "may be as the marvellous divine image of the `principium individuationis' and whose looks and gestures radiate the full delight, wisdom and beauty of illusion."(BT 22) Nietzsche claimed that when there has been a lifting of the veil and the man rapt in Apollonian illusion has apprehended the Dionysian element at the heart of nature, he is nauseated and desires annihilation. This insight undermines his will to live by revealing to him that, as an individuated part of the "original oneness", he is no more than an insignificant and ignoble victim of nature and chance. "The truth once seen," writes Nietzsche, "man is aware everywhere of the ghastly absurdity of existence, comprehends the symbolism of Ophelia's fate and the wisdom of the wood sprite Silenus: nausea invades him."(BT 52)[65]

Conrad shared this sceptical attitude towards the acquisition of knowledge and was all too aware of the threat which the unbridled scientific impulse of the modern world posed for mankind's emotional and spiritual well-being through "the unveiling of [...] those heartless

64 *Assorted Opinions and Maxims*. With the exception of *The Birth of Tragedy*, all Nietzsche quotations from here onwards are taken from *A Nietzsche Reader*, by R. J. Hollingdale; the number after the initials referring to the section of the book from which the passage is taken rather than to the page number.

65 The 'wisdom of Silenus' holds that "What would be best for [man] is quite beyond [his] grasp; not to have been born, not to *be*, to be *nothing*. But the second best is to die soon."(BT 29)

secrets which are called the Laws of Nature."[66] As he wrote to Cunninghame Graham about the prospect of Singleton with an education,

> Would you seriously tell such a man: `Know thyself. Understand that thou art nothing, less than a shadow, more insignificant than a drop of water in the ocean, more fleeting than the illusion of dream [...] Then he would become conscious - and much smaller - and very unhappy.[67]

Still, for both Conrad and Nietzsche, there were also advantages to be gained from an exposure to the "darkness" because, were the individual to survive his nausea and resist the death-wish, he would have entered into the most fertile ground for artistic creation and be initiated into tragedy. On the theme of tragedy Conrad wrote: "To be part of the animal kingdom under the conditions of this earth is very well - but as soon as you know of your slavery the pain, the anger, the strife - the tragedy begins."[68] This quotation expresses much of the essence of Nietzsche's conception of tragedy as the creative transfiguration of negative experience ("pain", "anger" and "strife" become "tragedy") suggesting, if not direct influence, at least a convergence of opinion between the two writers.

Nietzsche argued that in classical times tragedy arose from the need of man to overcome the knowledge which life afforded him, while for the ancient Greek, "so uniquely susceptible to the subtlest and deepest suffering"(BT 50), it constituted a strategy of survival, a means of holding the darkness at arms length. In "the supreme jeopardy of the will", Nietzsche writes, "art, that sorceress expert in healing approaches him; only she can turn his fits of nausea into imaginations with which it is possible to live."(BT 52) The whole genre is thus conceived as the balance between knowledge and illusion, Dionysos and Apollo: "the Apollonian embodiment of Dionysiac insights"(BT 56-7). The "veil of Maya" in the form of Apollonian art is seen by Nietzsche as a necessary prerequisite for tragedy because it prevents a submission to absurdity which would arise from too much Dionysian knowledge.[69] This theory is particularly useful

---

66 From the Preface to *The Nigger of the Narcissus*, The World's Classics, Oxford University Press, New York: 1984, xliii-iv.

67 *The Collected Letters of Joseph Conrad, Vol. I,* 14/12/1897, p422.

68 *The Collected Letters of Joseph Conrad, Vol. II,* 31/1/1898, p30.

69 The general thrust of my argument here can also be found in Daniel W. Ross, "*Lord Jim* and the Saving Illusion", but that essay remains almost entirely affirmative as regards Jim's

in appraising the career of Jim from nauseated transgressor of the seaman's code to `redeemed' tragic hero in Patusan.

After jumping from the Patna into the same boat as the officers, Jim can be said to feel precisely the "nausea" and jeopardy of the will" which Nietzsche describes in *The Birth of Tragedy*: "I wish I could die"(125), he confesses to Marlow, "I was confoundedly cut up. Sick of life."(140)[70] At the same point in the narrative, the officers begin a verbal commentary on events designed to make their desertion of duty appear more rationally justified than it actually was: "I knew from the first she would go,'`Not a minute too soon,'`A narrow squeak, b'gosh [..] She was gone! Not a doubt of it. Nobody could have helped. They repeated the same words over and over again as though they couldn't stop themselves."(127-28) This impulsive fictionalizing is based on the assumption that the Patna has sunk along with all the pilgrims - an outcome which is regarded by the crew as most "comforting"(142) because it "justifie[s] their haste"(142-43) and makes them appear less cowardly in their own eyes. This same need for rational self-justification also accounts for Jim's mysterious "impulse"(128) to "jump out of the boat and swim out to see - half a mile - more - any distance - to the very spot"(127) where the Patna was supposed to have sunk.

But there is a subtle difference between Jim's need to fictionalize his conduct on the Patna and the rest of the crew's. When they are picked up by the *Aden* and deliver their previously agreed account of the ship-wreck for the eyes of the world, this account is regarded by Jim as wholly unsatisfactory - not because it is untrue, but because it fails to address the one crucial fact of the case for him - his own personal failure: "They made up a story and believed it for all I know. But I knew the truth and I would live it down - alone, with myself [...] `I had jumped - hadn't I?' he asked dismayed. `That's what I had to live down. The story didn't matter."(140-41) Since, "of all mankind, Jim had no dealings but with himself"(293), it is above all his own self-image that he feels the need to restore after the jump, more than his public reputation. Jim's personal sense of inadequacy is also more harrowing to him than the social implications of his crime because, as we have already seen, Jim's reality is essentially subjective and

---

Patusan experiment and illusion in general thus failing to point out the novel's deeply ambivalent and sceptical stance towards both.

70 "It is at moments such as this", writes Tony Tanner, "that Conrad wants to know how a man behaves, how a man should behave, how he can find sanctions and supports to resist the insidious gravitational pull towards the base, beetle-like, irresistible argument that "nothing matters."(p137).

limited to his individual consciousness. This is why the questions he has to answer before the court of inquiry "came to him poignant and silent like the terrible questioning of one's conscience"(63) and even in the `unofficial inquiry', Jim "was not speaking to [Marlow], he was only speaking before"(111) him.

Jim would appear to have some justification then in distinguishing the "truth" of his personal failure from the "story" of the events leading up to the Patna's supposed ship-wreck. Yet on a deeper level, the novel regards this too as a bogus distinction for both the crew's story and Jim's way of explaining the events of the night in question can be seen as a deliberate or unconscious fabrication designed to cover up "the true horror behind the appalling face of things."(65) In *The Birth of Tragedy*, Nietzsche suggested that the "inquiring mind" might be no more than "a clever bulwark erected against the truth, [...] a dodge"(BT 4-5) and Jim's decision on the boat to "face it out [...] find out"(140) turns out to be precisely that for, as Marlow points out, "no man ever understands his own artful dodges to escape from the grim shadow of self-knowledge"(103). This is just as well considering "the grim shadow" is normally associated with death and Marlow's imagery here would seem to support Nietzsche's claim that "to deny false judgements would be to renounce life"(BGE 4). Seen from this perspective Jim's fictional distinction between "the truth" and "that wretched story they made up"(138) is actually life-affirming for, if there were an essential difference between himself and the other officers which did not emerge during the accident, it may yet show itself and redeem him - in his own eyes at least.

Still, these 'fictions' which Jim and the crew construct to justify their actions are in accord with the facts which they observed - even if those `facts' depended on their position and pre-disposition. "As a matter of fact", explains Marlow, "nobody lied; not even the chief engineer with his story of a mast-head light dropping like a match you throw down. Not consciously at least."(142) Thus, we have a perfect example of the inseparability of fact from fiction and the inherent untrustworthiness of appearances which for Schopenhauer constituted the essence of Maya: the world as representation. It is interesting to note that Jim later admits his own interpretation of events was "something like that wretched story they made up. It was not a lie - but it wasn't truth all the same [...] There wasn't the thickness of a piece of paper between the right and wrong of this affair."(138) The metaphor employed is thematically appropriate because "a sheet of paper," is precisely the difference between a page of prose of the kind a novel like *Lord Jim* is comprised of and the meaningless, formless experiences of life which such fictions are intended to impose order and meaning on. "A bit of ass' skin"(162), as Chester calls the seaman's certificate, is another such "sheet of paper" but it represents the difference between Jim's right to the life of the sea, and being "condemned to toil without honour like a costermonger's donkey."(154) The code itself which Marlow and Brierly have based their lives on is even less substantial than "a sheet of paper" because it is just "the name for that kind of decency"(93) and, as Marlow points out in a different context, "from the name to the thing itself is but a step."(189)

Jim has more explaining to do when he realises that the Patna hasn't sunk. He is "partly stunned by the discovery he had made - the discovery about himself - and no doubt was at work trying to explain it away to the only man capable of appreciating all its tremendous magnitude." The significance of this as of every other discovery for the ego-centric Jim is entirely self-referential: he has to account for it to himself because no one else can "appreciate all its tremendous magnitude". As Conrad wrote in "The Return" regarding the fictionalizing tendency in everyday life:

> there is a moment of dumb dismay, and the wanderings must begin again; the painful exploring away of facts the feverish raking up of illusions, the cultivation of a fresh crop of lies in the sweat of one's brow, to sustain life, to make it supportable, to make it fair [71]

This happens to be the best possible description of Jim's struggle back on shore after being picked up by the *Aden*. Jim's theory of a missed opportunity ("What a chance missed! My God! What a chance missed! p104) is an ingenious way of sustaining life since it assumes and reasserts the identity that, in fact, is problematical.

While attending the official inquiry, Jim doesn't speak to anyone, holding instead "silent, incoherent and endless discourse with himself"(67). Yet this inner dialogue is not sufficient to "save from the fire his idea if what his moral identity should be"(103) so Jim needs Marlow as his "ally", "helper", and "accomplice"(111). Marlow helps Jim restore the "veil of Maya" and conceal "the true horror behind the appalling face of things"(65) by acting as his confessor and confidant rather than impartial judge: "I don't want to excuse myself; but I would like to explain", says Jim, "I would like somebody to understand"(103) and Marlow is prepared

---

71 *Tales of Unrest*, p134

to provide such understanding. The compassionate captain suspends his critical judgement in favour of an attitude of sympathetic forbearance for the younger man's vital fictions: "Don't you believe it?" [Jim] inquired with tense curiosity. I was ready to make a solemn declaration of my readiness to believe implicitly anything he thought fit to tell me"(136), replies Marlow. What becomes Marlow's main priority during the `unofficial inquiry' is not to ascertain the objective truth about the Patna affair but to keep Jim alive and for this he must resort to a few deliberate fabrications of his own: "You said you would believe", says Jim, "Of course I do." Marlow protested in a matter of fact tone which produced a calming effect"(139). Previously Marlow has claimed: "I had no intention for the barren sake of truth to rob him of the smallest particle of saving grace that would come in his way"(102).

Jim knows in his heart that he is "responsible"(130) for his desertion yet he cannot live with this knowledge so he tries to find excuses for his actions and, by convincing Marlow, hopes to deceive himself regarding his lapse of nerve on the Patna: "Oh yes, I know very well - I jumped. Certainly, I jumped; but I tell you, they were too much for any man. It was their doing as plainly as if they had reached up with a boat-hook and pulled me over. Can't you see it? You must see it"(134). While Jim portrays himself as the helpless victim of suggestion and circumstance, Marlow acts as self-appointed audience in Jim's fictional reconstruction: "From his relation", remarks Marlow, "I am forced to believe he had not acted but had suffered himself to be handled by the infernal powers who had selected him for the victim of their practical joke."(123) This interpretation is obviously just another way of removing responsibility from himself.

As "an aesthetic phenomenon", wrote Nietzsche, "existence is still endurable to us and through art we are given an eye and hand, and above all a good conscience to enable us to make of ourselves such a phenomenon."(GS 107) This is precisely what Jim attempts to do after his jump so as to render his existence "endurable" once more. By narrating the incident to Marlow, he gains artistic distance from his own acts while, by presenting himself as no more than a role-player in an event conceived by an external intelligence for its own amusement (a "practical joke" of "the infernal powers"), he attains to the feeling, if not the fact, of "innate blamelessness"(101). Life thus becomes associated with and dependent on artistic representation in the novel and for Jim to deliver his redemptive fictions, both before the court and before Marlow, becomes literally a matter of life and death: "He wanted to go on talking for truth's sake, perhaps for his own sake also"(65); "He could no more stop talking now than he could have stopped living by the mere exertion of his will"(117), claims Marlow.

Marlow can indeed be said to approach Jim like art approaching the Apollonian Greek "in the supreme jeopardy of the will"(BT 52) but the captain also has his own reasons for befriending this young dreamer and taking an active interest in his fortunes. Just as Jim needs Marlow to help him restore his heroic illusions by covering up the fact of his failure on the Patna, so Marlow needs Jim to help dispel his doubts regarding the fixed standard of conduct and rekindle those illusions about the life of the sea which he had thought "gone out, extinct"(137). By virtue of his trustworthy and likeable appearance Jim represents for Marlow "all the parentage of his kind": "men and women [...] whose very existence is based upon honest faith, and upon the instinct of courage"(74). But Jim has been "found out" - not so much "in a crime but in a more than criminal weakness" - and there is "nothing more awful" for Marlow because "the knowledge of [Jim's] weakness" resemble "a hint of destructive fate ready for us all"(80). Marlow's interest in Jim is thus based on the need to find "some profound and redeeming cause, some merciful explanation, some convincing shadow of an excuse" for the fact that Jim's base actions have completely belied his virtuous appearance.

Jim represents not only a test case for the validity of the seaman's code when set against the instinct of survival, but also for the whole epistemology of western civilization, "so often concerned with mere surfaces"(286). As Daniel R. Schwarz points out, "Marlow's initial response to Jim, reveals his original epistemology: rational, logical, and deriving from a belief in the value of a few simple notions you must cling to if you want to live decently and die easy."[72] Like the Patna incident for Jim, Jim's case for Marlow stands as a terrifying lifting of the veil and glimpse into the darkness beyond, "like one of those grotesque and distinct visions that scare and fascinate one in a fever"(77). Jim has the disconcerting ability to undermine each one of Marlow's sustaining illusions - from the efficacy of the seaman's code and the reliability of surface appearances to the ability of reason to comprehend life and language to express that understanding.[73] Thus, Jim's life and death struggle to find a path to personal redemption is equalled only by

[72] "The Journey to Patusan: The Education of Jim and Marlow in Conrad's *Lord Jim*" *Studies in the Novel* 4, (Fall 1972: pp442-58) p450.

[73] As Royal Roussel points out, "in the same way Jim experiences the darkness as a shipwreck of the visible world, Marlow experiences it as the destruction of language."(p107).

Marlow's need for Jim to succeed or, alternatively, for his failure to be buried in some sort"(204), it being one of those "reminders of our folly, of or weakness, of our mortality" which "makes against our efficiency"(170) as civilised beings. The restoration of Jim's veil is a necessary precondition, in other words, for the restoration of Marlow's.[74]

From the start Marlow is prepared to entertain Jim's most prized illusions: that he is different from the rest of the crew and that there is more to him than his actions on the Patna might suggest. Describing his first glimpse of the Patna renegades, Marlow remarks: "They chatted together as they strolled and I did not care any more than if they had not been visible to the naked eye. They were nobodies"(77) - the implication being that Jim is a somebody, "one of us". Following Marlow's conversation with Brierly in which the captain of the Ossa challenges Jim's "courage" in attending the official inquiry and Marlow's right to the name of "seaman"(92) all in the same breath, Marlow is quick to defend Jim as though his own honour and credibility were indeed at stake along with Jim's: "I became positive that the inquiry was a severe punishment to that Jim, and that his facing it - practically of his own free will - was a redeeming feature in his abominable case. I hadn't been so sure of it before."(93) The tenuous sub-clause of this sentence ("practically of his own free will") betrays the uncertainty which Marlow is trying to conceal from himself here, while the fact that "he hadn't been so sure" of his position before suggests that Marlow is beginning to reappraise facts in order to re-confirm appearances. In other words, Marlow wants Jim to be "as genuine as a new sovereign"(76)[75] and as promising a boy as the sun ever shone on"(72) so he has to smooth over the contradictions in his own mind before thy can disappear in actuality.

Just as Jim would like Marlow to admit that things are not quite as clear as they appear with his jump, Marlow "can't bring [himself] to admit the finality"(159-60) of Jim's failure and is "always eager to take opinion on it, as though it had not been practically settled" by the official inquiry. These second, third and fourth opinions which Marlow obtains from the chief engineer, Jim, the French Lieutenant and Stein respectively are really no

---

74 Anthony Winner has rightly observed that "Marlow's own dream is involved [...] in Jim's dream."(*Culture and Irony*, p25)

75 Arnold E. Davidson has also made the point that Marlow "wishes to claim at least partial success with Jim, to find him in some saving way, "as genuine as a new sovereign"and not "nothing more rare than brass."("The Abdication of *Lord Jim*", *Conradiana* 13, 1981: 19-34) p30.

more than unconscious attempts to confuse[76] the moral import of a case which, as Marlow himself confesses, is all too clear: "He was guilty - as I had told myself repeatedly, guilty and done for"(154). Nietzsche points out that "Art makes the sight of life bearable by laying over it the veil of unclear thinking"(HA 151), and both Marlow and Jim can be said to be engaged in this sort of equivocation and artistic blurring after Jim's jump:

"I strained my mental eyesight", says Marlow, "only to discover that, as with the complexion of all our actions, the shade of difference was so delicate that it was impossible to say [whether Jim was] shirking his ghost or facing him out."(187) Yet, if the truth is that "it is impossible to lay the ghost of a fact", Jim is doomed to ignominy whatever he does following his desertion and, what is more, Marlow in his heart knows it: "A clean slate, did he say? As if the initial word of our destiny were not graven in imperishable characters upon the face of a rock."(179)[77]

Indeed, the whole community of the sea is likewise engaged as Marlow and Jim "ever since that mysterious cable message came from Aden to start us all cackling."(68-9) Although the fact contained in this is said to be "about as naked and ugly as a fact can well be"(69), Marlow still calls it "mysterious" because it has not yet been fully rationalized, that is to say linguistically appropriated by the community of the sea so that it poses no treat to "the fixed standard of conduct"(80) on which that community is based. This is, after all, the function of the official inquiry, its object being "not the fundamental why, but the superficial how of this affair."(84) As Marlow notes, "Complete strangers would accost each other familiarly, just for the sake of easing their minds on the subject"(69) - an observation which could well be applied to his own interviews with Jim, the chief engineer and the French Lieutenant for, as Nietzsche pointed out, "the man who `communicates' gets free of himself; and he who has `confessed' forgets"(GS 331).

The need to mystify unpleasant realities would partially explain not only Marlow's wish to tell Jim's story to his after-dinner audience of old sailors who are all too willing to "let that Marlow talk"(68) but also Conrad's desire to write *Lord Jim* and even our pleasure in reading it, despite its indirections and obscurities. As Nietzsche perceptively pointed out, "One does not want only to be understood when one writes but just

---

76 "There are many [...] passages", writes Douglas Hewitt, "which give the impression of a man ruminating to obscure the issue than of one thinking to clarify it."(p38).

77 See also Conrad's letter to Marguerite Poradowska; "Each act of life is final, and inevitably produces its consequences despite all the weeping and gnashing of teeth". (*The Collected Letters of Joseph Conrad, Vol. I,* 15/9/91, p95).

as surely not to be understood. It is absolutely no objection to a book if anyone finds it unintelligible: perhaps that was part of the author's intention."(GS 381) Marlow's tragic narrative can thus be said to act as a life-sustaining veil, covering up the darker facts of human experience; the darkest being death, the inevitable ship-wreck awaiting every traveller on the voyage of life, to employ the novel's own metaphor.[78] For, although life requires constant "exertion"(68) and only "the steadfastness of men"(132) can keep the "Dark Powers" from triumphing at any moment...

> it is easy enough to talk of Master Jim [...] on a blessed evening of freshness and starlight that would make the best of us forget we are only on sufferance here and got to pick our way in cross-lights watching every precious minute and every irremediable step, trusting we shall manage yet to go out decently but not so sure of it after all (68).

Just as this sentence is so long that one has forgotten what was said at the beginning by the time one has reached the end, so the novel attempts to conceal its original revelations regarding the precariousness of life and happiness by a lengthy and peripatetic narrative[79] which ends not only in a completely different setting from the white men and sea-ports in which it began but also in the opposite literary genre (romance as opposed to realism).

The difference between Conrad and Marlow is that Marlow is unaware of the deeper function of his own narrative and Conrad exploits this irony to subvert the Socratic ethos of his western narrator[80]: the rule that "no man ever understands quite his own artful dodges to escape from the grim shadow of self-knowledge" (102) applies as much to Marlow as it does to Jim. "I wanted to know"(101), claims Marlow, but when he interviews the delirious chief engineer in hospital in order to obtain "some exorcism

---

[78] The very same metaphor can also be found in *The World as Will and Representation*: "life itself", writes Schopenhauer, "is a sea full of rocks and whirlpools that man avoids with the greatest caution and care, although he knows that [...] at every step he comes nearer to the greatest, the total, the inevitable and irremediable shipwreck [...] namely death"(WWR I 312-13).

[79] "In *Lord Jim*", observes Thomas Moser, "the reader circles and circles the fact of Jim's jump for 111 pages, evading that fact just as Jim tries to evade it"(p42).

[80] As Ian Watt has argued, "Conrad's austere scepticism would probably have rejected the idea that complete self-knowledge is possible in this veil of tears and the question therefore arises whether Jim, or indeed anyone, should be judged and found wanting by standards derived from the unsupported modern dogma that full self-knowledge is possible and that it can deliver us from the ignominious fate of being what we are."(p340).

against the ghost of doubt"(80), he confesses himself "fairly routed"(83) and, before long, is forced to make his escape into the outside gallery. For, what attracts Marlow about the Patna case while simultaneously repelling him (as though he were indeed watching a tragedy in the Aristotelian mould) is not the facts, which can't explain anything"(63), but "the expectation of some essential disclosure as to the strength, the power, the horror of human emotions"(84) - the same reason why "everyone in any way connected to the sea"(68) attends the inquiry.

Marlow also has to retreat "a little cowed"(279), when he attempts to dispel Jewel's irrational doubts regarding Jim's constancy while she stubbornly clings to "incertitude" and "fear" as though they had been "the safeguards of her love"(274). "The winged words of truth"(276) about Jim not being "good enough"(278) to return to white civilization are said to drop at Marlow's feet like lumps of lead"(276) because Jewel simply doesn't believe them. What Marlow needs to make Jim predictable and safe ("he was too much like one of us not to be dangerous", Marlow has said) is not the truth but "a lie too subtle to be found on earth"(276), a fiction that will never be seen through: "an enterprise for a dream" indeed. Since language for Conrad is part of the Apollonian realm of surface illusions and words belong to that "sheltering conception of light and order which is our refuge"(274) against the "darkness", Marlow's desire "to know"(101) the truth about Jim rationally and communicate it through language is no more than a "clever bulwark against the truth [...] a dodge"(BT 5), to use Nietzsche's terms. "I am fated never to see him clearly"(221), remarks Marlow, but this is not as disadvantageous as it may appear because it gives Marlow the possibility of fictionalizing those aspects of Jim which are most mysterious and threatening to the seaman's code and to his civilized assumptions in general.

At first we see Marlow desperately clinging to Jim like a man not wanting to wake up from a reassuring dream in the night. After the "wretched cur" incident, it is Marlow who feels he has made a fool of himself, and failed to say the right thing in a difficult situation, so he rushes after Jim to reaffirm his own faith in "the power of language"(175) in a parody of Jim's earlier demand for `honourable satisfaction': "I was thinking of something to say, but I could find nothing on the spur of the moment, and [...] I said hurriedly that I couldn't dream of leaving him under a false impression of my - of my - I stammered."(98)[81] Later,

---

[81] "Those moments when Marlow approaches closest to the darkness", writes Royal Roussel, "are precisely those moments when speech fails him."(p107) Indeed, as long as the

Marlow will remark: "It was borne upon me suddenly and with unaccountable force that should I let him slip away into the darkness I would never forgive myself."(175) The captain is loathe to lose Jim to the darkness not only because "as soon as he left [his] room, that `bit of shelter', he would [...] begin the journey towards the bottomless pit"(175) but also because Jim pleasurably reminds Marlow of his own lost youth and innocence:

> He was a youngster of the sort you like to see about you; of the sort you like to imagine yourself to have been; of the sort whose appearance claims the fellowship of those illusions you had thought gone out, extinct, cold, and which as if rekindled at the approach of another flame, give a flutter deep, deep down somewhere (137).

The reference to "those illusions you had thought gone out, extinct, cold" links Jim to Apollo[82] "who is etymologically the `lucent' one, the god of light"(BT 21) and indeed, Jim can be said to represent the entire Apollonian realm for Marlow - especially those illusions which, unlike "the sombre contemplation of actuality"(BT 31), beautify life and make it worth living.[83] As Nietzsche claimed, Apollo reigns over "the fair illusion of our inner world of fantasy. The perfection of these states in contrast to our imperfectly understood waking reality [...] furnishes a symbolic analogue [...] to the arts which make life possible and worth living."(BT 21) Marlow might not be able to apprehend Jim rationally but, like a work of

---

misunderstanding lasts, Marlow observes that "To watch [Jim's] face was like watching a darkening sky before a clap of thunder [...] It was blackness without a single gleam."(95-6)

[82] Daniel Ross has made the same observation: "Jim's Apollonian qualities", he writes, "are reinforced by Marlow's frequent associations of him with the sun."(p164). In Patusan "He appeared like a creature not only of another kind but of another essence. Had they not seen him come up in a canoe they might have thought he had descended upon them from the clouds"(211). In the Rajah's court, the Apollonian theme is again evoked by Jim's colour, physical attractiveness and general awe-inspiring effect on the Bugis: "In the midst of these dark-faced men, his stalwart figure in white apparel, the gleaming clusters of his fair hair, seemed to catch all the sunshine that trickled through the cracks in the closed shutters of the dim hall." Jim's sun-like qualities would also explain why Marlow has such difficulties seeing him at times -"My eyes were too dazzled by the glitter of the sea below his feet to see him clearly" - as well as the leitmotif "under a cloud", which recurs for the last time after Jim's death: "And that's the end. He passes away under a cloud."(351)

[83] "Jim stands for our best illusions", remarks Tony Tanner, "those exercises of the imagination which we allow to guide our conduct in order to give it purpose, dignity and, in Conrad's word glamour."(p134). As I argue below, Jim can conversely be associated with darkness and the Dionysian realm.

art, Jim has symbolic significance and a suggestive charm which survives the "condemnation"(74), the "halter" of facts and endears him to the older man: "in the rifts of "the immaterial veil" he would appear to my staring eyes distinct of form and pregnant with vague appeal like a symbolic figure in a picture."(140) This would suggest that the only knowledge which can penetrate "the immaterial veil" without nauseating the knower is that afforded by art, despite the fact that, as Nietzsche points out, "our consciousness of our significance does scarcely exceed the consciousness a painted soldier might have of the battle in which he takes part."(BT 42)

Ironically, this aesthetic consolation which Jim offers Marlow is itself an illusion - like Jim's belief "that age and wisdom can find a remedy against the pain of truth"(138) - and neither can finally keep the darkness at bay which is waiting to engulf Jim like the night waiting to swallow the sun: "the night seemed to wait for him very still, as though he had been marked down for its prey [...] The candle spluttered out, and the thing was over at last, [...] The night swallowed his form."(157) Just as an innocent Jim represents the life-giving light of Apollonian illusion for Marlow and his civilization, so an undeceived and "unconsolable"(175) Jim threatens them with the destructive darkness of Dionysian self-knowledge for Jim is both an object of narcissistic contemplation and a terrible reminder of human mortality and fallibility. Thus, when the various temporary jobs fail to placate Jim's "wounded spirit" or satisfy his "adventurous fancy"(154), the only option left for Marlow is to "bury" Jim in accordance with "the wisdom of life"(170): "The position struck me as hopeless, and poor Brierly's saying recurred to me, `Let him creep twenty feet underground and stay there.' Better this, I thought, than this waiting above ground for the impossible."(190-191)

This must be regarded as a confession of failure on Marlow's part, for whereas he was previously determined to resist Brierly's and Chester's cynical plans in the hope of finding some positive avenue of rehabilitation for Jim, now he is "glad enough to dispose of him in any way"(190) he can. "I don't defend my morality", says Marlow, "There was no morality in the impulse which induced me to lay before him Brierly's plan of evasion - I may call it - in all its primitive simplicity."(155) Ironically, the "evasion" which Marlow is contemplating for Jim has also a personal significance because he is thinking of going home himself and wants a clear consciencewith which to enjoy his domestic pleasures: "you must touch your reward with clean hands", he says, "lest it turn to dead leaves, to thorns, in your grasp."(206) At the time, Marlow claims to want Jim "out of his own way" but later he admits "it may be I desired, more than I was aware of myself, to dispose of him [...] before I left"(206). Like Jim with regard to self-knowledge then, Marlow begins by chasing Jim and ends by running away from him; he begins with the idealistic hope of fostering the light in the young dreamer and is finally content to conceal the darkness at all costs. As Jim himself observes: "this thing must be buried"(182).

Stein, Patusan, and the final disillusionment

With Stein, the artistic solution which the novel has unconsciously espoused as a strategy of survival against the darkness becomes conscious and deliberate. In response to Marlow's inquiries, Stein says, "So if you ask me - how to be? [...] follow the dream and again follow the dream"(200-01) and the dream, as Nietzsche points out, is the one sphere in which "every man proves himself an accomplished artist."(BT 20) Stein himself bears all the hallmarks of the archetypal artist: a one time actor on the stage of life, he has acquired much experience of things and men but knows too much to want to participate any longer in the `play' of life or influence its course. Like some stoic sage or Prospero figure,[84] he is now content to observe the spectacle from a distance and live the life of the spirit where "the might of nature and the seductive corruption of men"(75) cannot obtrude. As befits an artist, he expresses his will and reveals himself through his work, the world-famous collection of butterflies and beetles he intends to bequeath to his small native town when he dies: "So you see me - so,'[...] `Something of me. The best."(193) Like his own Janiform personality as man of action/ man of knowledge, Stein's insect collection, filled with "horrible miniature monsters"(192) and beautiful butterflies, can be seen as a symbol for the balance of opposites in life: "look at the accuracy, the harmony. And so fragile! And so strong! And so exact! This is Nature - the balance of colossal forces [...] the great artist."(195) Implicit in Stein's statement is the idea of art as *mimesis*: that all artists aspire to reproduce the perfect balance which Nature, "the great artist", effortlessly achieves.

Nature may be inherently balanced but man, as Stein points out, is full of contradictions: he wants "in so many different ways to be, [...] He wants to be a saint and he wants to be a devil and every time he shuts his eyes he

[84] Like the sprites attending Prospero, the elderly Javanese servant who shows Marlow to Stein's study is said to vanish "in a mysterious way as though he had been momentarily embodied for that particular service."(192).

sees himself as a very fine fellow - so fine he can never be...In a dream..."(199) Stein's diagnosis suggests that the only way human beings can reach an equilibrium between their inner yearnings and their outer condition is in the realm of fantasy ("In a dream"). Interestingly enough, the very same argument can be found in *The Birth of Tragedy*: "If we could imagine an incarnation of dissonance", writes Nietzsche, "and what is man but that? - that dissonance in order to endure life would need a marvellous illusion to cover it with a veil of beauty"(145). The conflict between man's Apollonian need for beauty and contemplation, and his Dionysian desire for action and experience cannot be resolved except through death ("one thing alone can us from being ourselves cure"); it can only ever be assuaged, covered up, "buried". This is what Marlow has discovered through his own endeavours and the two men proceed to "bury" Jim in Patusan which has been used once before as "a grave"(204) for some dark secret in Stein's past.[85]

The two apparently disparate solutions that Marlow has previously considered to Jim's problem are brought together in Patusan and it becomes both Jim's personal art-world where he establishes order over "people in a book"(235), and an enormous grave where his fallen and dishonoured nature - the "fact"(46) he was originally seen fleeing from - is hidden. Because Jim's "romantic"(199) appeal, like the beautiful but fragile wings of a butterfly, depends on his retaining his youthful innocence, the task facing Marlow and Stein is somehow to take Jim out of the temporal world and arrest him at the height of his splendour, like an insect preserved in a glass case. The timeless and insular world of Patusan serves this purpose while its dream-like, ideal quality constitutes the perfect setting where someone like Jim ("The youngest human being now in existence"p204) can find some measure of success and fulfilment. By placing Jim in Patusan, Stein does that which Conrad considered the prerogative of the artist: "To snatch in a moment of courage from the remorseless rush of time, a passing phase of life" and "to hold up [...] the rescued fragment" - in this case, Jim.[86] In *Lord Jim* this is quite literally "rescue work"(NLL 13) and also coincides with Schopenhauer's image of art as plucking "the object of its contemplation from the remorseless stream of the world's course and hold[ing] it isolated before it."(WWR I 185)

---

85 "It was impossible to suspect Stein"(204), claims Marlow, but it might also be self-defeating for him to doubt the moral rectitude of the last man "eminently suitable"(192) to give advice on Jim's case.

86 See the Preface to *The Nigger of the Narcissus*, xlii.

Patusan too seems to have been "plucked" from the current of life at some point in its history and "the stream of civilization, as if divided on a headland a hundred miles north" is said to branch "east and north-east, leaving its plains and valleys its old trees and its old mankind neglected and isolated"(209). Although it is once said to have attracted considerable attention from some English and Dutch pepper merchants about the time of James the First, "nobody cares for it now, the glory has departed"(210). Patusan's history thus echoes not only Jim's fall from grace in the merchant marine but also Stein's self-sought isolation following his reversal of fortunes at Celebes. Stein once had everything a man could desire: youth, strength, friendship, a woman, a child and even the rare butterfly which he had dreamt of had come into his hand, but, in an instant, "Friend, wife, child, [...] phoo!' The match was blown out"(198). The thing to note here is that, of all life's gifts, only the rare butterfly has remained in Stein's possession. As Richard C. Stevenson points out, "the butterfly acts as an emblem of the ideal for which man strives, an emblem frozen in a timeless moment that both enchants man and reminds him of his own subjection to the world of process."[87] If Patusan, like Stein's insect collection, offers Jim a last "refuge"(212) against the corroding effects of time; it can also be said to reflect the world of art which for Conrad represented the only place where the magic and beauty of life could be preserved from the irresistible march of science and progress. It is appropriately situated "some three hundred miles beyond the end of telegraph cables and mail-boat lines [...where] the haggard utilitarian lies of our civilisation wither and die, to be replaced by pure exercises of imagination, that have the futility, often the charm, [...] of works of art"(251).

Patusan "being situated internally"(221), Jim finds himself in "total and utter isolation"(243) there, and "no externals"(209) can be detected to his successes despite the fact that they afford him "greatness as genuine as any man ever achieved."(223) This suggests that the daring deeds which Jim is said to perform in his new domain are still more the products of imagination than historical fact. But, as we have already seen, far from

[87] "Stein's Prescription for "How to Be" and the Problem of Assessing *Lord Jim*'s Career", *Conradiana Vol.* 7, (1975: 233-43) p236. Jim's ambivalent significance for Marlow is comparable to that of the butterfly in *Lord Jim;* his "last flicker of superb egoism"(349) is the most enduring emblem of his glory in Patusan - just as Stein's prize butterfly is the only remnant from the Celebes phase of his life.

regarding such fictions as lacking in substance,[88] Jim views them as life's "secret truth, its hidden reality"(58). As Conrad claimed in A Personal Record: "Only in men's imagination does every truth find an effective and undeniable existence"(p25) and the subjective quality of Jim's successes (he is called "an obscure conqueror of fame"p351) lends it a "deep hidden truthfulness"(251) which is lacking from a more public achievement such as Brierly's - for all his "inscribed gold chronometers and silver-mounted binoculars".[89]

Patusan's essentially fictive nature would also account for its greater clarity and durability in Marlow's eyes: "like a picture created by fancy on a canvass" it is said to remain "in the memory motionless, unfaded, with its life arrested, in an unchanging light."(286) The advantage of Patusan over the world of white men and sea-ports which Jim has left behind is like that of art over life. As Conrad pointed out, "The demand of the individual to the artist is, in effect, the cry `Take me out of myself!' meaning really, out of my perishable activity into the light of imperishable consciousness"(NLL 13) which recalls Jim's joyful outburst before setting off for Patusan: "I've been dreaming of it...Jove! *Get out of this.*"(my italics) Marlow confirms that Jim's escape in Patusan is as complete as any escape from the world can be: "had Stein arranged to send him to a star of the fifth magnitude the change could not have been greater. He left his earthly failings behind him [...] and there were a totally new set of conditions for his `imaginative faculty' to work upon."(203-4) Indeed, Jim's "imaginative faculty" transforms Patusan into the stuff of the "light holiday literature"(47) he had read as a boy and projects him into his cherished role of "hero in a book"(47).[90]

As Schopenhauer claimed, the object of art is "only the essential, the Idea"(WWR I 185) and in Patusan, besides discovering the essential Jim, Jim also finds idealised love (Jewel); devotion (Tamb Itam); friendship (Dain Waris); leadership (Doramin); and enmity (Cornelius). Indeed, the

---

[88] J. Hillis Miller defines *Lord Jim* as an attempt on Conrad's part to understand the real by way of a long detour through the fictive."(*Fiction and Repetition*, p36).

[89] Elliot B. Gose Jnr. rightly points out that *Lord Jim* addresses itself to the question "where does reality lie: in the objective actual or in the mind; in the conscious orientation to sense data or in the unconscious forms of the creative imagination?" ("Pure Exercises of Imagination: Archetypal Symbolism in *Lord Jim*", *PMLA*, LXXIX, March 1964: 137-47) p140.

[90] "Just as the artist seeks to bring to life the truth of the 'visible universe'," writes Daniel Schwarz, "to discover what is enduring and essential in the objective world, Jim's fantasies and visions shape the raw material of Patusan into a fulfilment of his dreams of conquest, fame, love, sexual fulfilment."(p445) Anthony Winner has claimed also that "the fate [Jim] dreams for himself is in its way parallel to the early modern vision of self-creation: to the idea of selfhood as art in Proust or The Great Gatsby's desire to live out a platonic idea of himself."(p19).

difference between Jim and all these personae is like the difference between the artist and his fictional characters: "they exist as if under an enchanter's wand", observes Marlow, "But the figure round which all these are grouped - that one lives"(287). This recalls Conrad's remarks about the novelist in A Personal Record: "a novelist lives in his work. He stands there, the only reality in an invented world, among imaginary things, happenings, and people. Writing about them he is only writing about himself"(A Familiar Preface, xiii). Like that of the tragic artist, Jim's self-appointed task in Patusan is to reconcile "antagonistic forces"(210) and this "experiment"(213), as Marlow describes it, is to be "his own doing; he was responsible for it and no-one else." Even the skills which bring Jim success in his new sphere seem more suitable for creative writing than trading or social reforming: "He had proved his grasp of the unfamiliar situation; his *intellectual alertness in that field of thought*"(226) (my italics).

Jim's status for the Bugis is something between that of a god[91] and a magician. After the successful storming of Sherif Ali's stockade which establishes him as a force to be reckoned with in Patusanian politics, various myths are constructed around his person in order to explain these remarkable achievements: "there was something occult in all this no doubt for what is the strength of ropes and of men's arms? There is a rebellious soul in things which must be overcome by powerful charms and incantations."(239) Another legend attributes supernatural powers to Jim: "the simple people of the villages [...] believed and said (as the most natural thing in the world) that Jim had carried the guns up the hill on his back - two at a time."(239) "The popular story has it that Jim with a touch of one finger had thrown down the gate."(242) Jim's power seems to stem more from the respect and love he inspires in the hearts of the Bugis than from anything tangible, such as wealth or social status: "his fame was the greatest thing around for many days journey. You would have to paddle, pole, or track a long weary way before you passed beyond the reach of its voice."(244) As is the case with Kurtz in the Congo, this white demigod of Patusan comes across as more of a voice than a flesh-and-blood human being and his word is said to be "the one truth of every passing day."(244) Even the artillery pieces which bring Jim a resounding victory over the

91 The fishing village which is subsequently taken "under that lord's special protection"(222) is greatly disturbed by Jim's first arrival as though having witnessed an epiphany with ominous implications: "The appearance of the being that descended upon them and demanded to be taken to Patusan was discomposing; his insistence was alarming; his generosity more than suspicious."

Sherif and spread his fame throughout the land seem merely to have echoed the true nature of Jim's appeal for the Bugis which is essentially aesthetic: "The sound of his fresh young voice [...] floated lightly, and passed away over the unchanging face of the forests like the sound of the big guns on that cold dewy morning"(242).[92]

Like an artist over his work or a god over his people, Jim wields absolute authority in Patusan:[93] "Jim had the power; in his new sphere there did not seem to be anything that was not his to hold or to give."(245) Rajah Allang, one of Jim's chief rivals in the land, is said to have "owed his life and such authority as he still possessed [...] to Jim's idea of what was fair alone."(244) Jim's power seems to extend even to the movement of the astral bodies over Patusan as though the entire land and everything in it were no more than a series of aesthetic phenomena produced and directed by himself. Showing Marlow the moon rising over the twin hills opposite his house, Jim remarks, "Wonderful effect [...] Worth seeing is it not?' And this question was put was put with a note of personal pride", observes Marlow, "as though he had a hand in regulating that unique spectacle."(205) The same seems to apply to Doramin's court with all its "solemn formality of greetings and leave-takings"(235): "It's well worth seeing', remarks Jim, "They are like people in a book, aren't they?' he said *triumphantly*." (my italics)

Yet despite Jim's successes and the unequalled power he enjoys in his new sphere, all is not well with the fictional world of Patusan and its author: it is not easy being a god - even over "people in a book"(235). To begin with, Jim has the unenviable task of overcoming years of accumulated fear and prejudice which keep the Bugis helpless under the twin subjection of the Rajah and Sherif Ali:

> When he got his idea he had to drive it into reluctant minds, through the bulwarks of fear, of selfishness. He drove it in at last. And that was nothing. He had to devise the means. He devised them - an audacious plan; and his task was only half done. He had to inspire with his own confidence a lot of people who had hidden and absurd reasons to hang back. (235)

---

92 Compare Jim's appeal in Patusan with the appeal of the artist in the Preface to *The Nigger of the Narcissus*: "The artist speaks to our capacity for delight and wonder"(xl), Conrad wrote.

93 Royal Roussel has made the same connection: "Jim's control suggests the absolute power the consciousness of the artist exercises over the world he has brought into being."(p100).

Jim's difficulties in Patusan are comparable to those which confront the aspiring creative artist. As Conrad wrote to Ford Madox Ford, "What creature would be mad enough to take upon himself the task of the creator? [...] braving heaven itself, [..] giving form to an idea, [...] clothing the breath of life with day. How fine and how insane."[94] And the order and harmony which Jim achieves in Patusan come at a high price: this hermetically sealed art-world[95] comes to resemble a stagnant, lifeless, mirror-image of the real world where "events move, men change, light flickers, life flows in a clear stream."(286) The "imperishable light of consciousness" in which art was said to preserve the object of its contemplation is associated with the deathly light of the moon[96] that dominates the landscape in Patusan: "All was silent, all was still; even on the river the moonbeams slept as on a pool [...] vague, grey, silvery forms mingled with black masses of shadow, were like a spectral herd of shapeless creatures pressing forward to drink in a lifeless stream."(224-25) Jim and Jewel resemble "knight and maiden meeting to exchange vows amongst haunted ruins"(273), but "the starlight is good enough for that story" because it serves to conceal the death-like stasis and perfection which is aspired to in the romantic genre.[97] Life may be deeply unsatisfying due to its fleeting, chaotic nature but art, by removing from it the element of unpredictability, can be said to kill the thing it beautifies, just as the rare butterflies and beetles must be dead before they can gain entrance into Stein's prize collection.

Jim is himself trapped in this world he has rescued from the stream of life and captured in his entomologist's net, "Jim the leader was the captive in every sense. The land, the people, the friendship, the love were like the jealous guardians of his body. Every day added a new link to the fetters of that strange freedom."(236) As Jim tells Marlow, "I must go on for ever holding my end to feel sure that nothing can touch me [...] I must stick to their belief in me to feel safe."(289) Thus, Jim may look "with an owner's eye"(225) at the land and the people, "but it was they that possessed him and made him their own to the innermost thought, to the slightest stir, to

---

94 *The Collected Letters of Joseph Conrad, Vol. II*, 23/4/1902, p409.

95 As Daniel R. Schwarz has claimed, "Jim shares with Dorian Gray and Jude Fawley, those other great fictive characters of the 1890's, the dream of hermetically sealing himself in an immutable state unaffected by the vicissitudes of an unknown future."(p446)

96 Elliot B. Gose argues that, after the jump, Jim "switched his allegiance from the temporal world of day alternating with night to a timeless world which Conrad characterizes both as deathly and as eternal."(p139).

97 As Thomas Moser has pointed out, "Conrad dramatizes the idea that man, with his egoistic longing to escape reality, desires [...] irresponsibility, peace, even death itself."(p34).

his last breath."(226) As Marlow points out, in Patusan Jim is "imprisoned within the very freedom of his power"(252).

With power comes responsibility and Jim soon discovers that he has bitten off more than he can chew with the Bugis who "had got into the habit of taking his word for anything and everything"(240). One of the consequences of Jim's legendary victory over Sherif Ali is that he is transformed virtually over-night into a moral and legal authority in Patusan so that he could "settle the deadliest quarrel in the country by crooking his little finger."(241) As Jim explains, the "trouble was to get at the truth of anything. Was not sure to this day that he had been fair to all parties [...] An awful responsibility [...] Rather storm a twenty-foot-high stockade any day", he confesses to Marlow.

This legislative duty which is thrust upon Jim is comparable to the social function of the artist in the post-Darwinian age. As a result of the moral vacuum left in Western culture by the decline in religious faith, the modern artist found himself having to play the role of law-giver and priest for society besides the more traditional one of story teller/entertainer. Yet Jim's history in Patusan suggests that it is very dangerous for a "creature" to play the role of "creator" and for man to try and fill the place traditionally occupied by God in the hearts of men. For, whereas God resides outside the world of "accident, hazard, Fortune"(279), man is very much part of that world and hence no more constant, reliable or imperishable than that which he would reign over. Jim may have the "reputation of invincible, supernatural power"(31) among the Bugis; he may be considered "invulnerable" to harm and the "visible, tangible incarnation of unfailing truth and unfailing victory" but these are only mythical attributes arising from the needs of the community and his own desire to overcome his ignominious past.

As Cornelius suggests, were it not for Jim's good fortune, he would hardly have the ability to "save himself"(284), let alone be "responsible for every life in the land"(335). "He knows nothing, honourable sir", Cornelius tells Marlow, "nothing whatever [...] He throws dust into everybody's eyes [...] He is a big fool, honourable sir"(284). This cynical assessment is lent credence by the mistake which Jim makes in trusting Brown and letting him go. In contrast to the omniscience of God, for mortal men "there is no more reading of hearts than touching the sky with the hand"(334),[98] as Doramin characteristically puts it, so that it is

---

[98] Anthony Winner has also drawn attention to the importance of Jim's limited perspective in Patusan: "Because Jim cannot know", he writes, "Dain Waris and others are killed."(p39).

practically impossible to predict Brown's movements after he is allowed to escape. Anyone may have made the mistake that Jim makes because, as Marlow affirms, there was no reason "to doubt [Brown's] story, whose truth seemed warranted by the rough frankness, by a sort of virile sincerity in accepting the morality and the consequences of his acts." The secular order which Jim's Patusan exemplifies is inherently unstable.

Despite Jim's successful rebirth as Tuan Jim, like the moon rising above the twin hills as though "escaping from a yawning grave in gentle triumph"(205), the memory of his past transgression makes it impossible for him to attain complete satisfaction in his new realm[99]: "What more can I want? If you ask them who is brave - who is true - who is just - who is it they would trust with their lives? - they would say Tuan Jim. And yet they can never know the real truth..."(268) Jim's 'reincarnation' possesses the Karma, as it were, of his previous existence and the arrival of Brown who calls himself "the scourge of God"(317) suggests that his "breach of faith with the community of mankind"(158) has not yet been atoned for. As Jim confesses, "The very world outside is enough to give me a fright because I have not forgotten why I came here. Not yet!"(208) and Marlow shares Jim's apprehensions when recalling the past: "I don't know whether it was exactly fair to him to remember the incident which had given him a new direction to his life, but at that very moment I remembered very distinctly, it was like a shadow in the light."(238)

Patusan's ultimate failure to satisfy Jim and make him forget the stain on his reputation reflects the inability of art to 'mend the clock' of existence by offering man a lasting haven against the consciousness of a flawed and fallen nature. The "experiment"(213) fails and Jim is unable to finally reconcile the "contradictory forces"(210) present both in Patusan and in himself. Interestingly enough, his predicament at this point is presented as an artistic failure - the drying up of inspiration: he tries to write to someone but "the pen had spluttered and that time he gave it up. There's nothing more; he had seen a broad gulf that neither eye nor voice could span. He was overwhelmed by the inexplicable; he was overwhelmed by his own personality"(294). Thus, the "destructive element"(200) of Dionysian knowledge cannot be resisted indefinitely, suggests *Lord Jim* and Patusan reveals itself as no more than "an insignificant islet before the branches of a mighty and devouring

---

99 "More than anyone else", observes Daniel Schwarz, "Jim feels that his accomplishments are apocryphal, that beneath the surface can be found 'the secret truth of his pretences'."(p447).

stream"(209). As Conrad remarked, "Everything is relative" and the realm of art is "merely the most enduring of the things of this earth"(NLL 13).

In accordance with the *coincidentia oppositorum,* where the dream ends, reality begins and in trying to realize his romantic visions, Jim cannot keep his "eyes shut".[100] With Brown's arrival and the massacre of Dain Waris' party, Jim discovers the same coward lurking in his breast,[101] the same failure to foresee every eventuality, the same "joke hatched in hell"(122) which had previously deprived him of his honour and peace of mind. Brown represents Jim's *döppelganger,* the 'secret sharer' of his personality, his Jungian alter-ego which is "the part of the self which the conscious mind seeks to cut off and deny."[102] But, as the image itself suggests, Jim can no more deny his solidarity to Brown than one can run away from one's shadow. Having once encountered the darkness, man cannot return to a state of innocence and Brown's sickening" solicitations to Jim, like those of the Patna's crew, force him to look once more inside himself and acknowledge his kinship with egoism and evil - the necessary concomitants of an earthly existence: "there ran through their conversation, a vein of subtle reference to their common blood [...] a sickening suggestion of common guilt, of secret knowledge that was like a bond of their minds and hearts."(239)[103] The resulting identification and merging of opposites which destroys Jim's position in Patusan is essentially the same which brought about Brierly's downfall, only now it is the former's turn to admit to himself that "men act badly sometimes without being much worse than others"(235).[104]

---

[100] "The irony of [Jim's] story", writes Paul L. Wiley, "lies in the fact that this attempt to transcend the brutality of existence involves him ever more deeply in the trials of a universe offering no support for such a dream."(*Conrad's Measure of Man,* p55) Also H.M. Daleski, echoing this idea, remarks : "it is precisely a man's submission to the destructive element that leads to the opening of the eyes, 'because you cannot always keep your eyes shut' and so to 'real trouble'."(p97).

[101] One of the reasons why Jim lets Brown go is that he was "anxious that some misunderstanding should not occur, ending perhaps in collision and bloodshed."(335).

[102] John Batchelor, *Lord Jim,* p151.

[103] "Gentleman Brown, with his appropriate name", writes C. B. Cox, "acts as a mirror for the dark side of Jim's consciousness, his involvement with the beetles which he has tried to forget."(p43) Then, Wilfred S. Dowden has pointed out that Brown and Jim "are in a sense kindred spirits in that it is supreme egoism which has brought about their downfall."(p70) Elliot B. Gose also links Brown and Jim in this way: "Like Jim's central attribute", he writes, "Brown's evil is 'derived from intense egoism'."(p143).

[104] The originator of the now widely accepted theory of identification between Brown and Jim, is Gustaf Morf, *The Polish Heritage of Joseph Conrad,* (1930). As Daniel Schwarz has also noted, "Once Jim recognises a mirror image in Gentleman Brown, the social fabric that he has woven on Patusan collapses. The world he has internalised in his imagination disappears to be

The truth in Conrad does not bode well for man and is rarely beneficial for life[105] so that the enlightenment and moral coming-of-age which is signalled by Jim's acceptance of the double is shortly followed by his death: "We shall have to fight [...] for our lives"(346), Tamb Itam informs Jim. "I have no life", replies Jim; "Will you fight?" asks Jewel. "There is nothing to fight for"(348), replies Jim. Yet, this "cruel, little awful catastrophe"(283) which finally wrings the truth out of Jim is merely the *coup de grace* to a will already fatally undeceived regarding life's allurements. The fact that Jim mercifully lets Brown go when the outlaw's life is in hands - like the fact that he has patiently tolerated the effrontery of Cornelius and the open enmity of the Rajah when it was within his power to do away with all opposition in Patusan - suggests that towards the end of his life, Jim is beginning to overcome the "*principium individuationis*" which is responsible for the "antagonism of the will with itself"(WWR I 253). Schopenhauer claimed that, "the veil of Maya has become transparent for the person who performs works of love and the deception of the "*principium individuationis*" has left him. Himself he recognizes in every creature, and hence in the sufferer also."(WWR I 373) As Jim says to Marlow regarding his relationship with Jewel, "You take a different view of your existence when you realise it is necessary, absolutely necessary, for another human being."(267) Also, the compassionate identification between Jim and Brown can be said to work as a catalyst on Jim, making conscious a process of maturity and self-discovery which had began with his first glimpse through the veil during the cutter incident.[106]

What is discovered at the end of the novel by Jim and also by those who have placed their trust in him, casts a negative verdict on both life and illusion, corresponding to the pessimistic conclusions drawn by Schopenhauer in *The World as Will and Representation*. "Every error must do harm", writes Schopenhauer, "He who cherishes the individual error must one day atone for it and often pay dearly"(WWR II 68). Yet, it is not only

---

replaced by cosmic emptiness [...] Gentleman Brown undercuts [Jim's] credo in a way which deliberately echoes how Jim affected Marlow, and even more radically, Brierly."(p448).

[105] As Tony Tanner has observed, "truth is always referred to as "painful" or "sinister" in the later Conrad."(p135).

[106] "Paradoxically, it is Jim's imaginative response to Gentleman Brown", claims Schwarz, "that intrudes flux into Jim's aesthetic realm."(p447) Thomas Moser has also claimed that *Lord Jim* enjoins us to "recognise our potential weaknesses, our plague spots, in order to achieve a perceptive moral life."(p24) Yet, it is this very process which, instead of making Jim a more responsible and contented citizen, destroys him and the community he has idealistically sought to help.

Jim who pays dearly for his persistent error, nurtured on the reading of romantic fiction, that it is possible for one to be "always an example of devotion to duty, and as unflinching as a hero in a book."(47)[107] By successfully inspiring the Bugis with this vision of himself to the point where they effectively base their social existence on his idea of what is right and wrong alone, Jim renders Patusan vulnerable to the disaster which overtakes it when the illusion is finally seen through and he goes "to conquer the fatal destiny itself"(346).[108]

The apprehensions which are first felt by the populace when Brown and the Rajah appear to make a pact in Jim's absence are fully realised with the death of Doramin's son: "There would soon be much bloodshed, and thereafter great trouble for many people. The social fabric of orderly, peaceful life, when every man was sure of to-morrow, the edifice raised by Jim's hands, seemed on that evening ready to collapse into a ruin reeking with blood."(319) Jewel, for whom Jim's existence is said to be "absolutely necessary"(267), is similarly abandoned in favour of a "shadowy ideal of conduct"(351) thereby confirming her darkest fears about the constancy of white men and the durability of earthly happiness: "They always leave us,' she murmured. The breath of sad wisdom from the grave which her piety wreathed with flowers seemed to pass in a feint sigh..."(271).

The final lifting of the veil for Jim is signalled by his hitting the shutter after Tamb Itam has awakened him with the news of the massacre: "The room was made light [...] Then Jim understood. He had retreated from one world for the small matter of an impulsive jump, and now the other, the work of his own hands, had fallen in ruins upon his head."(345) Brown's unforeseeable treachery confirms for Jim that what happened on the Patna was no aberration of fate and that, either through adverse fortune or human error, life will destroy the works of man and frustrate his desires."[109] As Schopenhauer wrote, "Whenever a man is struck down by misfortune, [...] or grows angry, or loses heart, he shows in this way that he finds things different from what he expected, and consequently that he laboured under a mistake, did not know the world and life, did not know

---

[107] As Anthony Winner has pointed out, "Jim is no longer alone in his dream. With him are Jewel, Dain Waris, and the entire 'social fabric of orderly, peaceful life, when every man was sure of tomorrow'."(p39).

[108] "Jim makes amends to himself", writes David Daiches, "by going to his certain and useless death in a gesture of purely romantic histrionics."(p32).

[109] As Tony Tanner states, "The horizons Jim dreamed of are unattainable, the heroic deeds he imagined for himself he cannot realize in action, [...] he comes to see an abysmal absence of meaning in the world."(p134-46).

how at every step the will of the individual is crossed and thwarted"(WWR I 88).

Jim decides to "defy the disaster in the only way [...] such a disaster could be defied"(345) and willingly goes to surrender the life he owes to Doramin. Yet, in so doing, he acknowledges the wisdom of Silenus which has run as a pessimistic undercurrent throughout the novel - that the best thing for man "is quite beyond [his] grasp: not to have been born, not to *be*, to be *nothing*. But the second best is to die soon."(BT 29) Through this final desperate gesture it becomes apparent that what Jim has been seeking all along - with his escapist day-dreams as a trainee officer; his self-satisfied aloofness as chief mate of the Patna; his romantic purity as the "white man who protected poor people"(314) in Patusan - is death. "Death is certainly to be regarded as the real aim of life", writes Schopenhauer, it "is the result, the *resume* of life, or the total sum expressing at one stroke all the instruction given by life in detail and in piecemeal, namely that the whole striving [...] was a vain and self-contradictory effort to have returned from which is deliverance."(WWR II 637). "Is he satisfied now, I wonder?"(351), asks Marlow after Jim has been killed, and we would have to reply in the affirmative.

Having presented illusion as "the only possible mode of redemption"(BT 10), the novel finally subscribes to Schopenhauer's conception of tragedy which considers "the greatest misfortune not as an exception, not as something brought about by rare circumstances or by monstrous characters, but as something which arises easily and spontaneously out of the actions of men as something essential to them."(WWR I 254) As Marlow observes, there is "a terrifying logic"(296) discernible in the final events of Jim's life - "something of the sort had to happen" - and the Malay who brings Tamb Itam and Jewel to Stein's house after Jim's death admits to being awe-struck by the "suddenness of men's fate, which hangs over their heads like a cloud charged with thunder"(347). Yet, all that Jim can ostensibly be charged with in Patusan is showing pity and courtesy to a man at the lowest ebb of his fortunes - no more, in fact, than what Marlow has done for him. In having deserted a ship full of people, Jim can be accused of a serious neglect of duty but in trusting Brown's word and letting him go Jim is committing no crime, breaking no bond; nevertheless, he has pledged his life as surety for any harm that comes to Patusan as a result and he proves as good as his word.[110] "The true sense of the tragedy", writes Schopenhauer, "is the deeper insight that what the hero atones for is not his own particular sins, but original sin, in other words, the guilt of existence itself: 'For man's greatest offence/ Is that he has been born,' as Calderon frankly expresses it."(WWR I 254)

Yet, despite Jim's final disillusionment regarding earthly existence, the novel stresses that as long as one is alive, one is always subject to deception and, although Jim has seen through he collective illusions of Maya - that fulfilment is possible, that one can master one's fate, that life is worth our attachment - he is still loathe to give up his personal delusions of grandeur, as is testified by his "last flicker of superb egoism"(349).[111] The grosser "passions of this earth" may indeed have no power over Jim, as Marlow asserts, but he is still "ready to surrender himself faithfully to the claims of his own world of shades."(352) The question then arises, has Jim finally redeemed himself[112] and attained the heroic status he has always aspired to? For Jewel, the victim of his emotional betrayal who pronounces a harsh judgement on that brand of Western idealism which it typifies, the answer must be 'no': "Ah! you are hard, treacherous, without truth, without compassion. What makes you so wicked? Or is it that you are all mad?"(300) The 'privileged reader' also harbours grave doubts regarding the efficacy of Jim's self-sacrifice and his whole role in Patusan. As Marlow reminds him, "You had said [...] giving your life up to [...] all mankind [...] was only endurable and enduring when based on a firm conviction in the truth of ideas racially our own. [...] Without it the

---

110 As Ian Watt has argued, "the code of chivalric honour requires that an adversary be treated with charity and as a human equal [...] When Brown agrees [to leave the coast], and then breaks his word, it isn't Jim who is dishonoured, as he would have been had he gone against his conscience."(p353).

111 Ian Watt has also noted a Schopenhauerian quality in the ending of *Lord Jim*. "Jim's state of mind before going to Doramin", he writes, "is consistent with Schopenhauer's view of the tragic protagonist who eventually refuses to be deceived by "the phenomenon, the veil of Maya" and whose "complete knowledge of the real nature of the world, acting as a quieter of the will, produces resignation, the giving up of not merely life, but of the whole will-to-live itself"."(p350) But, as I argue in the present work, the reappearance of Jim's "exalted egoism" in his last "proud and unflinching glance" suggests that Jim's "knowledge" of the world is still not "complete" and, although he gives up "life", he is still clinging to the "will-to-live". For, Jim is neither wholly undeceived as regards the "phenomenon" of his individuality, nor entirely resigned to "non-willing" as would have been the case had he approached his death with greater humility. As Schopenhauer pointed out, if it is to 'cure' us, "death must be taken with unconcern as is any other medicine."(WWR I 91).

112 Albert Guerard has focused on the same question, claiming that the novel "legitimately asks us to decide whether Jim, still at the call of his "exalted egoism", is really in the clear at this moment: whether he is truly redeemed."(p129).

sacrifice is only forgetfulness, the way of offering no better than the way of perdition."(293) As for the Bugis, some say: "He has worked all the evil"(350); others remark: "He hath taken it upon himself", but for most he remains simply "under a cloud." Yet there can be little doubt that Jim believes he has finally proved his mettle beyond any doubt and joined the ranks of those fearless heroes and adventurers which are the very stuff of legend.[113] For Marlow at least, this is the important thing because Jim, "having no dealings but with himself"(239), is finally true to the only thing he can be true or false to: his own romanticconscience.[114]

Stein's verdict is that Jim was "Not false!", but "True! true! true!"(200) while Marlow, standing up once more "like an evoked ghost, to answer for his eternal constancy", affirms that...

> not in the wildest days of his boyish visions could he have seen the alluring shape of such an extraordinary success! For it may well be that in the short moment of his proud and unflinching glance, he had beheld the face of that opportunity which, like an Eastern bride had come veiled to his side. (351)

This reference to Jim's veiled opportunity is ironical in the extreme because the complete lifting of the veil which accompanies death, rather than revealing to Jim the desirability of life - what Marlow assumes is the Eastern bride's beautiful face - would have disclosed instead Schopenhauer's "nothing" (WWR I 411), the total disillusionment/ enlightenment which, for Conrad too, was man's final reward.

Thus, adapting Schopenhauer's philosophy to the ending of *Lord Jim,* we can say that anyone who tries to assess Jim's career must necessarily pronounce a partial verdict because, being still alive, their eyes remain "clouded [...] by the veil of Maya"(WWR I 352). Viewed from this perspective, Marlow's affirmations of Jim's "constancy"(351) and "greatness"(209) can be read as part of the 'artistic solution' which he has consistently applied throughout the novel,[115] while Stein's vindication of

---

113 "Perhaps at last Jim felt himself metamorphosed into a hero", suggests C. B. Cox (p43). Conversely, Wilfred S. Dowden has stated that Jim's death "perhaps would have been to him an 'extraordinary [private] success' but in reality is a public failure."(p70).

114 Marlow is [finally] concerned with responding to Jim's psychic needs and understanding his consciousness, rather than with measuring Jim by fixed standards shared by the community", observes Daniel Schwarz, (p457).

115 J. E. Tanner makes the important point that "Marlow's remarks [...] reveal - or ought to reveal - more about the nature of his own involvement with Jim than about the nature of Jim's death."("The Chronology and Enigmatic Ending of *Lord Jim*", *NCF* 21, 1967: 369-80) p370.

Jim's submission to the dream - his own formula for "How to be" - can be regarded as self-justifying to a large degree. Marlow himself has claimed that "the last word"(208) about Jim "is not said - probably shall never be said" and "there will be no message, unless such as each of us can interpret for himself"(293).[116] As Conrad wrote to Marguerite Poradowska, "The Creator knows his creatures. We others raise a corner of the veil and look at the denizens of his imagination through the fog of our faults, or disappointments, and our regrets."[117]

---

116 "What we as readers are likely to think of [...] Jim as a person", suggests Albert Guerard, "will depend partly on the persons we are."(p145).

117 *The Collected Letters of Joseph Conrad, Vol. I,* 2/2/1894, p148.

2

Heart of Darkness: "Will" and Wilderness

The emergence of the darkness: uncovering the "will"

Whereas in *Lord Jim* the appearance of the darkness coincided with a momentary lifting of "the veil of Maya" which, for the most part, stood firmly in place, in *Heart of Darkness* the Dionysian element comes menacingly to the fore. Like the mist on the Essex marshes, "draping the low shores in diaphanous folds"(28),[118] the Apollonian illusions of Marlow's civilization have become transparent and can barely conceal the suffering and horror of life. With the death of Jim "who seemed to catch all the light left in a darkened world"(LJ 291), humanity seems to have lost its last spark of idealism and to be plunged in an all-pervasive gloom. This is reflected in the melancholy mood of the passengers on the Yawl who "exchanged a few words lazily" but "felt meditative and fit for nothing but placid staring." The novel begins with the same image which attended Jim's last moments in Patusan - a blood-red sunset symbolizing the death of God in the hearts of men and the approach of the night of nihilism and despair: "the sun sank low and from glowing white changed to a dull red without rays and without heat, as if about to go out suddenly, stricken to death by the touch of that gloom brooding over a crowd of men". Just as in Nietzsche's *The Gay Science* it is European culture as a whole which is deemed responsible for `killing' God through scepticism, so in Conrad's passage it is the "gloom brooding"[119] over the passengers on the *Nellie* which seems to have mortally wounded the sun, immersing the world in darkness.

Heart of Darkness reflects the post-Darwinian idea that at the heart of man is not a metaphysical soul but a blind and instinctive natural force, the object of which is to maintain the individual in life at all costs.[120] This ironic reversal echoes Schopenhauer's translation of Kant's essentially moral "thing-in-

---

[118] All quotations from the novel refer to the Penguin Twentieth Century Classics, *Heart of Darkness*, edited with an introduction by Paul O'Prey, 1989.

[119] "One obvious reason for this pessimism", writes Cedric Watts, "was the decline of religious belief as a consequence of the rising prestige of science and the resultant growth of the sense of loss." (*A Preface to Conrad*, p51)

[120] "In Conrad", observes Cedric Watts, "there is a keen post-Darwinian sense that man and his struggles are but part of a Nature, red in tooth and claw."(Ibid., p50)

itself" into the amoral and savage "will".[121] The jungles of the Congo can be seen as a metaphor for a society where men have been reduced to beasts through the loss of that ethical and rational order which their religious beliefs used to provide. What becomes important in this "God-forsaken wilderness"(40) is not "moral ideas of some sort" but self-preservation and profit.[122] When Marlow asks one of his flabby white companions what he meant by coming to Africa at all, he is told, as the most natural thing in the world: "To make money of course. What do you think?"(48) In such an environment it might even be an advantage not to have any moral or intellectual `content' which might render one vulnerable to `corruption' from within. As the irrepressible but vacant manager of the central station claims, "Men who come out here should have no entrails.' He sealed the utterance with that smile of his, as though it had been a door opening into a darkness he had in his keeping."(51), observes Marlow.

Instead of being set apart from the rest of creation through the possession of a soul, human beings are now intimately allied to the wilderness of life through a dark primeval force, comparable to Schopenhauer's "will", which constitutes the hidden essence of both nature and man. Like the explored Congo in contrast to the uncharted region on the map of Africa, man's centre has "ceased to be a blank space of delightful mystery - a white patch for a boy to gloriously dream over. It had become a place of darkness."(33) Echoing the transcendent nature of the "will", the darkness is presented as both universal and beyond the direct apprehension of the senses so that it often takes the form of an inner vacuum or absence.[123] The manager makes one suspect that there was "nothing within him"(50) while the brickmaker gives Marlow the impression that he "could poke [his] forefinger through him and would find nothing inside but a little loose dirt, maybe."(56) The Cartesian duality of body and soul which used to underpin Western thought is thus replaced by a conception of life as a phenomenon entirely physical, albeit incorporating an abstract "will-to-live" which has nothing spiritual about it. As Nietzsche pointed out, "the thing in itself [...] *appeared* to be so

---

121 For a fuller discussion of this theme, see Linda M. Hall's Introduction to *The Theme of the Outcast*, p9.

122 As Cedric Watts points out, "If one is brought up to believe that the existence of God makes moral sense of the universe and gives a happy ending (regeneration in Paradise) to all virtuous lives on earth, then the loss or absence of faith may entail a grim awareness that the universe is no longer man's homeland but a ruthlessly amoral territory on which man, with his ideals, sensitivities and aspirations is an intruder."(Ibid., p51)

123 "The chief contradiction of *Heart of Darkness*," writes Albert Guerard, "is that it dramatizes evil as an active energy [...] but defines evil as vacancy."(*Conrad the Novelist*, p244)

much, indeed everything and is actually empty, that is to say empty of meaning."(HA 16)

As life loses the meaning it was once thought to possess, so surface appearances are deprived of support and come more and more to be viewed as hollow and deceptive masks. In *Heart of Darknes* all the ennobling and virtuous aspects of man are regarded as mere illusions, beautifying "rags that would fly off at the first good shake."(69) Besides a "universal genius"(115), Kurtz was supposed to be "an emissary of pity, and science, and progress"(55) - some of the best things which civilization has to offer. For Marlow he personifies the divine gift of *logos* which more than any other attribute was thought to distinguish men from animals: "of all his gifts", observes the captain, "the one that stood out pre-eminently, that carried with it a sense of real presence, was his ability to talk"(83) Yet, when he is "assaulted by the powers of darkness"(85) and needs to show a little "restraint in the gratification of his various lusts"(97), none could be found "under his magnificent eloquence" and he succumbs.[124] When Marlow first perceives Kurtz's enormous ascendancy amongst the savages, he exclaims: "Let us hope that the man who can talk so well of love in general will find some particular reason to spare us"(99). The case of Fersleven is another example of the superficiality of human virtue and its inability to combat what the novel regards as a profound viciousness at the heart of man. "Fersleven was the gentlest, quietest creature that ever walked on two legs", observes Marlow, "but he had been a couple of years already out there engaged in the noble cause, you know, and he probably felt the need at last of asserting his self-respect in some way. Therefore he whacked the old nigger mercilessly."(34) The "noble cause" referred to above doesn't seem to accord well with the basic impulses of even the "gentlest" and "quietest" of men.[125]

The collection of middle-class professional types which constitute Marlow's audience on the *Nellie* are also meant to represent some of the best products of European civilization. We have the grand Director of Companies "who resembled a pilot, which to a seaman is trustworthiness personified."(27) There is also a Lawyer - "the best of old fellows" who "had, because of his many years and many virtues, the only cushion on deck"(28). Marlow meets the same basic types in the Congo but with the darkness as

---

124 As Jacques Berthoud remarks, "for all Kurtz's [gifts], he had proved incapable of restraint, and thus of fidelity to the values he has professed."(*The Major Phase*, p57)

125 The "evolutionary view", writes Jacques Berthoud, "holds that civilization is something merely imposed on man's essential nature - that culture does not eradicate, but merely keeps in check his primitive instincts."(Ibid., p60)

back-drop, their respectable exteriors resemble an empty facade. The accountant may have retained "his collars, his vast cuffs, his brushed hair"(46) but that cannot conceal the fact that he has lost the essence of his humanity. Regarding the dying invalids groaning in his room, he remarks: "When one has got to make correct entries, one comes to hate those savages - hate them to the death."(47) The manager of the Central Station claims to be "very, very uneasy"(51) about the state of Kurtz' health, "the best agent he had", and goes to great lengths to show Marlow his eagerness to rescue him; but his real reasons for travelling to the Inner Station are quite different: "Save me!", exclaims Kurtz, "save the ivory, you mean."(102)[126] As Schopenhauer observed, "Our civilized world is [...] only a great masquerade. One meets with knights, parsons, soldiers, doctors, advocates, priests, philosophers, and what not! But they are not what they represent themselves: they are mere masks under which are hidden as a rule money makers."[127]

Heart of Darkness moves from the mask to the reality and this is reflected in the form which the narrative takes. Just as it begins with the evocation of the "great knights-errant of the sea"(29) and arrives at the ego-mania of the depraved Kurtz so we move from the frame narrator's superficial realism at the beginning to Marlow's expressionistic rendering of "the African nightmare feeling".[128] In contrast to *Lord Jim* where the narrative oscillates continually between light and darkness, the "phenomenon" and the "thing in itself", *Heart of Darkness* takes the form of a very gradual lifting and lowering of the veil. In moving from the river Thames to the Congo and then back to the Thames, Marlow is moving from the surface of life to the centre and back to the surface again. Nevertheless, there are two distinct instances in which the veil image is used as it was in *Lord Jim*. In the first instance Marlow sees the forest alive with moving natives as though it were one living being - an image which points to the deep affinity between nature and man: "suddenly, as though a veil had been removed from my eyes, I made out deep in the tangled gloom, naked breasts, arms, legs, glaring eyes, - the bush was swarming with human limbs in movement"(80). In the second instance it is the natural "will" at the heart of man which is revealed in the face of the dying Kurtz, signifying Marlow's arrival at the darkest point of his journey: "It was as though a veil had been rent. I saw on that ivory face

126 As Jacques Berthoud points out, "the rescue attempt, a task with which Marlow has been professionally entrusted and from which he had derived a modicum of self-respect, has proved itself from beginning to end a cynical masquerade."(Ibid., p51)

127 *Selected Essays*, p206.

128 *Collected Letters Vol. I*, to William Blackwood, 8/2/1899.

the expression of sombre pride, of ruthless power, of craven terror - of an intense and hopeless despair."(111) The "ruthless power" and "hopeless despair" seen simultaneously on Kurtz' face reflects the two aspects of Schopenhauer's "will to live" which, "failing to recognize itself, here in one individual enjoys fleeting and delusive pleasures, and there in another individual suffers [...] for these in return"(WWR I 373).

Nietzsche also placed the "will" behind all natural phenomena but for him it was not simply a "will to live" but a "will to power" striving always for self-aggrandizement and expansion rather than mere self-preservation. Nevertheless, both philosophers would have agreed that the violent excesses of nineteenth century colonialism depicted in the novel reveal human beings stripped of their ethical and cultural drapery and thus paint a true picture of life. "Exploitation", writes Nietzsche, "does not pertain to a corrupt or imperfect or primitive society, it pertains to the *essence* of the living thing as a fundamental organic function, it is a consequence of the intrinsic will to power which is precisely the will to life."(BGE 259) Seen in this light, Kurtz appears less of a degenerate, an aberration of nature, and more an exemplar of the "will" as the driving force behind the activities of man. His atavistic regression in the forests of Africa threatens to undermine completely the progressive, scientific and commercial myths with which colonialism in particular and Western civilization in general justifies itself. "Evidently the appetite for ivory had got the better" of his "less material aspirations"(96), observes Marlow. As for furthering the cause of knowledge, the harlequin affirms that Kurtz had indeed discovered lots of villages and even a lake "but mostly his expeditions had been for ivory."(94) "But he had no goods to trade with by that time," objects Marlow. "There's a good lot of cartridges left even yet," replies the harlequin.

As Nietzsche had written, "life is *essentially* appropriation, injury, overpowering of the strange and weaker, suppression, severity, imposition of one's forms and, at the least and mildest, exploitation."(BGE 259) Thus, if this is the case, Marlow is not just discovering the truth about colonialism in going to Africa, but also the truth about himself and life in general. "I felt as though, instead of going to the centre of a continent, I were about to set off for the centre of the earth"(39), he remarks. This journey will involve a gradual stripping away of cultural and temporal layers which have separated man from nature; civilization from savagery; London from the Congo. He compares travelling up the Congo river and encountering the dancing savages on its banks to "travelling back to the earliest beginnings of the world"(66) and meeting "prehistoric man"(68).[129] Yet, he does not regard their howling and leaping and "horrid"(69) grimacing as the expression of something essentially "inhuman": "What was there after all?", he asks himself, "Joy, fear, sorrow, devotion, valour, rage [...] but truth - truth stripped of its cloak of time." Marlow's recognition of his "remote kinship to [the] wild and passionate uproar" of the savages is closely related to the Roman commander's "fascination of the abomination"(31) which has formed an integral part of the colonizing impulse since the beginnings of civilization.

In a parody of Fersleven's and Kurtz' regression, Marlow himself begins to act impulsively after seeing the seductive Congo river on the map - "The snake had charmed me"(33), he recalls. As soon as he gets the idea of captaining a steamer for one of the European companies trading on the river we detect in him a lowering of the moral sensibilities and a rather different Marlow emerges from the restrained scrupulous individual we have been accustomed to expect. First he applies to his relatives on the continent to get him an appointment: "This was already a fresh departure for me", he admits, "I was not used to get things in that way [...] but then - you see - I felt I must get there by hook or by crook."(33) When the men fail to come up with anything, Marlow is shocked to recall that he went as far as to enlist female assistance: "Would you believe it? I tried the women, I, Charlie Marlow set the woman to work - to get a job. Heavens! Well, you see, the notion drove me."(34) Having arrived in the Congo, Marlow finds it increasingly difficult to control his nerves and remembers the doctor back in Brussels: "I felt I was becoming scientifically interesting"(49), he admits. The behaviour of the company agents irritates him intensely and, during his first meeting with the manager, he forgets his manners and interrupts twice: "Being hungry, you know, and kept on my feet too, I was getting savage"(51), he explains.

The closer Marlow gets to the centre of Africa, the more the latent "darkness" within his own personality comes to the surface. When his helmsman is wounded by a spear and Marlow's shoes are soaked in blood, panic seizes him and he lets go of the steering wheel signifying the surrender of conscious control: "I was morbidly anxious to change my shoes and socks", he admits[130]. Marlow's fear of death, implied in this scene, is one of the many forms which the "darkness" can take but there are also times when

---

[129] "A journey into the jungle", writes Jacques Berthoud, "can be seen as a descent into man's history, a return to his primordial origins."(Ibid., p43)

[130] As Albert Guerard has claimed, this "obscure human act [...] unites several interpretations beginning with the simple washing away of guilt. The fear of the blood may be however, a fear of the savage, not the civilized-rational. In any event it seems plausible," he concludes, "to have blood at this stage in a true initiation story."(*Conrad the Novelist*, p246)

this instinctive energy can actually prove useful. In a scene which recalls a hunter stalking his prey, Marlow exploits the latent power of the "will" to track down the invalid Kurtz at night and carry him back to the steamer single-handedly:

> I was strangely cocksure of everything that night. I actually left the track and ran a wide semi-circle (I very believe chuckling to myself) so as to get in front of that stir of motion I had seen - If I had seen anything. I was circumventing Kurtz as if it had been a boyish game. (106)

It is interesting that Marlow should call this deadly serious operation a "boyish game" because stalking prey can be said to constitute one of the earliest experiences of the human species and Marlow seems to be falling back here on a skill genetically acquired - relying on his 'collective subconscious', to use Jung's term. As Linda M. Hall has written: "What the rational individual is unaware of is that he is prompted and impelled to action by a totally non-rational impulse, which because it lies deeper than consciousness is beyond control."[131]

Colonialism and the civilizing impulse

Just as Marlow is unaware, before he goes to the Congo, of the primeval, irrational forces which motivate his personality, so the white "gang of virtue"(55) is under the misconception that it can bring the light of civilization to the jungles of Africa and transform all the natives into useful, disciplined Europeans. But, as Kurtz's painting of the blind-folded Europe bearing the torch into the wilderness suggests, all that the upholders of progress will succeed in doing in Africa is illuminate their own inner "darkness": the background on the painting remains "sombre - almost black"(54), yet "the effect of the torch-light on the face was sinister", observes Marlow.[132] *Heart of Darkness* suggests that not only are the forces of

---

[131] Introduction to *The Theme of the Outcast*, p13.

[132] Suresh Raval has pointed out that "if this [...] renders questionable Kurtz's status as an emissary of light and hope, it also discloses the problematical nature of the very idea of enlightenment."(*The Art of Failure*, p29) Cedric Watts, referring to the Faustian theme in the novel has also pointed out that "Conrad's tale has a strong and heavily ironic theme of light bearers heading into darkness."(*The Deceptive Text*, p78)

civilization and progress weaker than the "darkness" they are attempting to overcome but that the civilizing impulse itself may be no more than a sublimation of the same instinctive force it is pitting itself against.[133] Marlow's aunt talks about the company "weaning those ignorant millions from their horrid ways"(39) but even if this can be regarded as one of the goals of colonialism, it is fraught with contradictions. As Nietzsche pointed out, "*every* means hitherto employed with the intention of making mankind moral has been thoroughly immoral."(*The Twilight of the Idols*)

Thus, in trying to `civilize' the Congo natives, the Europeans are paradoxically resorting to the most savage of methods. When one of the company's store-rooms catches fire, the whites blame a negro and proceed to beat him to within inches of his life: "What a row that brute makes!", remarks one agent, "Serve him right", replies another, "This will prevent all conflagrations for the future." And a few moments later this same moralist reveals a rather different attitude towards the fire and the commotion it has caused in the night: "it's so natural. Ha! Danger - agitation." One of the more obese and unfit company agents who had to be carried everywhere in a hammock slung under a pole by a group of Negroes is abandoned at one point by his carriers in the bush: "The heavy pole had skinned his poor nose"(49) relates Marlow, "He was very anxious for me to kill somebody." It doesn't even strike this `specimen' of civilization that, not only is he morally in the wrong but that the punishment he is proposing far exceeds the crime that was supposed to have been committed at his expense - both in severity and wickedness. As Nietzsche pointed out, "the wild beast has not been slain at all, it lives, it flourishes, it has only been transfigured"(BGE 229) and this is clearly borne out by the behaviour of the Europeans in Africa.

Conrad wrote that there is "an implacable menace of death in the triumph of the humanitarian idea" and indeed, the natives of the Congo are being killed in the process of being `improved'. Shortly after landing on shore, Marlow sees a chain-gang of Negroes, the "raw matter"(43) of the civilizing process, which nevertheless don't seem to be obtaining much benefit from their `improving' experience. "All their meagre breasts panted together the violently dilated nostrils quivered, the eyes stared stonily uphill. They passed me within six inches without a glance, with that complete, deathlike indifference of unhappy savages." A little further on Marlow has the chance to observe at first hand the real `end-product' of the "work"

---

[133] "Since mind", writes Royal Roussel, "must draw its strength from the very force which contests its domination , it would seem that it would be impossible for mind ever to defeat this source. It would always lose in such a context. If this is true, then to attempt to subjugate this source is to invite inevitable destruction."(*The Metaphysics of Darkness*, p21)

which the Europeans are carrying out in Africa: "The work was going on. The work! And this was the place where some of the helpers had withdrawn to die [...] They were not enemies, they were not criminals, they were nothing earthly now - nothing but black shadows of disease and starvation"(44). Further on still, Marlow meets a man who claimed to be "looking after the upkeep of the road"(48). "Can't say I saw any road or any upkeep", declares Marlow, "unless the body of a middle-aged negro with a bullet hole in the forehead may be considered a permanent improvement"(48). The whole philosophy of colonialism is summed up in the famous post-scriptum of Kurtz's report to the International Society for the Suppression of Savage Customs: "Exterminate all the brutes!"(87)

Even in the rare instances where the Negroes survive their `improvement', any change is purely temporary and doesn't stand up to the test of the darkness which makes all "principles" appear like "Acquisitions, clothes, pretty rags [...] that would fly off at the first good shake."(69) The case of the chain-gang driver can be seen as a model for human progress in general and the superficiality of the changes brought about by civilization:

> Behind the raw matter one of the reclaimed, the product of the new forces at work, strolled despondently carrying a rifle by its middle. He had a uniform jacket with one button off, and seeing a white man on the path hoisted his weapon to his shoulder with alacrity (43).

It is clear that the only tangible difference between this "reclaimed" piece of wilderness and the other men in the chain-gang begins and ends with the military paraphernalia in his possession. Had Marlow not been passing by, this "product of the new forces at work" would have continued holding his rifle from the middle like a more elaborate spear. Another such 'improved' individual is Marlow's helmsman who "steered with no end of a swagger while you were by but if he lost sight of you, he [...] would let that cripple of a steamer get the upper hand of him in a minute."(79) When the steamer is attacked near Kurtz's station the entire native crew who he has taken great pains to instruct submit at once to their natural instincts and, like Jim on the *Patna,* abandon their posts: "I saw my poleman give up the business suddenly", recalls Marlow, "and stretch himself flat on the deck without even taking the trouble to haul his pole in. At the same time the fireman [...] sat abruptly before his furnace and ducked his head."(86) As Schopenhauer argued, "no system of ethics which would mould and improve the will is possible. For all teaching affects only *knowledge,* and knowledge never determines the will itself, in other words, the *fundamental character* of willing, but merely its application to the circumstances in question."(WWR II 223).

The folly of man's attempts to subjugate nature when he is no more than a sum of natural forces himself, taking his cue from wholly natural impulses, is clearly apparent in the attempts of the colonizers to conquer and mould in their own likeness the continent and people of Africa. Not only are the Europeans visibly weaker and less well adapted to the tropical environment than the natives, but they have lost all the power and incisiveness of the natural "will" as a result of their cultural 'over-refinement' - something which is regarded by the novel as a symptom of degeneration. As Nietzsche pointed out, "The disease of the will [....] is worst and most varied where civilization has longest prevailed"(BGE 145). Marlow has seen men driven by "violence", "greed" or "hot desire" but the colonial enterprise seems to him to be driven by "a flabby, pretending, weak-eyed devil of a rapacious and pitiless folly."(43) This also emerges from the description of the French man-of-war firing randomly into the bush as though trying to conquer the continent single-handed and take the wilderness prisoner by force of arms: "Pop, would go one of the six-inch guns; a small flame would dart and vanish, a little white smoke would disappear, a tiny projectile would give a feeble screech - and nothing happened. Nothing could happen."(41) The railway-building "work" which the colonizers are supposed to be engaged in is characterized by a similar absurdity and incomprehensibility: "A heavy and dull detonation shook the ground, a puff of smoke came out of the cliff, and that was all. No change appeared on the face of the rock."(42) The implication here is that man, especially when he has been long alienated from nature, stands as much chance of making an impression on Nature as this purposeless blasting has of changing the face of the rock.[134]

Heart of Darkness shows that, just as `civilized' man cannot hope to alter in essentials either nature or his fellow man, so the transformation he has achieved in himself is subject to erosion from within at any moment.[135] As Schopenhauer pointed out:

> Man is at bottom a wild horrible creature. We know him as merely broken in and tamed by civilization and hence the occasional outbreaks of his nature shock us. But where and when

[134] As Royal Roussel has pointed out, "Even man's apparently self-contained reason must maintain its roots in emotion and sensation in order to survive."(*The Metaphysics of Darkness*, p9)

[135] As Jacques Berthoud observes, *Heart of Darkness* "can be considered as an inquiry into how strong the hold of civilization is on its members."(*The Major Phase*, p45)

> the padlock and chain of legal order fall off and anarchy enters, then he shows himself for what he is. [136]

This is certainly revealed in the portrayal of the colonizers who in many respects behave more savagely in Africa where "there were no external restraints"(50-51) than the worst so-called `savages' they come across. The cannibals on Marlow's steamer, for example, exhibit remarkable self-restraint in not `tucking into' the pilgrims who, in stark contrast, reveal surprising depths of sadism. After the attack by Kurtz's followers, one of the pilgrims remarks to Marlow: "We must have made a glorious slaughter of them in the bush. Eh? What do you say?' He positively danced the bloodthirsty little gingery beggar"(89), observes Marlow. The manager also finds in the relatively lawless Congo an environment which allows his congenital power-lust and material aspirations a virtually free rein: "We will not be free from unfair competition till one of these [independent traders] is hanged for an example"(64), he tells his nephew. "Certainly,' grunted the other; [...] Anything can be done in this country."

The regression of the colonizers in the jungles of Africa suggests that their own society has merely held in check an innate viciousness which surfaces all the more powerfully when those long-standing legal and cultural restraints have been removed. As Schopenhauer argued, "human society only exists through the force of hatred, anger or fear. For the ferocity of our nature would probably make every one a murderer at once were it not mingled with the necessary dose of fear to hold it within bounds."(*Selected Essays*, p211) *Heart of Darkness* implies that the potential to become like Kurtz is present in all 'civilized' men for his complete abandon to every form of savagery and lust has clearly come about as a result of his total estrangement from everything that constitutes civilized society. How could we imagine, says Marlow,...

> what particular region of the first ages a man's untrammelled feet may take him into by way of solitude - utter solitude without a policeman - by way of silence - utter silence where no warning voice of a kind neighbour can be heard whispering of public opinion? These little things make all the great difference. (85)

Self-restraint has not been so cultivated in the society which produced Kurtz and this is one reason why, instead of converting the so-called savages to

---

136 *Selected Essays*, p207.

civilization, he ends up indulging in their practices himself, finally taking "a high seat amongst the devils of the land"(85). As Marlow points out, the heads stuck on poles around Kurtz' camp showed that "Mr Kurtz lacked restraint in the gratification of his various lusts"(97).

Just as all morality was regarded by Schopenhauer as "directly opposed to the natural will, which in itself is absolutely egoistic"(WWR II 215), so reason is seen in *Heart of Darkness* as incapable of grasping the essential nature of the "will". Marlow's attempts to impose some order and meaning on his Congo experience echoes the European project of civilizing the dark places of the earth and can be seen as a form of linguistic colonialism. But the deeper he penetrates to the "heart of darkness"(68), as he calls it, the more he discovers that his rational and linguistic tools are ineffectual there. He first compares the experience to watching a nightmare: "the general sense of vague and oppressive wonder grew upon me. It was like a weary pilgrimage amongst hints for nightmares."(41) But rather than increasing in frequency, these "hints" which might have provided some answer to the riddle of the darkness become more scarce until Marlow is forced to admit in Socratic fashion that the only thing he knows about this new environment is that he knows nothing: "We were cut off from the comprehension of our surroundings [...] We could not understand because we were too far and could not remember because we were travelling in the night of first ages, of those ages that are gone, leaving hardly a sign and no memories."(69)[137]

This failure of Marlow's to shed light on the darkness results in language which is more evocative than descriptive but it would be wrong, as some critics have done, to attribute this to an imaginative failure on Conrad 's part or some perverse tendency towards mystification.[138] What Conrad is attempting to convey by such phrases as "It was the stillness of an implacable force brooding over an inscrutable intention"(66) is the unknowability of the "will" as "thing-in-itself" rather than as mere "phenomenon". As Schopenhauer pointed out:

---

[137] Daniel R. Schwarz has opined that "Marlow's probing mind cannot impose an interpretation on Kurtz."(*From Almayer's Folly to Under Western Eyes*, p63)

[138] See F.R. Leavis' famous attack on *Heart of Darkness*'s "adjectival insistence" in *The Great Tradition*. Albert Guerard, on the other hand, defends Conrad saying, "The unspeakable rites and unspeakable secrets become wearisome, but the fact - at once literary and psychological is that they must remain *unspoken*. A confrontation with such a double and facet of the unconscious cannot be reported through realistic dialogue."(*Conrad the Novelist*, p247)

> a `knowledge of things in themselves' in the strictest sense of the word would be impossible, because where the being-in-itself of things begins, knowledge ceases, and all knowledge primarily and essentially concerns merely phenomena. (WWR II 275)

Thus, in moving from the phenomenon of civilization to the essence of nature, Marlow is not moving towards meaning but away from it. In order to make sense of his experience he is obliged to remove from the centre to the surface once more and reflect on what he has seen.[139] This would explain the frame narrator's rather odd statement that, for Marlow, "the meaning of an episode was not inside like a kernel but outside, enveloping the tale which brought it out only as a glow brings out a haze"(30).[140]

The quest for knowledge and the "saving illusion"

The voyage of discovery[141] which Marlow undertakes in *Heart of Darkness,* besides relating to the civilizing impulse of the colonial venture can also be seen as an allegory for modern man's scientific quest for empirical knowledge - what Nietzsche called a "Socratism bent on the extermination of myth"(BT 137). Having reduced all metaphysical, religious and ethical discourse to the realm of falsehood, science sought to replace them with objectively verifiable statements of fact. The novel dramatizes the resultant change in man's relationship with `truth' as a consequence of the suspicion that the beliefs which formed the foundation of Western culture were, at best, vital fictions and, at worst, errors. We trace the development of Marlow's moral outlook from a position where he "hate[s], detest[s], and can't bear a lie"(57) to the feeling that the naked truth is "too dark - too dark altogether"(121) and needs to be concealed behind a "saving illusion"(119). His culminating lie to the Intended reflects Nietzsche's theory that "illusion is the only possible mode of redemption"(BT 10), that both the need for

---

[139] As D. R. Schwarz points out, "Marlow has journeyed back from the inner reality to the surface world" and "learned that once he leaves the surface, there is no epistemological map for the inner truth."(Ibid., p68-70)

[140] As Surash Raval has observed, "The modernist quality of *Heart of Darkness,* [lies] in its subversion of the paradigm of romance." (*The Art of Failure,* p19) i.e. that meaning is to be found within or beyond the surface of things.

[141] Lee M. Whitehead disputes the idea that Marlow is on such a quest, claiming "There is more of the wanderer than the seeker in Marlow". ("The Active Voice and the Passive Eye: *Heart of Darkness* and Nietzsche's *The Birth of Tragedy*", p121)

transcendence and any hope of achieving it lies within man's imagination and not within the scope of his capabilities.

Initially, Marlow's voyage is prompted by the innocent curiosity of a child wishing to explore the world and gain first hand experience of its mysteries: "When I was a little chap," he explains, "there were many blank spaces on the earth and when I saw one that looked particularly inviting on a map [...] I would put my finger on it and say When I grow up, I will go there."(33)[142] But the dangers attending this desire are suggested by the imagery which Marlow uses to describe the Congo river and his subsequent obsession to travel down it to the heart of the 'Dark Continent':

> there was [...] a mighty big river that you could see on the map, resembling an immense snake uncoiled with its head in the sea, its body at rest [...] and its tail lost in the depths of the land. And as I looked at the map of it in a shop-window it fascinated me as a snake would a bird. (33)

Marlow's experience is placed within the larger context of the Biblical myth of forbidden knowledge with nature seen tempting man to lift the veil and look beneath just as the serpent tempted Eve and Adam to eat from the Tree of Knpwledge: "Watching a coast as it slips by the ship," says Marlow, "is like thinking about an enigma. There it is before you smiling, frowning, inviting, grand [...] with an air of whispering, Come and find out."(39)

Marlow is tempted to solve the "enigma" of the wilderness but were he to do so, the narrative suggests, he would fall like the Faustian Kurtz who, in return for ultimate knowledge about himself and life, loses his soul:[143] "the wilderness had whispered to him things about himself which he did not know, [...] and the whisper had proved irresistibly fascinating because he was hollow at the core."(97) Kurtz's loss of substance which also characterizes those individuals which have been longest engaged in the civilizing mission mirrors the "blank spaces"(33) on the map of the earth which fascinated Marlow when he was a boy. *Heart of Darkness* implies that in striving to know and possess the "blank spaces" of nature in his scientific quest, modern man may instead be risking the loss of his own identity and

---

142 David Daiches has claimed that Marlow's "experience was in fact his introduction to the adult world; it marked the end of his youth." (*The Novel and the Modern World*, p36)

143 As R. J. Andreach has observed, Marlow travels "as far as it is morally permissible, to the brink of the inscrutable mystery," but "refrains from invading it." (*The Slain and Resurrected God*, p48)

self-mastery to the darkness.[144] As Nietzsche pointed out, "if thou gaze long enough into an abyss, the abyss will also gaze into thee."(BGE 97) Kurtz's death-bed boast to the wilderness, "Oh but I will wring your heart yet!"(110) may seem a far cry from the young Marlow's natural excitement before the map of Africa but, as a glance at the former's idealistic beginnings shows, there is not such a great distance separating the will to knowledge from the will to power in man. As Martin Seymour-Smith points out, "man is bound to fall because he brings a power-seeking curiosity to natural knowledge so that he corrupts it."(Introduction to *Nostromo*)

By the time Marlow leaves for the real Congo, he is not as innocent as he was when he first put his finger on the abstract "blank space" on the map and this change is reflected in the transformation which the "blank space" itself has undergone in the interim: "It had got filled since my boyhood with rivers and lakes and names. It had ceased to be a blank space of delightful mystery - a white patch for a boy to gloriously dream over"(33). Before his departure, Marlow resembles the typical product of his sceptical age; he doesn't seem to possess any strong religious beliefs but neither does he have much faith in the secular myths of capitalism and progress: "I was going to take charge of a two-penny-half-penny river steamboat with a penny whistle attached!", he announces, "It appeared, however, I was also one of the Workers with a capital - you know. Something like an emissary of light, something like a lower sort of apostle."(38-39) He knows that the company was "run for profit" rather than for "weaning those ignorant millions from their horrid ways"(39) but he doesn't seem to believe in the profit-making philosophy of the enterprise either: "They were going to run an over-sea empire and make no end of coin by trade"(35), he remarks scathingly.

In going to Africa Marlow hopes to find something more genuine and true than the myths which his culture has to offer[145] even if he does go as part the "great cause of these high and just proceedings"(43), as he ironically calls Europe's civilizing mission. He is looking for the meaning of life which he has lost, the natural existence which his civilization has alienated him from: "The idleness of a passenger, my isolation amongst all these men with whom I had no point of contact, [...] seemed to keep me away from the truth of things"(40). He thinks at first that this "truth of things" may be found in

---

144 "If a man dare possess the core, the center," writes R. J. Andreach, "He dies morally and physically: he is no longer a man. Kurtz became the mystery he set out to conquer."(Ibid., p49)

145 "Marlow is careful to imply", writes Peter J. Glassman, "that he was attracted to the Congo primarily because he had been repulsed by the vapidity of modern Europe."(*Laguage and Being*, p199)

the noise of the surf along the coast and in the sight of the row-boat full of happy, paddling natives:

> Now and then a boat from the shore gave one a momentary contact with reality. It was paddled by black fellows [...] they had faces like grotesque masks - these chaps; but they had bone, muscle, a wild vitality of movement, that was as natural and true as the surf along their coast. (40)

But this illusion doesn't last long because Marlow is merely projecting here the idealized image of nature and the myth of the noble savage which his culture is fond of contemplating in its more romantic moments: "For a time I would feel I belonged still to a world of straight-forward facts; but the feeling would not last long. Something would turn up to scare it away", he recalls.

While the wilderness is enticing Marlow further into its mysteries, it is simultaneously warning him away which suggests that the quest for a deeper truth which man is embarking on is something dangerous. Marlow recalls that the coast was "bordered by dangerous surf, as if Nature herself had tried to ward off intruders"(41). In the Company headquarters in Brussels Marlow feels a vague sense of apprehension for the first time, as though the legal and commercial formalities he is obliged to complete were the prelude to an altogether different and far more sinister initiation awaiting him in the jungles of Africa: "I began to feel slightly uneasy. You know I am not used to such ceremonies, and there was something ominous in the atmosphere. It was just as though I had been let into some conspiracy - I don't know - something not quite right;"(36) As the two company women "guarding the door of Darkness"(37) suggest, Marlow is being initiated into the secrets of life and death: "An eerie feeling came over me [...] the one [was] introducing, introducing continuously to the unknown, the other scrutinizing the cheery and foolish faces with unconcerned old eyes." Once in the Congo, Marlow is shocked by his first glimpse of colonialism in action and stands "appalled, as though by a warning"(43-44). All these apprehensions can be traced to the idea arising from myth that the pursuit of knowledge in man is both a "crime committed on nature"(BT 61) and a form of hybris. As Nietzsche pointed out, "the myth [of Oedipus] whispered to us that wisdom [...] is an unnatural crime, "The edge of wisdom is turned against the wise man"(BT 61).

Heart of Darkness suggests that what nature is concealing from her creatures in order to protect them from nausea is the corruption and sordidness of life as well as their own intimate alliance with it - their mortality, in other words.[146] The "dangerous surf"(41) all along the coast which Marlow compares to a natural exclusion zone is containing "streams of death in life, whose banks were rotting into mud, whose waters, thickened into slime". Corruption and death are omnipresent in the "heart of darkness"(68) and everything, both natural and man-made, seems to be in a state of decomposition, returning to its origins. The "grass sprouting between the stones"(35) in the streets of Brussels echoes the "grass growing through the ribs" of Fersleven after his death and anticipates the rioting vegetation in the Congo. Marlow notices a railway truck lying "on its back with its wheels in the air [...] The thing looked as dead as the carcass of some animal"(42), he observes. Then he comes across some more pieces of "decaying machinery" and compares the wreck of his steamer to "the carcass of some big river animal."(50) But it is not just physical corruption that Marlow discovers in the jungle; Europe's whole colonial venture seems to reek of death and Marlow is disgusted more by the moral decay of the company than by the rankness of the tropical environment. The company agents "wandered here and there with their absurd long staves like a lot of faithless pilgrims bewitched inside a rotten fence [...] A taint of imbecile rapacity blew through it all like a whiff from some corpse"(52), he remarks.

Marlow's quest for truth unearths such sordid and demoralizing details about the baser activities of nature and man that it soon disintegrates into the desperate struggle to "hold on to the redeeming facts of life"(52), as Marlow calls them.[147] Marlow feels the need to forget what he finds just as he felt the need to "bury" Jim's failure in Patusan merely in order to carry on. In *Heart of Darkness*, the flattering idea of man's superiority over the rest of creation is parodied by a seemingly immortal hippo who would roam on the bank at night but could not be killed by all the bullets of the pilgrims: "That animal has a charmed life", observes the brickmaker, "but you can say that only of brutes in this country. [...] no man here bears a charmed life"(59). Ironically, it is the hippo who has the advantage now. However, just as in the modern wilderness the idea of man's spiritual immortality is regarded as a myth which has been exploded, so in the novel we find constant references to the smell of decaying hippopotamus - the same creature that was supposed to

---

146 As Peter J. Glassman points out, "Marlow is compelled to understand that the great adventure of life which he has attached himself to is really in the business of death."(Ibid., p203)

147 "Marlow has come to the Congo exactly to probe beneath 'the mere incidents on the surface," writes Peter J. Glassman, "exactly to discover [...] what life is like. Now that he is beginning to find out, now that life has shocked him by its "overwhelming realities", its "vengeful aspect' its suggestion of nightmare, is he to wish life to fade away behind the invulnerable shield of his culture's meaningless industriousness?" (Ibid., p213)

bear "a charmed life". The cannibals on Marlow's steamer bring along a provision of hippo-meat which goes off and makes "the mystery of the wilderness stink in [his] nostrils"(67). Marlow's desire to sustain the "saving illusion" that there is something in man that is beyond nature and incorruptible corresponds to the need to bury the offending dead-matter in the mud:

> The earth is for us a place to live in which we must put up with sights and sounds, with smells too, breathe dead hippo, so to speak, and not be contaminated. And there [...] your strength comes in, the faith in your ability for the digging of unostentatious holes to bury the stuff in. (86)

Besides burial in the mud (the equivalent of psychological repression) another possible method of resisting the demoralizing effect of the wilderness is through work. Although Marlow feels the appeal of the dancing savages and is keenly aware of the timeless truth which they represent, he nevertheless is able to resist joining them because he "had to watch the steering, and circumvent those snags, and get the tin-pot along by hook or by crook. There was surface truth in these things", he explains, "to save a wiser man"(70). One `wise man' man who could certainly have used such "surface truths" and whose whole `knowledgeable' culture proves particularly vulnerable to the "darkness", is Kurtz. *Heart of Darkness* suggests that, having been initiated into the mysteries of life as a result of his Faustian pursuits, European man has lost his "saving illusions" and would do well to occupy himself in more wholesome, less hybristic, activities than playing at God.

It is while engaged in superficial, mechanical work that Marlow admits for the first time that it may not be altogether beneficial to be aware of "the inner truth" of life and this realisation marks a clear departure from the Marlow who regretted being cut off from the truth of things African by his European cultural `baggage': "When you have to attend to [...] the mere incidents of the surface", he explains, "the reality [...] fades. The inner truth is hidden - luckily, luckily. But I felt it all the same."(68) Unfortunately, the strategy of work can't keep the "darkness" at bay for long[148] and this echoes Jim's inability to "keep his eyes shut" in Patusan while attempting to realize

[148] As Peter Glassman points out, "One must regard Marlow's paeans to labor as the moral equivalent to Europe's 'humbug' and 'rot' about the Congo, or as the correlative of what Marlow has called the 'beautiful' but fantastic self deception of women."(Ibid., p212)

his dream. As Marlow points out, "one must look about sometimes and then..."(52)

Then Marlow temporarily puts his faith in the myth of scientific progress to save him from the truth he discovers in the Congo but this solution proves no more efficacious than work. The modern scientific fallacy promoted by apparently miraculous technological advances that all human beings need to solve their problems are the appropriate material pegs to fit into the right material holes is echoed in Marlow's claim that "what I wanted was a certain quantity of rivets - and rivets were what really Mr Kurtz wanted, if he had only known it."(59) Of course rivets cannot help either Marlow or Kurtz resist the assault of the "darkness" which requires "a deliberate belief"(69) or "saving illusion"(119) of the kind which scientific materialism is opposed to. Yet the myth of scientific progress itself, suggests *Heart of Darkness*, can sometimes constitute such an inner bulwark in "the great demoralization"(46) of the modern wilderness. "We shall have rivets!", says Marlow to one of his engineers, "No! Rivets!", the other replied, "as though he couldn't believe his ears. `Good for you!"(60) But the promised scientific heaven proves to be a sham and fails to materialize. Instead of rivets there comes a caravan of worthless merchandise headed by a man on a donkey parodying Jesus' triumphant entry into Jerusalem on Palm Sunday: "each section [was] headed by a donkey carrying a white man in new clothes and tan shoes, bowing from that elevation right and left to the impressed pilgrims."(61) It is when his precious rivets don't arrive that Marlow begins to foster the idea that Kurtz might be able to offer some moral message or example that would redeem the sordidness of the Congo: "I was curious to see whether this man, who had come out equipped with moral ides of some sort, would climb to the top after all and how he would set about his work when there."(62)

Ironically, although Marlow never believed that the Company went to Africa to do anything other than make money, he is still looking for that "unselfish belief in the idea"(32) that would redeem colonialism. The idealistic Kurtz who first ventured into the heart of the Congo seems to offer the hope that corruption and greed are not the final words about life and that spiritual values still exist somewhere deep inside man.[149] Kurtz has said that "Each station should be like a beacon on the road towards better things, a centre for trade of course, but also for humanizing, improving, instructing"(65) and, if this were true, then those illusions which thrilled the

---

[149] As D. R. Schwarz points out, "Marlow, desperate to retain his illusions, wanted to meet a man reputed to be 'an emissary of pity and science and progress".(*From Almayer's Folly to Under Western Eyes*, p66)

young Marlow looking at the map of Africa and which prompted the older Marlow to leave the "whited sepulchre"(33) of Brussels are still tenable. Indeed, Kurtz presents himself as something of a living legend, a shining example for all the other company agents to follow. Marlow first hears about him from the accountant who says, "He is a very remarkable person [...] Sends in as much ivory as all the others put together."(47) The brickmaker calls him "a prodigy"(47) and adds, "We want [...] for the guidance of the cause entrusted to us by Europe [...] higher intelligence, wide sympathies a singleness of purpose [...] and so *he* comes here, a special being"(55) Clearly, it is not just the savages who look up to Kurtz as though he were a divinity; Marlow too comes to believe that Kurtz is a "remarkable man" and that his inevitable ascent to power will produce miraculous results: "Do you read the company's confidential correspondence", he asks the brickmaker, "When Mr Kurtz [...] is General Manager, you wont have the opportunity."

In keeping with his symbolic role as all things to all men, Kurtz is necessarily presented in a rather mysterious way so that he resembles more of a myth than a real person. As Marlow says:

> I had heard that Mr Kurtz was in there. Yet somehow it didn't bring any image with it than if I had been told an angel or a fiend was in there. I believed it in the same way one of you might believe there are inhabitants on the planet Mars (57).

Everyone who knows Kurtz finds it difficult to talk about him other than in very vague terms as though they are fictionalizing his character to fit their needs rather than describing it. "Tell me pray", says Marlow to the brickmaker, "who is this Mr Kurtz?' `The chief of the Inner Station he answered in a short tone [...] He is an emissary of pity and science and progress, and devil knows what else."(55) It's fortunate for Marlow too that he doesn't see Kurtz straight away because that gives him the opportunity to mythify Kurtz into whoever or whatever he wants him to be: "He was just a word for me. I did not see the man in the name any more than you do"(57) Yet, even after Marlow has met Kurtz, he still clings to this original vague impression of him as though refusing to accept what Kurtz really was rather than what he would have liked him to be: "I had taken him for a painter who wrote for the papers, or else a journalist who could paint - but even the cousin [...] could not tell me what he had been - exactly. He was a universal genius - on that point I agreed"(115). This is the same mystifying principle which prevented Marlow from seeing Jim clearly in *Lord Jim*.

Clearly, Kurtz seen from a distance is the sum of other people's idealistic expectations of him. The `real' Kurtz is as different from this living legend as the real conquerors of the earth are different from "the great knights errant of the sea"(29) which the frame narrator eulogizes at the beginning of the tale. Instead of representing something genuine and true in the face of the pilgrim's shallow mendacity, Kurtz turns out to be a paradigm of deception: "Kurtz - that means short in German", observes Marlow, "well, the name was as true as everything else in his life - and death. He looked at least seven feet long"(99) Marlow originally thinks that the corruption and decay in the Congo is emanating from the company's sordid activities and so turns to Kurtz "positively for relief"(103) but he discovers that it is in fact emanating from Kurtz[150] who is a sort of unburied corpse in the heart of the wilderness representing everything that Marlow is trying to forget and escape from: "It seemed to me I had never breathed an atmosphere so vile and I turned mentally to Kurtz for relief [...] I had turned to the wilderness really not to Mr Kurtz who I was ready to admit was as good as buried. And for a moment it seemed to me as if I also were buried [...] I felt an intolerable weight oppressing my breast the smell of the damp earth, the unseen presence of victorious corruption"(103).

The real Kurtz cannot save Marlow from the mendacity and corruption of life nor make him forget his mortality but having elevated Kurtz to the role of saviour, Marlow is obliged to sustain him there by any means possible - including lying. This realization marks the final phase of Marlow's quest for knowledge and corresponds to the idea of Nietzsche's that "without a continual falsification of the world [...] mankind could not live."(BGE 4) Marlow had originally thought that the `truth' at the heart of life was able to redeem the `lies' at the surface but he now arrives at the opposite position. "You know I hate, detest, and can't bear a lie"(57), he reminds us, yet within a short time in the Congo, Marlow becomes "as much of a pretence as the rest of the bewitched pilgrims. This simply because [he] had a notion it somehow would be of help to that Kurtz"(57). From very early on, Marlow shows his readiness to sacrifice the truth to the redeeming "idea" of Kurtz in the same way as the colonizers were said to offer sacrifices to the idea of "efficiency" in order to redeem the "conquest of the earth"(31). But even after Marlow has seen the atrocities which Kurtz is capable of, he still refuses to give up his faith in the man who had come out "equipped with moral ideas of some sort"(62). "I think Mr Kurtz is a remarkable man"(102), he will

150 "Ironically," writes D. R. Schwarz, "Marlow turned only to a different form of greed and egotism."(*From Almayer's Folly to Under Western Eyes*, p67)

remark, "with emphasis", and regardless of whether such a claim is justified or not, the fact that Marlow repeats it until the end of the novel would imply that he needs to cling to this image despite the mounting evidence to the contrary.[151]

In lying for Kurtz Marlow sacrifices what used to be his most prized belief - his belief in the truth - but *Heart of Darkness* suggests that there is no length to which human beings will go to keep their "saving illusions" alive which in turn keep them alive. A case in point is provided by Marlow's story of the Scotch sailmaker:

> I once knew a Scotch sailmaker who was certain, dead sure there were people in Mars. If you asked him for some idea how they looked and behaved he would get shy and mutter something about `walking on all fours'. If you as much as smiled, he would - though a man of sixty - offer to fight you. (57)

The vital need for illusion is something which seems to link all human the characters in the novel, regardless of culture or race. The harlequin, for whom Kurtz was "one of the immortals"(103) pleads with Marlow to protect Kurtz's memory until the other confirms, "All right [...] Mr Kurtz's reputation is safe with me." The attack which Kurtz' followers carry out on the steamer turns out to be merely a "protective"(78) measure prompted by the desire to keep hold of the man whom they are worshipping as a god: "They don't want him to go"(92), explains the harlequin. But when they hear the steam-whistle, they realize that the `magic' of their adversaries is stronger than their own and will finally wrest their white god away from them: "from the depths of the wood [there] went out such a tremulous and prolonged wail of mournful fear and utter despair", observes Marlow, "as may be imagined to follow the flight of the last hope from the earth"(82). For Marlow, the idea of not reaching Kurtz in time to hear his eloquent discourse fills him with a mysterious dread, the force of which surprises him:

> I thought, By Jove! it's all over [...] and my sorrow had a startling extravagance of emotion, even such as I had noticed in the howling of the savages in the bush. I couldn't have felt more of lonely desolation somehow, had I been robbed of a belief or missed my vocation in life. (83)

---

[151] As Jacques Berthoud has asked: "Is an essentially empty affirmation of value, like Kurtz's really preferable to the manager's open cynicism? Is Marlow's claim that Kurtz is a remarkable man really defensible?"(*The Major Phase*, p58)

The story of Kurtz exemplifies better than anything else in the novel the psychological importance of illusion and the dangers involved in the acquisition of knowledge for man.[152] Despite his enormous intellectual gifts, Kurtz is morally corrupted when the wilderness whispers to him things about himself he did not know because he has lost those illusions which *Heart of Darkness* regards as man's sole defence against demoralization in life. As he did with Jim, Marlow must somehow rescue Kurtz from the darkness of nausea and doubt if he wants to salvage his own faith in the power of civilizing illusions.[153] On the night when Kurtz leaves the steamer to return to his atavistic orgies, Marlow struggles not only for Kurtz's soul and his own, but also for the soul of a Europe which "knew no restraint, no faith, and no fear"(108). The fear that the appeal of the wilderness may be stronger for Kurtz than the desire to return home, as well as the terrible implications for western civilization if that were the case, is echoed in the moral shock which Marlow receives upon discovering Kurtz's absence from the steamer: it was "as if something altogether monstrous, intolerable to thought and odious to the soul, had been thrust upon me unexpectedly."(105)[154] He attempts to lure Kurtz back with the promise of fame - "Your success in Europe is assured in any case"(107) - but the only illusion which he can appeal to that Kurtz hasn't yet divested himself of is that of the self: "I had to deal with a being to whom I could not appeal in the name of anything high or low. I had even like the niggers to invoke him - himself - his own exalted and incredible degradation." The fact that Marlow succeeds in retrieving Kurtz from the jungle without having to "smash his head" or "throttle him" implies that there is still hope for illusion and that civilization is not irredeemable despite the latent savagery at the heart of man which such regressions as the brutal exploitation of Africa reveal.[155]

But to rescue the physical Kurtz from the darkness is not enough; in order for Marlow to sustain his "saving illusions", he must also salvage the myth of

---

152 This theme is closely linked to the Faustian myth which Cedric Watts examines in *The Deceptive Text*: Kurtz resembles both Faust and Oedipus," he writes, "who by challenging the unknown, seeks to bring great benefits but instead brings disaster to himself [...] The tale is a dramatization", he continues, "of the ways in which civilized man generally may be in the grip of a desire to know and to conquer which in the long run inflicts destruction on the environment and self-destruction on the moral nature of that civilization itself.(p82)

153 "Faith in humanity", writes Jacques Berthoud, "must look into a deranged mirror and overcome the mocking image."(*The Major Phase*, p58)

154 As Jacques Berthoud points out, "For Marlow to prevent Kurtz from returning to the jungle is not only necessary for his physical survival; it is also a last-ditch affirmation of the reality of the civilized against that of the primitive."(Ibid., p58)

155 "Marlow's success in bringing Kurtz back to the steamer", is rightly seen by Jacques Berthoud as "some sort of spiritual victory."(Ibid., p58)

Kurtz by interpreting his final verdict back on the steamer in such a way as would make its import safe for civilization. Kurtz' words themselves - "The horror! The horror!(111) - are poised between light and darkness and are as ambiguous as everything else about the man who utters them. They are said to embody a "strange commingling of desire and hate"(113) and, while Kurtz is uttering them, he seems to be "embracing, condemning, loathing all the universe."(117) Yet Marlow, wishing to stress their morally redemptive value, sees in them a "judgement" passed by Kurtz "on the adventures of his soul on this earth"(112). As many commentators have pointed out though, rather than constituting a moral reflection on his abominations, Kurtz' last words may simply be the expression of regret at the approach of death and the impossibility of indulging any longer in "the gratification of his various lusts."(97)[156] This interpretation is lent credence by the manuscript of *Heart of Darkness* where Conrad originally painted the picture of a totally unrepentant Kurtz: "I have lived supremely", says Kurtz, "I have been dead - and damned. Let me go - I want more of it...More blood, more heads on stakes, more adoration, rapine and murder."

Just as his author deleted these dark words from the manuscript of the novel, Marlow offers his listeners an optimistic rendering of Kurtz' verdict, reflecting the Conrad who felt it the artist's duty to sustain the illusions of civilization at a time when they were being undermined by the discoveries of science. "It was an affirmation", claims Marlow, "a moral victory paid for by innumerable defeats, by abominable terrors, by abominable satisfactions. But it was a victory! That is why I have remained loyal to Kurtz to the last, and even beyond"(113).[157] This attempt at rhetoric fails because the single noun at the end ("victory") is not strong enough to carry the long and laboured adjectival phrases that go before it ("innumerable defeats", "abominable terrors", "abominable satisfactions") and so the intended linguistic coup doesn't come off. Also, it is not really to Kurtz that Marlow remains loyal when he presents his report back in Europe with the post-scriptum torn off but to the bond of civilization. Like the "bond of the sea" which was said to make the passengers of the *Nellie* "tolerant of each other's convictions and even yarns"(27), the bond of civilization is seen to consist more in the preservation of the "saving illusions" of others than in the blind acquisition

---

[156] Peter J. Glassman, for example, claims that "Whatever he has done and been, Kurtz has hungered after life: so fiercely and freely has he lived that he has felt it a horror to die. [...] Kurtz whispers that it is horrible to have to die. That is all."(*Language and Being*, p232-33)

[157] "How credible is Marlow's interpretation," asks Schwarz, "that 'The horror! The horror!' is an affirmation, a moral victory, paid for by innumerable defeats, by abominable terrors, by abominable satisfactions."(*From Almayer's Folly to Under Western Eyes*, p69)

of knowledge which, if we are to judge from Kurtz', example is anything but "improving"(70).

What Marlow does consciously before the Intended - that is misrepresent Kurtz by stressing only his virtuous side - is what he has been doing subconsciously ever since lying to the brickmaker about belonging to the same "gang of virtue"(55) as his idol. "Every truth needs some pretence to make it live"[158] wrote Conrad and for the sake of the truthfulness in the Intended's love for Kurtz as well as the truth which the idealistic Kurtz represented, Marlow chooses to employ a lie: "the last word he pronounced was your name"(121), he tells her.[159] Yet this "lie", like Kurtz' verdict itself, is ambiguous. Although dark from the point of view of concealing the truth, it is nevertheless associated with light by virtue of its life-sustaining quality - the naked truth from this perspective would have been "too dark altogether."[160] Also, it consists of equal parts of fact and fiction because Kurtz may indeed have repented with his last words and so have finally expressed his allegiance to the values of Europe and the Intended rather than those symbolized by Africa and the Savage Woman.[161] Just as this possibility cannot be positively proved, so it cannot be categorically refuted.

There are many such irresolvable tensions in Conrad's work which can be said to reflect the balance which art achieves between opposites in life; between knowledge and illusion, fact and fiction, darkness and light. In misrepresenting Kurtz positively, Marlow is also doing what art does for life, that is cover up its more sordid aspects by "a great and saving illusion" so that it may be desirable still.[162]

As Nietzsche wrote:

---

158 *Collected Letters Vol. I*, to Edward Garnett, 7/8/1901.

159 Walter F. Wright argues that, "If he had told the girl the simple facts, he would have acknowledged that the pilgrims in their cynicism had the truth, that goodness and faith were the unrealities."(quoted in D. R. Schwarz, p70)

160 "Marlow's lie, arguably itself an act of darkness," writes Berthoud, "is also a means of keeping back the darkness."(*The Major Phase*, p63) Or, as Ian Watt puts it, "The lie to the Intended is both an appropriately ironic ending for Marlow's unhappy quest for truth, and a recognition of the practical aspects of the problem: we must deal gently with human fictions, as we quietly curse their folly under our breath."(*Joseph Conrad in the Nineteenth Century*, p332)

161 As Suresh Raval has argued, "to tell the truth would be to misunderstand the meaning of Kurtz's last struggle and final judgement [...] Marlow could not have told her the truth without recounting his entire Congo experience, culminating in Kurtz's final judgement; mere mention of Kurtz's immersion in savage passions would have been for Marlow a grievous slander."(*The Art of Failure*, p33.

162 As David Daiches points out, "the question of the morality of Marlow's conduct [towards the Intended] does not arise. The point is that the conventions of civilized life cannot bear too much reality."(*The Novel and the Modern World*, p42)

> He who has glanced with piercing eye into the very heart of the terrible destructive processes of so-called universal history as also into the cruelty of nature, and is in danger of craving for the Buddhistic negation of the will, Art saves him and through art life saves him for herself. (BT 61-62)

The mutual dependence of content and form which can be said to constitute the essence of art is reflected in the interdependence of Marlow and Kurtz, Europe and Africa, the Intended and the Savage Woman. The `lies' of Europe would have been too hollow and the `truth' of Kurtz too ugly to be lived but together they form a balanced whole which is echoed in Marlow's final "pose of a meditating Buddha"(121). Marlow seems to have transcended "The horror!" of his Congo experience by representing it artistically through the narrative; he has escaped the nausea afforded by knowledge through a coherent verbalization of his absurd and chaotic impressions of the wilderness. As in *Lord Jim*, this can be said to represent Conrad 's "Apollonian embodiment of Dionysiac insights"(BT 56-57), the exorcism of the Mr Kurtz's dark gifts "with a lie"(84).

Nietzsche's "superman" and Schopenhauer's compassionate man

Heart of Darkness shows how the traditional quest for union with God, life seen as a pilgrimage, has been subverted by materialism and western man's self-glorifying desire to play the role of God over nature and other men. In *The Gay Science* Nietzsche argued that having `killed' God through solipsism, we moderns would have to elevate ourselves to the status of gods merely in order to fill the vacuum left in the world. Kurtz, as representative of secular, scientific Europe seems to have succumbed to precisely this temptation in the "God-forsaken wilderness"(40) of the Congo. In his report to the "International Society for the Suppression of Savage Customs" he begins with the argument that, "We whites, from the point of development we have arrived at, must appear to them [savages] in the nature of supernatural beings - we approach them with the might of a deity"(86). Soon after writing this, Kurtz is seduced into believing that he really is "one of the immortals"(103) but it is not just the technological advances of his civilization which allow him to assume such a role in the jungle; he seems to have completely escaped the traditional moral restraints holding back ordinary men and become a law unto himself: "They adored him", says the harlequin,

"What can you expect?" [...] he came to them with thunder and lightning, you know - and they had never seen anything like it - and very terrible. He could be very terrible."(95)

In many respects Kurtz resembles the "superman", who was envisaged by Nietzsche as a being who had freed himself from ethical notions of right and wrong - what Nietzsche termed the "slave ethic" - and submits "only to the law which [he himself] has given."(D 187) The harlequin is certainly convinced that this is the case and says to Marlow, "You can't judge Mr Kurtz as you would an ordinary man." Besides ethical laws, Kurtz also seems to have rejected all external restraints, civilized customs, professional practices and even physical boundaries in the jungle. When Marlow finds him, "There was nothing either above or below him [...] He had kicked himself loose of the earth [...] he had kicked the very earth to pieces."(107) This self-appointed god of the Congo, is entirely egoistic - "everything belonged to him"(85) - and, like Nietzsche's "superman", follows the "master ethic" reserved for the natural aristocrats of life who refuse to accept any limits to their will to power and lust for life. "I had a small lot of ivory", relates the harlequin, "He declared he would shoot me unless I gave him the ivory and then cleared out of the country because he could do so, and had a fancy for it and there was nothing on earth to prevent him killing whom he jolly well pleased."(95) The phrase "nothing on earth" is more than idiomatic here because all absolute morality such as that which forbids murder presupposes the existence of a metaphysical plane from which an act or omission may be judged objectively. If there is no such plane, then all morality is merely relative and there is literally nothing to stop men doing what they please - except, of course, other men.

Heart of Darkness suggests that, in a context where men cease believing in the metaphysical origin for morality, complete anarchy of the kind which Kurtz exemplifies is not so far away. As Dostoyevsky pointed out, "If God is dead everything is permitted" and Kurtz, like the "superman", assumes this is the case and acts accordingly. "The modern cult of sinning", writes Charles I. Glicksberg - as it is portrayed in literature - is often a protest against a world that is emptied of moral order."[163] Kurtz's libidinous excesses would, according to this perspective, render him not a dangerous criminal or evil transgressor, but an existential hero. For the harlequin this is clearly the case: "You can't judge Mr Kurtz as you would an ordinary man"(95), he tells Marlow; "You don't know how such a life tries a man like Kurtz"(98). The petty shallowness of the pilgrims and moral pretensions of the manager are

---

[163] *Modern Literature and the Death of God*, p42.

so exasperating in fact, that, for a while, even Marlow prefers Kurtz's relatively straight-forward heads on stakes to the company's hypocritical posturings: "there was nothing exactly profitable in those heads being there"(97), he observes. Kurtz's final verdict will also be used by Marlow to support the theory that Kurtz was a `hero of the spirit' and a moral pioneer: "he had made the last stride, he had stepped over the edge [...] And perhaps in this is [...] all the wisdom, and all truth, and all sincerity"(113). In having lived irrationally, amorally, without restraint Kurtz could be said to have asserted the autonomy of the individual will and defied social and cultural conventions which have lost their relevance and validity in a world deprived of God. As Dostoyevsky argued, "caprice [...] preserves for us what is most precious and most important - that is, our personality, our individuality".[164]

But the novel suggests that there is a moral law which binds all men equally and arises from their common mortality.[165] It is while approaching the moment of death that Kurtz perceives the limits of his being and is moved to pass "judgement on the adventures of his soul on this earth."(112) The "truth of being", writes Charles I. Glicksberg, "is summed up in the truth of dying"[166] and, for Kurtz, the truth is that he has not been above the moral law which applies equally to all mankind. Fersleven, that other supposedly "supernatural being"(35), had also thought he could transgress moral bounds with impunity in the jungle but death puts an end to both illusions and the spear of the chief's son "went quite easily between the shoulder-blades"(34). Kurtz is not obstructed in his wrong-doing as directly as Fersleven, yet his excesses do bring about his downfall by destroying his physical and psychological health. By the time Marlow reaches him, he resembled a disinterred corpse with "the cage of his ribs all astir" and "the bones of his arm waving"(99); the darkness which he has surrendered to is said to have "consumed his flesh"(84). Even if he had wanted to continue participating indefinitely in those "midnight dances ending with unspeakable rites"(86), he would not have been able to and the limits of his physical, mortal nature bring him down to the earth he has arrogantly tried to kick "to pieces"(107). The knowledge of his lack of moral restraint "came

---

164 *Notes from Underground* quoted in *A Preface to Conrad*, p70.

165 "The moment of death", observes Jacques Berthoud, "has a meaning that is relevant to all mankind. So that what the dying Kurtz perceives may not only be true of himself as an individual, it may also be significant for humanity at large."(*The Major Phase*, p59)

166 *Modern Literature and the Death of God*, p142. Jacques Berthoud has also argued that "We have to take the moment of death, [...] as a condition of insight. As far as Kurtz is concerned, it is the instant in which, for the first and last time, he sees his past for what it truly has been."(*The Major Phase*, p59)

to him at last"(97), opines Marlow, but by that time the wilderness had taken on him "a terrible vengeance".

In desiring to be a human god adored by other men, Kurtz's "unlawful soul" has been "beguiled beyond the bounds of permitted aspirations"(107) and he has only succeeded in becoming a human devil: "He had taken a high seat among the devils of the land"(85), claims Marlow. The atavistic acts which he has indulged in, rather than being amoral, have been immoral and instead of constituting an heroic protest against a world deprived of moral order, they resemble "the inconceivable ceremonies of some devilish initiation."(84) They are not even acts of "pure, uncomplicated savagery"(98) such as those committed by animals that know nothing of the ethical law because man possesses consciousness of sin and has fallen from a state of grace.[167] As Conrad claimed:

> We can't return to nature, since we cannot change our place in it. Our refuge lies in [...] murder, thieving, reforming [...] in negation, in contempt [...] each man according to the promptings of his particular devil.[168]

Kurtz's abominations are merely the expression of that side of man which can enjoy inflicting cruelty on others out of no motive besides the feeling of power which it affords him. As Schopenhauer wrote, "no animal ever tortures for the sake of torturing but man and this constitutes the devilish character in him which is far worse than the merely animal."[169]

In striving to be more than a man, a "superman", Kurtz becomes much less than a man - a paradox which recalls Macbeth 's famous claim, "I dare do all that may become a man;/ Who dares do more is none."[170] As the novel progresses, Kurtz is gradually losing the essence of his humanity - seen to reside in the balance between the "angel" and the "fiend"(57) - until Marlow can say of him "the shade of the original Kurtz frequented the bedside of the hollow sham whose fate it was to be buried presently in the mould of primeval earth."(110) Gentleman Brown uses the same phrase to describe Jim who had opted for the other extreme in the angel/fiend dichotomy: "He

---

167 "A man cannot shed his inheritance of civilization with impunity," writes Jacques Berthoud, "for primitivism, like innocence, once outgrown or lost cannot be recovered. Kurtz has stripped himself of all the cultural values he took so ostentatiously into Africa. But he has not thereby regained the reality possessed by his primitive ancestors."(*The Major Phase*, p53)

168 *Letters to Cunninghame Graham*, p71.

169 *Selected Essays*, 'On Ethics', p197)

170 *Macbeth*, Act I, scene 7.

a man! Hell! He was a hollow sham."(LJ 297) When Kurtz has reached the height of his prestige amongst his worshippers, he doesn't look like a man/god overflowing with vitality and power as one would expect the "superman" to look, but a defeated and frail individual gesturing and talking loudly to conceal his own lack of substance and frailty before the forces he has attempted to conquer by force: "It was as though an animated image of death carved out of old ivory had been shaking his hand with menaces at a motionless crowd of men made of dark and glittering bronze."(99) So much for Kurtz's superiority over "them savages" - the deathly pallor of his skin, like "old ivory" turned yellow, associates him with a skeleton and is in stark contrast with the healthy-looking "glittering bronze" of his native followers.

The extreme solipsism of the "superman" results in his being "hollow at the core"(97) because, if everything exists only in consciousness, then so does the individual in whom consciousness resides who thus becomes a vacant reflection of a man and finally vanishes. Kurtz accordingly moves from being a "phantom"(99), to an "apparition", to a "shadow"(100). Marlow remarks that this "initiated wraith from the back of Nowhere honoured me with its amazing confidence before it vanished altogether."(86) When Marlow first sees Kurtz he looks like someone who, in order to stop himself from collapsing inwards, is trying in vain to swallow up everything outside of himself: "I saw [Kurtz] open his mouth wide", recalls Marlow, "it gave him a weirdly voracious aspect as though he had wanted to swallow all the air, all the earth, all the men before him."(99) Thus, in accordance with the *coincidentia oppositorum* which Conrad's work often reflects, complete self-sufficiency becomes the complete dependence of the self on external props and sanctions. As Hillis Miller points out, "When Kurtz's will has expanded to boundless dimensions, it reveals itself to be what it has secretly been all along: nothing."[171] The self-appointed demigod of the Congo is actually more reliant on the adoration of his subjects to bolster up his empty ego than they are reliant on him - the supposed master of the wilderness is really its servant: "my ivory, my station, my river [...] Everything belonged to him", says Marlow, "but that was a trifle. The thing was to know what he belonged to, how many powers of darkness claimed him for their own."(85) This ironic reversal recalls how Macbeth thought he was using the powers of darkness for the furtherance of his ambitions when, in fact, they were using him as a pawn in a far greater game.

Viewed from a Schopenhauerian rather than a Nietzschean perspective, Kurtz's life would exemplify, not the liberating effects of knowledge but the

---

171 Introduction to *Poets of Reality*, p6.

terribly destructive effects of self-delusion. "A foolish man", writes Schopenhauer,

> often tries to escape by wickedness, in other words, by causing another's suffering, from the evil, from the suffering of his own individuality, involved as he is in the *principium individuationis*, deluded by the veil of Maya (WWR I 352).

Kurtz's extreme cruelty, encapsulated in the phrase "Exterminate all the brutes!"(87), can be regarded as the supreme example of the will being deceived by its own reflection and not recognizing itself in all creatures around it but fighting with them egotistically and amorally. The mistake which Kurtz makes in thinking he is "one of the immortals"(103) and a law unto himself can also be traced to what Schopenhauer called the "illusion of multiplicity". Schopenhauer argued that because man is the only creature to possess consciousness of the will which, in itself, is infinite and self-determined, he sometimes harbours the feeling that he himself, a limited and finite being, is entirely free and boundless. But "the fact is overlooked that the individual [...] is not will as thing-in-itself but as phenomenon of the will, is as such determined and has entered the form of the phenomenon"(WWR I 113). The will as phenomenon is governed by the laws of cause and effect and is subject to decay and death but Kurtz is so deluded by the will as "thing-in-itself" that he goes on boasting right until the end, imagining great future exploits even on his death-bed:

> Sometimes he was contemptibly childish. He desired to have Kings meet him at railway stations on his return from some ghastly nowhere where he intended to accomplish great things [...] `Oh but I will wring your heart yet!' he cried at the invisible wilderness. (110)

Whereas Kurtz uses the knowledge which the wilderness whispered to him to become a "superman" and take "a high seat amongst the devils of the land"(85), Marlow uses his privileged knowledge of the will to tame its wild excesses and become a compassionate man. In desiring to inflict no suffering on others, even if that means temporarily alleviating his own, he escapes most of the misery inherent in his human condition as knowledgeable bearer of the will. Linda M. Hall has pointed out that, "The first step in defeating and transcending will, which Schopenhauer also sees as the first step in the ethical world, is to recognize its universality"(p16). Marlow achieves this first step by identifying and sympathizing with both colonizer and colonized, victimizer and victimized in *Heart of Darkness*. He can imagine the Roman commander's "growing regrets, the longing to escape, the powerless disgust, the surrender, the hate"(31) but he can also see that taking the earth away "from those who have a different complexion or slightly flatter noses than ourselves, is not a pretty thing"(31-2) Indeed, according to Schopenhauer, victim and victimizer are but two sides of the same will to live which, divided into opposites, produces the phenomenon of the world with all its extremes of pleasure and pain. As Conrad himself wrote to Marguerite Poradowska, "But you are afraid of yourself, of the inseparable being always at your side - master and slave, victim and tormentor - who suffers and causes suffering."[172]

Marlow has perceived the victim and tormentor within his own being and this makes him restrained and compassionate towards others rather than cruel and rebellious. He doesn't unburden himself of his knowledge before the Intended, thereby shattering the life-sustaining illusion of a fellow sufferer for only the slightest benefit to himself but keeps back what he has learnt in the wilderness "for the salvation of another soul."(116)[173] As Schopenhauer pointed out, "The person who performs works of love [...] is free from the perversity with which the will [...] inflicts misery and endures misery not knowing that like Thyestes it is eagerly devouring its own flesh."(WWR I 373) The civilization which Kurtz represents - that "weak-eyed devil of a rapacious and pitiless folly"(43) - can feel no qualms about raping a whole continent in its lust for wealth and power but the humanity which Marlow comes to represent is able to respect a single individual's touching naiveté.[174] Yet Marlow doesn't only see himself in the innocent Intended, he also sees himself in the fallen Kurtz - "I am Mr Kurtz's friend - in a way"(113), he tells the harlequin and this will enable him to keep Kurtz's reputation safe back in Europe. He doesn't show Kurtz the justice "which was his due"(121) and which he claimed was all he wanted, but mercy and

---

172 *Collected Letters Vol. I*, 20/7/1899, p162.

173 Cedric Watts has claimed that "the salvation of another soul' can be regarded as a metaphor whose literal tenor is quite secular (the preservation of the Intended's faith in Kurtz and thus in life)".(*The Deceptive Text*, p83) But this is too uncomplicated an explanation of Marlow's ambiguous choice of words. Albert Guerard argues that the first 'soul' to be redeemed by Marlow was Kurtz and that "though no priest was in attendance, Kurtz can repent." He adds, "*Heart of Darkness* combines a Victorian ethic and late Victorian fear of the white man's deterioration with a distinctly Catholic psychology."(*Conrad the Novelist*, p243)

174 As Cedric Watts points out, "If civilization is represented by a humane fellow like Marlow, then Conrad can see it is indeed a worthy achievement. If it is represented by jingoistic statesmen and the commercial exploitation of Africa, Conrad can see it is a hypocritical fraud."(*A Preface to Conrad*, p91)

this reflects the difference between himself and Kurtz. Kurtz acts as if there were no God but Marlow's behaviour throughout the novel suggests that, for some men at least, not all things are permitted.

3

The Secret Agent: Linguistic Explosions and the "Death of God"

Stevie as the last righteous man

At the heart of *The Secret Agent* lies an explosion the shock waves of which reverberate through every sphere in the novel revealing the deeply interdependent yet very precarious nature of the characters and institutions depicted therein. J. Hillis Miller has suggested that Conrad viewed the city as "an arbitrary set of rules and judgements, a house of cards built over an abyss"[175], so the explosion at Greenwich Common can be said to disclose this "house of cards". To shift the image, the destruction of Stevie removes the foundations from a structure reminiscent of the 'house that Jack built' for Stevie is the *raison d'être* of Winnie, who is the wife of Verloc, who is the informer of Chief Inspector Heat, who is the right hand man of Sir Ethelred, who is answerable to the House of Commons.

Many commentators have noted Stevie's important moral position in the novel. Irving Howe has suggested that Conrad intended Stevie to represent " the humanitarian impulse in its most vulnerable form"[176], while D. R. Schwarz claims that he "is the one character who idealistically observes the world with the expectation that right and wrong should exist."[177] He goes on to say that "Stevie is the last righteous man, the heir to the Christian tradition of mercy, charity and love" but adds that "Significantly, the character described as a moral creature is retarded, incoherent to his fellows and dead [...] Stevie's concepts of justice and goodness have become anachronisms." It appears that, in *The Secret Agent,* to be sensitive and moral is to be abnormal while to be normal, like Verloc, is closer to being monstrous.[178]

Claire Rosenfield has suggested that Stevie "becomes the scapegoat or pharmakos of the society, an arbitrary victim of the wasteland that is modern London. Traditionally, the death of the hero preliminary to his

---

175 J. Hillis Miller, *The Poets of Reality*, p6.

176 Irving Howe, "Order and Anarchy", in *The Secret Agent Casebook*, edited by Ian Watt, p45.

177 D. R. Schwarz, *Almayer's Folly to Under Western Eyes*, p170.

178 For the disturbing implications of "normality" in *The Secret Agent* see J. Berthoud, *The Major Phase*, p152.

bodily or spiritual rebirth and the regeneration of the community may take the form of tearing to pieces.[179] In this context, it is tempting to read the cannibalistic references in *The Secret Agent* as "the sacramental feast in which the hero's body is eaten by his followers in order to revitalise the community."[180] Yet for Heat, the Greenwich case "lacked all suggestion but that of atrocious cruelty."(108) Stevie's death is totally devoid of any heroism nor is any rebirth - either individual or generic - promised for this city lost in night. Clearly, this parody of a religious rite is devoid of transcendent qualities leaving only the unredeemed fact of physical annihilation.

As Avrom Fleishman has pointed out, "a society that regards human beings as things [...] can easily see them as mere meat once their bodies are reduced to fragments."[181] Also there is Karl Yundt's imaginative interpretation of the economics of capitalism:" They are nourishing their greed on the quivering flesh and the warm blood of the people."(80) "In this form", says Fleishman, "the image seems an accurate description of the relationship among men in a fragmented society."Human beings no longer form the basis of a vital community and, once dead, they may be seen as "raw materials for a cannibal's feast"(106). The phrase "raw materials" acquires an additional meaning in the context of Stevie's reduction to meat while also implying a latent cannibalism within the modern industrial impulse.

C. B. Cox has argued though that "to take Karl Yundt's outright condemnation of industrial conditions as Conrad's own position would presuppose a firm moral stance incompatible with the extreme irony of the cannibalistic references."[182] He claims that their "tone does not imply a prescriptive alternative to the devolution of civilization described in the novel and the return of men to savages or wild beasts."[183] Chief Inspector Heat, examining Stevie's remains, is compared to " an indignant customer bending over what may be called the by-products of a butcher's shop with a view to an inexpensive Sunday dinner"(107). Here we find another

---

179 Although Conrad had travelled extensively, he is more likely to have acquired a knowledge of fertility rites or vegetation myths from his reading of Frazer. For the anthropological connection see R. G. Hampson, "Conrad, Frazer and the truth of primitive passion" in Robert Frazer (ed.), *J. G. Frazer and the Literary Imagination*.

180 Claire Rosenfield, *Paradise of Snakes*, pp105-7.

181 Avrom Fleishman, *Conrad's Politics*, p202.

182 C. B. Cox, *The Modern Imagination*, p91.

183 Fleishman notes that the "entire society can be seen as a jungle of animal forms obeying the laws of predatory survival. Alien to this world, forced to live in it yet inevitably devoured, men acquire the character of beasts." *Conrad's Politics*, p201.

industrial term ("by-product") being used in conjunction with Stevie's remains suggesting the gradual incorporation of human beings into the manufacturing process, not as labour, but as raw materials. The main effect of the passage though is to convey a sense of debasement. The celebrant of the ritual is displaced by the "indignant customer", the sacrifice is overtaken by strictly utilitarian, gastronomical ends, and the overriding concern is to pay as little as possible for the modern 'sacrament' of the Sunday roast.

Winnie's later contemplation of her brother's violent death re-introduces a religious perspective. Her mental picture of Stevie as "bits of brotherly flesh and bone"(233) may be seen to contain the Biblical allusion of Cain and Abel: brother is still killing (half)brother many centuries after the primal sin. Also, if Stevie is seen as the scapegoat of modern London, then his tender age and disposition associate him with the original sacrificial 'lamb', Isaac. In the Old Testament story, the intended victim had to be dismembered and burnt very much as Stevie is exploded into smoking fragments by Verloc's bomb. But whereas Abraham's God spares Isaac's life, substituting him at the last moment with a real lamb, the revolutionary cause for which Stevie unwittingly gives his life is blind and unfeeling - no substitution takes place safeguarding the innocent 'scapegoat'. Furthermore, Verloc is a very faithless Abraham and does not even believe in the cause for which he is working, let alone in any metaphysical deity. Also, the joy of Isaac's mother, Sara, when her son is returned to her alive in the Old Testament story is in stark contrast to Winnie's reaction when the murderer of the boy returns "like any other man would come home to his wife."(233)

The violence of the explosion at Greenwich Common might be seen to reflect the immensely destructive effects on western culture of the event which Nietzsche termed the "death of God" with the consequent loss of unity from nature and meaning from existence. Hillis Miller employs the same metaphor of the explosion to describe this event in the history of ideas: "What once was a unity gathering all together, has exploded into fragments [...] subject, objects, words, other minds, the supernatural - each of these is divorced from the others and man finds himself one of the poor fragments of a broken world." [184] There is an interesting parallel between this description of this metaphorical event and Heat's description of Stevie destruction: "limbs, gravel, clothing, bones, splinters - all mixed up

184 See the Introduction to *Poets of Reality*, p1.

together."(196) This "perverse god",[185] as Claire Rosenfield has called Stevie, disappears in paradoxically apocalyptic fashion - a nearby policeman is reported to have seen "something like a heavy flash of lightning in the fog" (106) - leaving a perplexing puzzle for Heat who would have liked to " trace this affair back to its mysterious origin"(108). For Conrad, there is only one possible discovery which such an investigation can lead to, as we have seen in the previous chapter: modern man's heart of darkness.

While Conrad does not refrain from depicting in full the "utter desolation, madness and despair" (43) afflicting the modern world, there is no suggestion in the novel that a return to an age of faith is either possible or desirable. As Nietzsche argued, due to our greater understanding of the workings of nature "the door to the religious life [is] once and for all closed to us."(HA 111) Although religious language is used quite frequently by Conrad, this only serves to highlight the absence of religious faith as a continuing source of personal and collective values.[186] Like Stevie's face cropping up unexpectedly after his death, this type of language intrudes largely to reveal its own incongruity in the atmosphere of extreme doubt which pervades the novel.[187]

The Secret Agent is pervaded by an atmosphere of moral nihilism largely ignored by its characters. As Eloise Knapp Hay pointed out, Winnie and Verloc "are not prepared to explore moral or political questions".[188] Yet, as Hillis Miller has argued, it is only by admitting to the nihilism unleashed by the "death of God" does Western culture stand a chance of avoiding self-destruction. The "special place of Joseph Conrad in English literature", writes Miller, "lies in the fact that in him the nihilism covertly dominant in modern culture is brought to the surface and shown for what it is."[189]

Conrad 's artistic aim in *The Secret Agent* finds an interesting parallel in Nietzsche's own iconoclasm for both writers attempted to 'explode' the myths supporting modern social structures by exposing the decay and corruption which these structures serve to conceal. As Martin Seymour-Smith has argued "the structure of an entire society [is] not just questioned

---

185 *Paradise of Snakes*, p122.

186 For a survey of religious language in *The Secret Agent*, see John Lester, *Conrad and Religion*, and R. G. Hampson, "Conrad and Frazer", pp183-84. For Biblical allusions see James Purdy, *Conrad's Bible*.

187 For a discussion of the function of Biblical and mythical allusions in *The Secret Agent*, see D. R. Schwarz, *Joseph Conrad: From Almayer's Folly to Under Western Eyes*, pp171-3.

188 *The Political Novels of Joseph Conrad*, p235.

189 *Poets of Reality*, p5.

but exposed and destroyed [...] the infected corpse of society is dragged out into the open and shown for what it is."[190] Being by its very nature non-prescriptive, Conrad's art does not offer any alternative to the social structures depicted in the novel but in making us "see" them clearly it prepares the way beyond them. As R. J. Hollingdale claimed with regard to Nietzsche, "the delineation of the nihilist world is a necessary preliminary to transcending it."[191] The Professor claims that "what's wanted is a clean sweep and a clear start for a new conception of life. That sort of future will take care of itself if you will only make room for it."(97) Conrad's relentless irony in the novel can be seen as a form of linguistic terrorism with his words acting as linguistic bombs designed to "make room" for this abstract "clear start" without resorting to real violence. Writing to Edward Garnett on the explosive potential of words, Conrad remarked:

> your words [...] they exploded like stored powder barrels - while another man's words would have fizzled out in speaking and left darkness unrelieved by a forgotten spurt of futile sparks. An explosion is the most lasting thing in the universe. It leaves disorder, remembrance, room to move, a clear space.[192]

There is a clear resemblance between the tone and language of this extract and the Professor's words above which would suggest that, like Nietzsche, Conrad believed that "he who wants to be a creator [...], truly has first to be a destroyer and break values." [193]

This would support C. B. Cox's claim that "the purpose of the novel is anarchic".[194] Other commentators have come to a similar conclusion although there is some debate about this. Fleishman proposes that "Conrad needed 'clear space' in the artistic realm" but dismisses the idea that this made him " a concealed anarchist in art or politics."[195] He sees Conrad's aim in *The Secret Agent* as being the far more constructive one of "reorder[ing] the substance of the fragmented world into an organic

---

190 The Introduction to *The Secret Agent*, p36.

191 Introduction to *A Nietzsche Reader*, p11.

192 *Collected Letters Vol. I*,

193 *Thus Spoke Zarathustra*, p139.

194 *The Modern Imagination*, p86.

195 *Conrad's Politics*, p186.

community."[196] Martin Seymour-Smith, on the other hand, picks up on Frederick Karl's suggestion that Conrad "had well hidden anarchic tendencies" and concludes that " the anarchism, idealism and romanticism of the young Conrad were well hidden in the elder Conrad, but they were merely covered over by a world-weary cynicism." [197]

It may be more than just a world-weary cynicism on Conrad's part which led him to question the effectiveness of supposedly humanitarian acts of violence: "there can be no evolution out of a grave" he asserted.[198] This suggests not that Conrad doubted the possibility of social change *per se*, but that he had little faith in violence to bring it about - a position inextricably linked with his hatred of Czarism, conveyed in the novel through the character of Vladimir.[199] However much he may have been repelled by extreme political methods though, he could not help respecting the sincerity and commitment of extremists. As he wrote to Joseph Blackwood:

> Of course I do not defend political crime. It is repulsive to me by tradition, by sentiment, and even by reflection. But some of these men had struggled for an idea openly, in the light of day, and sacrificed to it all that to most men makes life worth living.[200]

This is what sets the Professor apart from the other anarchists - even while, as Jacques Berthoud points out, his "systematic rejection of normality costs him his sanity."[201] The most damning aspect of the social revolutionaries that congregate in Verloc's shop is that they have neither enough integrity to acknowledge the price of living in an organised society, nor the courage to sacrifice anything towards an imagined utopia. "For obviously one does not revolt against the advantages and opportunities of that state", observes the narrator, "but against the price which must be paid for the same in the coin of accepted morality, self-restraint and toil."(82) If we view social morality as a kind of modern faith,

---

196 Ibid., p189.

197 Introduction to *The Secret Agent*, p10.

198 *Notes on Life and Letters*, p199.

199 For Conrad's position on the Russian situation see "Autocracy and War", *Notes on Life and Letters*, p101.

200 *Collected Letters Vol. I*, 29/10/1897, p401.

201 *The Major Phase*, p137.

these men are neither believers nor true heretics; they are merely blasphemers.

Through a series of linguistic bombs, *The Secret Agent* explodes almost every belief and ideal held by its characters. The indiscriminate way in which this is done reflects the arbitrary destructiveness of time for which no illusion is sacred. It also supports Nietzsche's argument in *Beyond Good and Evil* that all human ideals are vital fictions primarily designed to sustain life and not reflections of timeless or metaphysical truth. Conrad 's demythifying tendency in this novel does not even differentiate between full-scale "saving illusions" - like the Intended's in *Heart of Darkness* - and minor prejudices. The Assistant Commissioner's revelations about Vladimir explodes Toodles' idea of the Explorer Club's "extreme selectiveness" and "social purity"(201), while Verloc's discussion with Vladimir explodes the latter's misconceptions regarding anarchist practices ("Anarchists don't marry [...] It would be apostasy." p69). When Verloc is approached by Heat, he threatens to "tell the whole story"(196) in a spontaneous release of suppressed information that would destroy the illusions and shatter the peace of many minds: "It shall all come out of my head and hang the consequences [...] it will upset many things" (197). The Chief Inspector compares this to "the laying waste of fields of knowledge" (197) but is unaware of the damage caused by his own words on the normally incurious Winnie who overhears his conversation with Verloc:

> Ofcourse. Blown to small bits: limbs, gravel, clothing, bones, splinters - all mixed up together. I tell you they had to fetch a shovel to gather him up with. Mrs Verloc sprang suddenly from her crouching position, and stopping her ears, reeled to and fro between the counter and the shelves (196).

The above account of a real explosion accidentally triggers off a psychological explosion in Winnie who attempts in vain to stop Heat's destructive words from entering her consciousness.[202] Her sudden reflex movements, first upwards, then from side to side, offer a dramatic representation of the explosion which has taken place in her mind. The "supreme illusion" of Winnie's life is revealed to her the instant it was destroyed - as if caught in the illuminating flash of an explosion before

---

202 Jeremy Hawthorn first put forward the idea of linguistic bullets in *Language and Fictional Self-Consciousness*: "A word is like a "bullet". Its meaning is not necessarily the intention of the person who utters it [...] The bullet means what it does to the recipient as well as what the person who pulls the trigger intends."

disappearing altogether: "an appalled murmur [...] died out on her blanched lips. 'Might have been father and son.'" (221) This experience is described in geo-historical terms suggesting a significance for Mrs Verloc far exceeding a normal event: "this creature's moral nature had been subjected to a shock of which, in the physical order, the most violent earthquake of history could only be a faint and languid rendering." (229)

Vladimir and Verloc

The linguistic bomb which triggers off the whole chain-reaction of illuminating explosions is spoken by Vladimir. It shatters Verloc's mistaken impression that the value of individuals consists in what they are in themselves"(213), thus anticipating his "single amiable weakness: the idealistic belief of being loved for himself."(252) In challenging and exposing Verloc's false sense of security, Vladimir's shock tactics have precisely the effect which he intended. As Vladimir announces to Verloc:

> 'The good old Stott-Wartenheim times are over. No work, no pay.' Mr Verloc felt a queer sensation of faintness in his stout legs. He stepped back one pace and blew his nose loudly. He was in truth, startled and alarmed. The rusty London sunshine struggling clear of the London mist shed a luke warm brightness into the first secretary's private room and in the silence Mr. Verloc heard against a window-pane the faint buzzing of a fly - his first fly of the year heralding better than any number of swallows the approach of spring. The useless fussing of that tiny, energetic organism affected unpleasantly this big man threatened in his indolence. (62)

Verloc's shock and disillusionment, interestingly manifest themselves as a change in the colour of his surroundings. Forgotten are the "powdered old gold" overtones and the "red coppery gleams"(51). Now, the same light barely manages to break through the mist and shed a lukewarm brightness into the room. Also, Verloc seems to have suddenly become aware of the "rusty" aspect of things which had previously eluded him. On his way through Kensington, earlier, we were told: "There were red coppery gleams [...] on the broad back of Mr Verloc's overcoat, where they produced a dull effect of rustiness. But Mr Verloc was not in the least conscious of having got rusty."(51) The metal imagery suggests that London's "opulence and luxury" are now seen to be far less secure and permanent than they had earlier seemed, as incorruptible gold is replaced by corruptible copper. Verloc's view of London, it is subtly suggested, shifts as he is made to reconsider his sense of his own value. In keeping with Verloc's new perception of things following the loss of his illusion of permanence, what was once a pleasant city has now become very sinister.[203]

The "faint buzzing of a fly" that Verloc hears has both psychological and symbolic significance. Firstly, it reflects the state of heightened sensitivity which accompanies a moral shock of the kind which Verloc has just been subjected to. Secondly, it reflects the process by which a simple yet disturbing idea can disrupt a peaceful state of mind and begin to overturn it. The unpleasant effect of the fly's buzzing acts as an "objective correlative"[204] to the threat to Verloc's indolence. The idea which, like a time bomb, destroys his life many days after it is evoked is Vladimir's "When you cease to be useful you shall cease to be employed."(64) The narrator will later comment on the autonomous nature of some ideas: "a notion grows in a mind sometimes till it acquires an outward existence, an independent power of its own and even a suggestive voice."(216) Besides Verloc, Winnie will be hounded to death by the words "the drop given was fourteen feet"(238), while Ossipon finds himself haunted by the newspaper report on Winnie's death: "An impenetrable mystery is destined to hang forever over this act of madness and despair."(266) Verloc's response to Vladimir's threat is the first instance of this phenomenon where words appear to possess the power to haunt individuals and even influence their destinies.

The fly "heralding better than any number of swallows the approach of spring" also becomes an anti-romantic symbol for blind natural cycles. For an instant the veil is lifted and Verloc, whose "mission in life being the protection of the social mechanism"(54), is made to see that, beyond the social mechanism, he is struggling against time itself. Time is the ultimate "secret agent" in the novel, imperceptibly yet irresistibly undermining both natural and man-made structures from within till they are reduced to their original constituents. For Verloc, the approach of spring is linked to the passing of the "good old Stott-Wartenheim days" when his position in the embassy seemed assured. Now, the indolent life-style he has worked

---

203 For the simultaneous coexistence of pleasant London with sinister London in *The Secret Agent*, see Jacques Berthoud, *The Major Phase*, p147.

204 This term comes from T. S. Eliot, "Tradition and the Individual Talent", *Selected Essays*.

so hard to maintain seems threatened by the irritating "fussing" of a "silly, jeering, dangerous brute"(216). Verloc's fatal flaw, like his culture's in general, is his infinite complacency before the forces of nature and the passage of time which unleashes their blind fury. This is one aspect of" scientific man" which Nietzsche criticizes in *Untimely Meditations*, saying: "scientific man behaves like the proudest idler of fortune, as though existence were not a dreadful and questionable thing but a firm possession guaranteed to last forever."(p35)

Verloc suffers "an extremely rude awakening"(203) from the romantic age of French field-guns and Grand Ducal visits. Vladimir's 'linguistic bombs' transport him to a scientifically yet absurdly violent world where the individual is insignificant and society itself seems tottering on the edge of an abyss. There is however, a further possible level of meaning in the juxtaposition of Vladimir's words with the buzzing of the fly" heralding [...] the approach of spring". European civilization can be said to be going through a winter of nihilism and doubt, but for every winter there is a spring. Vladimir's world of scientific terrorism does not represent an improvement on" the good old Stott-Wartenheim days" but is merely the last phase of the romanticism which grips western culture. Yet, like the unromantic fly which signals the end of winter better than any attractive sparrows, Vladimir's world of scientific terrorism paradoxically heralds a new age for mankind.

Miller claimed that "Conrad's work does not turn the malign into the benign but leads to a reversal".[205] Certainly, in *The Secret Agent* there is no attempt to depict the new order that will succeed romanticism; Conrad did not see the writer's task as being prescriptive.[206] As Michaelis points out: "No one can tell the form the social organisation may take in the future. Then why indulge in prophetic fantasies? At best they can only interpret the mind of the prophet and can have no objective value. Leave that to the moralists" (73). This echoes Nietzsche's psychological argument in *Beyond Good and Evil* that "all great philosophy has up to now consisted of [...] the confession of its originator, and a species of involuntary and unconscious autobiography."(p10) Of course, it was Nietzsche who more than anyone else was advocating the destruction of the old morality to make way for the new, and Conrad can here be read as ironically using

---

[205] Introduction to *Poets of Reality*.

[206] As La Bossiere writes, quoting the Preface to *Tales of Hearsay*, "Conrad's art never preaches but only holds the mirror up to nature, for men to see themselves, and draw such moral as they can from their own faces." (*The Science of Unknowing*, p6)

Nietzsche's own argument against Nietzsche.[207] Whereas the latter was to go on to prophesy the coming of the superman, Conrad gives a vision of the superman to the Professor and discloses its psychological roots in the Professor's biography.

Mutually opposed systems

Conrad is unmistakably modern in the critical attitude he maintains towards a variety of systems that were influential at the turn of the century. As regards Marxism, Martin Seymour-Smith writes: "Conrad certainly shared Marx's view that men and women should not be treated as merchandise. But he did not share his historical determinism: still less his dialectical materialism." Scientific positivism is generally viewed in *The Secret Agent* from a Nietzschean perspective - as representing an alternative religion and satisfying man's need for certainty: "Some still have need for metaphysics but also the longing for certainty which at present discharges itself in scientific positivist fashion among large numbers of the people."[208] This need is exemplified in Ossipon who, following the fashionable theories of the Italian criminologist Lombroso, (1836-1909), labels Winnie a "murdering type" on the basis of her physiognomy: "He gazed scientifically. He gazed at her cheeks, at her nose, at her eyes, at her ears... Bad!... Fatal! [...] Not a doubt remained... a murdering type."(259)[209] The irony is that he right, as Winnie's subsequent actions will confirm, yet in the description of Ossipon there are clear signs that would classify him too as a degenerate. Karl Yundt has previously put forward a plausible Marxist critique of Lombroso's tautological theories: "Teeth and ears mark the criminal? Do they? And what about the law that marks him still better - the pretty branding instrument invented by the

---

207 As George Butt has argued, "Conrad's responses to Nietzsche were contradictory, and included unwilling sympathy and hostility, imitation and parody". "What Silenus Knew: Conrad's Uneasy Debt to Nietzsche", *Comparative Literature*, 41 (1889, pp155-169) p155.

208 *The Gay Science*, p285. Eloise Knapp Hay has also pointed out that in *The Secret Agent*, "science, like religion is all things to all men. From a means of destroying society to way of labelling criminals." *The Political Novels of Joseph Conrad*, p244.

209 As R. J. Andreach writes, "on the train Winnie lifts her veil granting her would-be saviour a glimpse into the mystery. There is no mystery for him, though only a simple scientific explanation." *The Slain and Resurrected God*, p83. Andreach argues quite convincingly that Conrad resented the scientific denial of the mystery behind the veil which the heroine embodies.

overfed to protect themselves against the hungry?"(78) In the first case Conrad is turning the same system against itself and in the second he is playing off one system against another.

Ossipon, like his society in general, may have moved away from a morality based on religious belief, but he is clearly no closer to resembling an ethically self-determined being. As the narrator points out, "He was free from the trammels of conventional morality - but he submitted to the rule of science."(259) Regarding the fact that Ossipon invokes Lombroso "as an Italian peasant recommends himself to his favourite saint", Nietzsche would argue that one form of 'slave morality' has merely replaced another. By comparing Ossipon to an Italian peasant, Conrad mocks the former's progressive pretensions while suggesting that superstition and fear may be as much an integral part of science as of religion.[210] Religious feeling and scepticism are similarly placed in dialectical opposition to one another. Appropriately enough, the character most sceptical about the soul's survival after death is said to feel "hope" at the approach of his body's ruin on earth. Like Stevie's spirit turning up "with a vengeance"(211) in a de-spiritualized world to participate in the undoing of Verloc, the moral aspect of Ossipon's actions return to hound him to an early grave: "I am seriously ill' he muttered to himself with scientific insight."(269)

Linguistic effects and the shortcomings of linguistic communication

Vladimir's threats would not have produced the psychological explosion which they do, had Verloc not believed in the first secretary's readiness to carry them out. The Professor's power is based on the same principle: "I have the means to make myself deadly, but that by itself, you understand, is nothing in the way of protection. What is effective is the belief those people have in my will to use the means. That's their impression. It is absolute. Therefore I am deadly."(93) Verloc will later feel an irresistible need of confessing - of making a clean breast of it to somebody - to anybody"(202) as if the knowledge he has been carrying is too heavy for him to bear alone and needs to be shared amongst his fellow men in a spontaneous verbal outpouring. This relates to the impulse which prompts

---

[210] For the way Conrad depicts an age of science that has not escaped from magical or religious ways of thought, see R. G. Hampson, "Frazer and Conrad", *The Modern Language Review*, Vol. 85, part 1. pp184-85.

Coleridge's Ancient Mariner to pass on tainted knowledge to the reader or Marlow's need to re-tell the story of Kurtz and Jim.[211] However, both Verloc and Ossipon find it difficult to express this 'tainted knowledge' they possess because it implicates them in murder. The Assistant Commissioner acts as Verloc's confessor in the same way Marlow does for Jim and Kurtz, revealing a spiritual need in man not catered for by science, the modern religion.

The Assistant commissioner then confesses the confession to Sir Ethelred, echoing the chain-reaction set off by Stevie's death. However, the change in perspective as well as the diminished importance which Heat attaches to Verloc's and Vladimir's exchange defuses any linguistic explosions that may have been set off. As Heat relates: "He had been driven out of his mind by an extraordinary performance, which for you or me it would be difficult to take as seriously meant, but which produced a great impression on him."(202) This also reveals the subjective nature of linguistic effects: a deeply unsettling conversation for one person in a certain state of mind can appear no more than a "ferocious joke" for someone else in a different state of mind. 'Linguistic bombs' also depend for their effect on the ignorance or sensitivity of the recipient as well as the desire to shock or the lack of tact on the part of the person who utters them. Verloc ironically finds Heat's description of Stevie's dismemberment unsuitable for Winnie's ears ("He's a brute blurting it out like this to a woman" p211) reflecting the hypocrisy of a society which can perpetrate atrocious acts but finds speaking about them tactless.[212]

The unpredictability of linguistic effect must have been a problem that occupied Conrad's mind not a little. This would explain why in *The Secret Agent* words seem to have a power and a will of their own as if mocking the authority of their human creators.[213] An anarchic state of affairs seems to have been produced in the realm of language too by the "death of God", so that meaning is random or impossible to ascertain while the effect of a communication often entirely unpredictable. The following passage can be read as enacting an authorial uncertainty regarding language and an attempt to reaffirm authorial control:

---

211 For this theme see Peter Brooks, *Reading for the Plot*.

212 The hypocrisy of Verloc's tactfulness here is in stark contrast to Marlow's profoundly humane gesture towards the Intended in *Heart of Darkness*

213 For the way inanimate objects also show signs of rebelliousness in the novel, see C. B. Cox, *The Modern Imagination*, p84.

> The Assistant Commissioner gave this definition in an apologetic voice. But in truth there is a sort of lucidity proper to extravagant language and the great man was not offended. A slightly jerky movement of the big body [...] accompanied an unremittent stifled but powerful sound. The great man had laughed. (203)

Suspense is created here by the "delayed decoding"[214] of Sir Ethelred's reaction suggesting the outcome to the Assistant Commissioner's report was not a foregone conclusion. The explosions of laughter which are provoked in Sir Ethelred could easily have been explosions of shock or displeasure instead as is testified by the Assistant Commissioner's" apologetic voice". The reassuring last line though, confirms the narrator's theory of appropriate candour, and certainty is restored to the paragraph by the epigrammatic: "The great man had laughed" .

Unlike Vladimir whose words can have a powerfully disturbing effect on his interlocutor, Stevie is " no master of phrases" (168) and his words remain unexploded bombs when they are spoken to Winnie:

> 'Poor! Poor!' he ejaculated appreciatively. 'Cabman poor, too. He told me himself.' The contemplation of the infirm and lonely steed overcame him. [...] 'Poor brute, poor people!' was all he could repeat. It did not seem forcible enough, and he came to a stop with an angry splutter: 'Shame!' (168)

Stevie's explosive exclamations are potential detonators for the compassion of anyone listening but Winnie, " who could not pretend to such depths of insight", remains unmoved. His passionate phrases cannot penetrate to her inner consciousness where they would have the most effect for, as Conrad tells us, " She was in the dark as to the inwardness of the word 'Shame'." Her philosophy which" consisted on not taking notice of the inside of facts"(156) protects her when having to handle potentially explosive language so that she is able to avoid incurring any damage herself. This is the case when she explains the role of the police in society using the revolutionary terms she has heard the anarchists employ:" They are there so that them as have nothing shouldn't take anything away from them who have."(170) Winnie is said to convey this unexploded bomb

---

214 For the way this device is employed by Conrad see Ian Watt, *Conrad in the Nineteenth Century*, also Cedric Watts, *Deceptive Texts*.

"with the equanimity of a person untroubled by the problem of the distribution of wealth." .

Stevie, on the other hand, could be "filled with horror" by the "mere names of certain transgressions"(170). After apprehendingthe discrepancy between his ideal conception of the metropolitan police "as a sort of benevolent institution for the suppression of evil"(169) and Winnie's revolutionary version, he is said to be "impressed and startled"(170). But the extreme sensitivity and "delicate honesty" which allow him to perceive moral incongruities and transgressions keenly,[215] also render their verbal communication difficult: "he felt with great completeness and some profundity", we are told, but "his thoughts lacked clearness and precision".(170)

Not only does the faculty of perception appear to be at odds with that governing expression, but the inadequacies of language can often lead to linguistic frustration. Stevie's "subversive act"[216] of letting off fireworks on the stairs of the preserved milk firm is the result of the "two other office-boys work[ing] upon his feelings by tales of injustice and oppression till they had wrought his compassion to the pitch of that frenzy."(50) This episode shows that where a verbal release of tension is impossible, a more physical form of self-expression may be resorted to with far more destructive results. One could argue that the fireworks which Stevie employs to demonstrate his moral outrage at social injustice are more appropriate than words, for they reflect not only the explosive quality of the feelings stirred up in Stevie, but also the cruelty and violence of what he is protesting against.[217] In the end, however, they are less socially acceptable than linguistic symbols, and after Stevie's "altruistic exploit"(50) he is dismissed as "likely to ruin the business". This desperate

---

215 Clare Rosenfield has compared Stevie to the archetypal "child-god" who is characterised by "superior powers of perception" (*Paradise of Snakes*, p10). Avrom Fleishman, on the other hand, suggests that Stevie "is in the tradition of the comic jester who is free to reveal the madness and corruption of society with impunity."(*Conrad's Politics*, p196) If the latter were true though, his gruesome death suggests that the time-honoured immunity enjoyed by the fool is not respected by the society depicted in *The Secret Agent*.

216 Jacques Berthoud has argued in *The Major Phase* that Stevie and the Professor are two different types of revolutionary.(p90)

217 Clare Rosenfield has suggested an archetypal connection between the cruelty of the system on the one hand and the type of firework which Stevie lets off in the preserved milk firm: "The catherine wheels which Stevie, in a fit of vicious sympathy, sets off on the stairs of the milk firm [...] recall the martyrdom of St. Catherine and that wheel from whose circumference spikes project. They suggest that the circles of modern society are wheels of torture."(*Paradise of Snakes*, p90) This accords with Jacques Berthoud's comment on Stevie's "momentary but appalling vision of society as some kind of pain generator."(*The Major Phase*, p140)

but essentially well-meaning attempt at communication sets the stage for the tragicomedy of human misunderstanding which follows.

Stevie's verbal indictment of social injustice during the cab-ride scene reveals the shortcomings of linguistic communication. The problems of conveying the full internal force of an idea externally seem almost insurmountable to Stevie so he resorts to repetition: "it was very difficult. 'Poor brute, poor people!' was all he could repeat. It did not seem forcible enough"(168) But repetition merely increases the linguistic tension rather than relieving it and, like the build up of pressure in a bomb, his frustration finds an outlet in the exclamation "Shame!". Stevie then tries to juxtapose the proposition "Poor people" with the proposition "Bad world" and arrives at the new proposition: "Bad world for poor people." Now this attempted fusion of two truths, instead of producing an even greater single truth, produces only a half-truth: it is not a bad world exclusively for poor people although it is also bad for them. This highlights the non-logical nature of language as does the ambiguity of the word "poor"(168). Stevie has not taken into account that 'poor' meaning 'without funds' is not necessarily synonymous with the same word meaning 'deserving pity'. As the narrator suggests, "these words would have been whole if they had not been made up of halves that did not belong to one another."(168) In his quest for the perfect expression, Stevie has panicked and tried to fit in "all the words he could remember" so that his final verdict on social conditions has lost the immediacy and explosive purity of his original observations.

Winnie's stabbing of Verloc can be seen as another instance of linguistic frustration. Ironically, Verloc, whose profession relies on an ability to use language deceitfully or selectively, is killed by a woman "of singularly few words either for public or for private use."(219) Also, the Verlocs' mutual habit of " not going to the bottom of facts and motives"(222) which safeguarded their marriage prior to Stevie's death, seals its doom once communication becomes essential: "Mrs Verloc's philosophical almost disdainful incuriosity, the foundation of their accord in domestic life, made it extremely difficult to get into contact with her, now this tragic necessity had arisen."(216) This is said very much from Verloc's point of view but in a later statement the narrator hints at Verloc's own responsibility for the state of secrecy which has existed in the Verloc household: "For the first time in his life [Verloc] was taking that incurious woman into his confidence."(218)[218] It soon becomes apparent, though, that Winnie is in no position to reciprocate this long-overdue gesture on Verloc's part, finding words singularly inappropriate to express her state of mind: " She did not see any alternative between screaming and silence, and instinctively chose the silence."(222) Verloc senses that Winnie's unwillingness to communicate her feelings is an ill omen under the present circumstances and " would have been more satisfied if she had been moved to throw herself upon his breast"(277) which of course she does - though not quite in the way he would have liked.[219] However, the "law of individuality"[220] which governs the novel makes it impossible for him to understand his wife's position. "And in this" , observes the narrator, "he was excusable, since it was impossible for him to understand it without ceasing to be himself."(213) When Winnie finally stabs Verloc, the unsettling revelation is not so much that the normally placid Winnie is capable of savage rage but that the maternal instinct itself might be violent by nature. As the narrator casually yet disturbingly remarks: "Mrs Verloc's temperament [...] when stripped of its philosophical reserve was maternal and violent."(219)[221]

The "death of God" and role-playing

In *Modern Literature and the Death of God,* Charles Glicksberg claims that a characteristic of modern fiction is that "the writer can discover no unitary enduring self."(p17) In *The Secret Agent,* the "death of God" has brought about not so much a disintegration of personality as the ability of characters to assume an almost infinite variety of personas. Verloc simultaneously plays the part of *agent provocateur,* revolutionary anarchist, seller of pornography and respectable husband, but the conflicting

[218] Fleishman has pointed out that "Despite the integrative function of knowledge in *The Secret Agent,* it destroys those who have become inured to a life if secrecy."(*Conrad's Politics,* p193)

[219] There is a grim use of puns in this scene e.g. Verloc's "strike me dead"(227) which suggest that Verloc is in a way inviting his own death. So, we could say that, on a subliminal level, the shortcomings of linguistic communication are momentarily and fatally overcome.

[220] J. Hillis Miller, discussing the philosophy of *The Secret Agent,* writes: "the world is dominated by a law of individuality." (*Poets of Reality,* p54)

[221] On the theme of Winnie's maternal 'explosion', D. R. Schwarz writes, "Winnie is an example of how the potential for fidelity and pathos becomes warped and destroyed both by human brutality and economic conditions. Ironically her rage at Stevie's demise enables her to discover in an act of homicide the atavistic energy that modern man seems to have lost."(*From Almayer's Folly to Under Western Eyes,* p168)

demands which these roles place on his personality bring about his downfall. By employing Stevie in his terrorist activities, he makes the proverbial error of mixing his private with his public functions, producing an explosive compound which destroys the entire Verloc household.

The narrator ironically describes Verloc as "a rock - a soft kind of rock"(53) which suggests an oxymoronic type of character, lacking in any fixed or reliable qualities. It also ironically refers to Nietzsche's claim that "man only has value and significance in so far as he is a stone in a great building for which purpose he has to be[...] Above all not a stage-player! [...] no one of us is any longer material for a society."(GS 304) Verloc certainly seems to be unfit as " material for a society" , encompassing as he does so many contradictory roles while being too indolent and cynical to commit himself to any one single occupation. As the narrator observes:

> He might have been anything from a picture-frame maker to a locksmith; an employer of labour in a small way. But there was also about him [...] the air of moral nihilism common to keepers of gambling hells and disorderly houses; to private detectives and inquiry agents; to drink sellers and, I should say to the inventors of patent medicines. (52)

Like Kurtz who had a vast range of talents and "could get himself to believe anything"(HD 115) because he had no real faith in anything, Verloc can counterfeit the appearance of honest and dishonest professionals alike, all work appearing equally futile to him: "he was the victim of a philosophical unbelief in the effectiveness of every human effort."(52) This makes him a perfect example of Nietzsche's "stage-player" .

After Verloc's murder, he adopts yet another role. His corpse appears to Ossipon to have real potential as a public attraction of the fair-ground type:

> the true sense of the scene came to Ossipon through the contemplation of the hat [...] it lay on the floor before the couch as if prepared to receive the contributions of pence from people who would come presently to behold Mr Verloc in the fullness of his domestic ease reposing on the sofa. (250-51)

Ironically, this posthumous role which Verloc adopts is presented as no less valid than any of the many roles he played while still alive. Indeed, the only essential difference is that there is no possibility of him suddenly revealing yet another persona. Death is seen to bring all contradictions to a close guaranteeing the lasting peace which life denies: Verloc is finally said to "look comfortable"(236).

Winnie's own multiple roles seem to be triggered off by Verloc's Jekyll and Hyde transformations from intimate spouse to murderer and then back to intimate spouse again: "He was lying on the couch quite easy - after killing the boy - my boy. [...] And he says to me like this: 'Come here'."(254)[222] This only confirms her philosophy that "things didn't bear much looking into", but deprives her character of its former "single purpose" and "noble unity of inspiration"(219). The lack of essential coherence in Verloc's character, like the attempt to blow up Greenwich Observatory, is "impossible to fathom out [...] by any reasonable or even unreasonable process of thought."[223] It points to a universe where essence has been banished leaving only an incoherent array of surface appearances.

Conrad claimed that "the ethical view of life involves us in [...] many cruel and absurd contradictions" adding, "I have come to suspect that the aim of creation cannot be ethical at all. I would fondly believe that its object were purely spectacular."[224] Nietzsche held similar views claiming that "the existence of the world is justified only as an aesthetic phenomenon."(BT 8) It is perhaps significant that Stevie's meaningless yet literally spectacular death in a "pyrotechnic display"(233) impresses upon Heat "the absurdity of things human"(110). Still, nothing is affirmed in Conrad without some qualification and this non-ethical ontology is at least rendered problematic by the Stevie's vengeful reappearance in the end of the novel to participate in his murderer's undoing.

Before Stevie's death, Winnie is content to play the role of "respectable woman"(243). Thus, when Verloc feels "not at all well" , "Mrs Verloc with all the placidity of an experienced wife, expressed a confident opinion as to the cause, and suggested the usual remedies."(85) When Verloc considers emigrating though, she unwittingly offers him a glimpse of another side to her character but immediately covers up this momentary indiscretion: "If you go abroad you'll have to go without me. You couldn't, you would miss me too much."(186) The ploy works. "Verloc's idealistic belief in being loved for himself"(252) and not for his protection of Stevie

---

222 For the "simultaneous coexistence of the commonplace and the catastrophic" in the novel, see Jacques Berthoud, *The Major Phase*, p138.

223 Author's Note, p62.

224 *A Personal Record*, p22.

stops him from seeing through Winnie's 'loyal wife' pose. In fact Winnie admirably manages to sustain this pose right up until the moment she stabs Verloc, ironically marking "the formal closing of the transaction between them".

With the death of Stevie, Winnie experiences the nausea and absurdity of existence which is normally concealed beneath the Apollonian illusions of nature and man. The quasi-maternal imperative, which previously furnished her life with meaning, is suddenly made redundant and with it vanish any feelings of allegiance towards her husband. She is not yet able to define herself anew, for her marriage 'contract' with Verloc, although essentially null and void, is still formally binding, mocking her newly acquired sense of freedom:

> Mrs Verloc was a free woman. She had thrown open the window of the bedroom either with the intention of screaming Murder! Help! or of throwing herself out. For she did not know exactly what to make of her freedom. [...] Mrs Verloc closed the window and dressed herself to go out another way. She was a free woman. (228)

Although the narrator repeatedly calls Winnie a "free woman", she is not actually free while her husband is still alive. His restrictive authority operates from within her very name which constitutes her social identity (the formal "Mrs Verloc" is preferred to "Winnie"). Ironically, it is at this point that she perceives her marriage bond most keenly. The options open to her are, therefore, unacceptable but her desperation is not yet powerful enough to overcome her will to live: "The street repelled her by taking sides with that man [and] Her instinct for self-preservation recoiled from the depth of the fall."(228) In accordance with social etiquette she resolves to dress in respectable attire and exit through the door instead. This further undermines the narrator's claim that "she was a free woman" as do the symbols of her old contract which she drapes around her like chains: her black veil and little red handbag.

Arriving downstairs, she naturally discovers that even the door will not allow her to escape into a new role: "There must have been something imperfect in Mrs Verloc's sentiment of regained freedom. Instead of taking the way of the door she leaned back with her shoulders against the tablet of the mantlepiece."(232) Winnie's turning her back on the "tablet" of her domestic hearth symbolizes the " formal closing of the transaction"(232) between herself and Verloc. The word " tablet" has Biblical overtones and this gesture of Winnie's is clearly symbolic: in killing Verloc, Winnie can be said to be re-enacting the modern world's conscious rejection of the absolute morality signified by the tablets of stone on which the Ten Commandments were engraved. Her act can therefore be seen as an early instance of existentialist revolt:

> 'Winnie.' 'Yes, 'answered Mrs Verloc the free woman. She commanded her wits now, her vocal organs; she felt herself to be in an almost preternaturally perfect control of her body. It was all her own, because the bargain was at an end. (233)[225]

Indeed, the bargain is at an end but it is her resolve to kill Verloc which will earn Winnie her freedom. Part of the problem for Winnie is that, in gaining her freedom, she has broken social laws which threaten to deprive her of her freedom and her life.[226] Her extreme act of self-determination carries the seeds of its own failure within it. The 'Furies' that afterwards torment her are not those of divine law or personal guilt but impersonal social justice: "she imagined herself all alone amongst a lot of strange gentlemen in silk hats who were calmly proceeding about the business of calmly hanging her about the neck [...] 'The drop given was fourteen feet' No! That must never be. She could not stand that."(238) It is not the abstract concept of death which is abhorrent to Winnie, but the scientifically impersonal form her execution would take at the hands of the state.

The blood leaking out of Verloc's body, like the ticking of a clock, will become the symbol of her new freedom - a new servitude dictated by the social and physical repercussions of her deed." It was a trickle dark, swift, thin...Blood! [...] with a sudden shriek she ran to the door as if the trickle had been the first sign of a destroying flood."(236)[227] This deed has earned Winnie a momentary glimpse of eternity as time speeds up in her mind

---

[225] Eloise Knapp Hay argues that "Winnie does not mean to murder her husband any more than Jim means to desert the Patna."(*Paradise of Snakes*, p258) But Winnie breaks her "contract" with Verloc far more self-consciously and deliberately than Jim breaks his with the merchant marine. This is testified by Winnie's unrepentant confession to Ossipon in which she accepts full responsibility for her actions: "I came - for the last time...with the knife"(258) Jim, on the other hand, tries to claim diminished responsibility for his crime: "Certainly I jumped! [...] but I tell you they were too much for any man. It was their doing as plainly as if they had reached up with a boat-hook and pulled me over."(LJ 134)

[226] Martin Seymour-Smith suggests that Winnie acts out a tragic paradox: "Awakened suddenly to her own humanity [...] by Verloc's treachery, she denies it by killing him."

[227] As Fleishman has pointed out, "Winnie substitutes her husband's body for the ordinary clock of public chronology." (*Conrad's Politics*, p209)

like drops of liquid becoming a constant flow. But Winnie's temporal existence is strictly incompatible with eternity and she is terrified by the lack of parameters in her new existence. In attempting to escape a defunct marriage she has placed herself in the temporal predicament described by Heidegger as the 'time trap': "caught in a trap of time man reaches out eagerly to the future fleeing from nothingness and yet rushing headlong toward the death that is nothingness."[228]

Finally, Winnie cannot cope with the "dreadful gift of freedom" , as Charles I. Glicksberg calls it, and seeks refuge in suicide after she has desperately tried to play the role of mistress to Ossipon, whom she tenderly addresses as Tom.[229] This signals her ultimate failure as an existential heroine for she proves incapable of determining herself independently of men who have hitherto given meaning to her life and then deprived her of it. Characteristically, "Tom" abandons her to commit suicide in utter despair after robbing her of all her family's savings - a pathetic and futile end to a quietly heroic life of self-sacrifice and toil.[230]

The Secret Agent suggests that it is far easier to free oneself from restrictive or redundant roles than to define the purpose of one's own existence afresh. If the attainment of freedom is regarded as an end in itself, then, in the words of the Assistant Commissioner, one might come to resemble" an impulsive man who after committing suicide with the notion that it would end all his troubles, had discovered that it did nothing of the kind."(203) This analogy is finally more appropriate to Winnie's condition although it was originally intended for Verloc. Nietzsche, himself, stressed more the self-defining aspect of existentialism than the self-liberating: "Do you call yourself free?" he asked, "I want to hear your ruling idea and not that you escaped from a yoke [...] can you furnish yourself with your own good and evil and hang your own will above yourself as a law?"[231] This novel shows that Conrad understood well the existentialist concept of freedom, even if the characters it depicts are finally unable to bear freedom's "dreadful" burden.

---

[228] Quoted in Charles I. Glicksberg, *Modern Literature and the Death of God*, p8.

[229] In *The Tragic Vision*, Murray Krieger argues that although Conrad creates a tragic vision, his characters are unable to rise to the level of tragic action - suicide is the only way out for them.

[230] Eloise Knapp Hay claims that, in *The Secret Agent*, "women dramatize the grim fortitude of urban humanity and men are their parasites."(*The Political Novels of Joseph Conrad*, p260)

[231] *Thus Spoke Zarathustra*, p89.

4

Under Western Eyes: Reason and Feeling

Objectivity and the fictionalizing tendency

Schopenhauer argued that the intellect does not reflect the world objectively nor can it ever do so for "Nature has produced it for the service of an individual will [...] not to fathom out or comprehend [the] inner essence [of things]"(WWR II 192). According to Schopenhauer, the world which a person observes is necessarily his "representation": that is the projection of the viewing subject's mind onto the empirical world, and nothing more.

Under Western Eyes reflects this idea in various ways. Firstly, it depicts Russia as a "monstrous blank page awaiting the record of an inconceivable history"(78) - a statement reminiscent of Bismarck's claim, "La Russie - c'est le neant." Various attempts are made by various characters in the novel to define Russia and the Russian character but, as can be seen from the diversity of opinion which results, this object cannot easily be pinned down. Revealing is Razumov's claim to Peter Ivanovitch that "We are Russians, that is - children; that is - sincere; that is cynical"(214). No definition will quite do here, and the final adjective is strangely incongruous with the original noun: "children [...] that is - cynical". Equally contradictory is the characterisation of Ziemianitch: a man intended to represent the undifferentiated mass of the Russian people. Haldin famously calls him "A bright spirit! A hardy soul!"(66) but this reflects more his own idealism than the actual qualities of the peasant and is also in stark contrast with the opinions of others on the same subject. We should not be surprised to hear the proprietor of the drinking-house Ziemianitch frequents wax cynical on the merits of this "proper Russian man - the little pig [...] Bring out the bottle and take your ugly mug out of my face [...] that's the fellow he is ."(75) When Razumov finds Ziemianitch unconscious with drink and beats the senseless body of this "little pigeon" he exclaims ironically: "A true Russian man! Razumov was glad he had beaten the brute - the bright soul of the other."(77) Haldin's father is also called "a true Russian in his way"(71) but he appears as neither "a bright spirit"(75) nor a "brute"(77) - "His was the soul of obedience"(70) says Haldin who has himself committed murder out of "resignation" yet remarks interestingly, "I am not like him. "Razumov himself who claims "Russia *can't* disown me [...] I am *it*!"(215) is ironically reproached by Haldin for his "frigid English manner"(65). "Ah! You are a fellow," he tells him, "Collected - cool as a cucumber. A regular Englishman."(69) Clearly, what is or is not typically Russian depends largely on the character and disposition of the person attempting to fill "the monstrous blank page"(78) of Russia.

The character who tries hardest to define Russia and through whom we obtain most of our information about its distinguishing marks is the English teacher of languages. Although he confesses to having "no comprehension of the Russian character"(72), he repeatedly attempts to define what is unique or typical about it and does this mostly by contrasting it with the West. At one point he is moved to remark that "the psychological secret of the profound difference of that people consists in this, that they detest life, the irremediable life of the earth as it is, whereas we westerners cherish it with perhaps an equal exaggeration of its sentimental value"(134). But this polarization in which "that people" appear to hate one thing and "we westerners" appear to love it is itself part of the western, rational way of viewing the world by splitting it up into opposites. This is Russia and the West seen precisely under western eyes and not what it appears to be: the balanced and mature observation of an impartial observer. The English teacher of languages can be said to display what Schopenhauer regarded as a central facet of human perception - the impossibility of its being objective. Unfortunately this lack of objectivity can be traced to Conrad 's own technique in *Under Western Eyes*. As Douglas Hewitt points out, despite Conrad's attempts to "strike and sustain the note of scrupulous impartiality"(49), "His animus against Russia - his belief that it is fundamentally more evil than the rest of Europe - has been introduced into the novel."[232] I would not go as far as that critic by suggesting that this "animus" has "not been subjected to any process of imaginative re-creation" by Conrad but indeed, to a great extent, "evil is given a local habitation and a name in Russia."[233]

The narrator insists on two things that a) the Western mind is congenitally incapable of understanding fully the Russian mind and b)

---

232 *Conrad: A Reassessment*, p82.

233 Ibid., p81.

"this is not a story of the West of Europe"(72).[234] Yet the deeper reasons for both claims lie within the teacher's personal and cultural disposition, for were he to admit that there is any affinity between the Russian and western minds or between the Russian and western political situations, he would be implicated in "the moral corruption of an oppressed society where the noblest aspirations of humanity, the desire of freedom, an ardent patriotism, the love of justice, the sense of pity, and even the fidelity of simple minds are prostituted to the lusts of hate and fear"(58). Like Razumov, the teacher of languages can be said to be shrinking from the fray "as a good natured man might shrink from taking definite sides in a violent family quarrel."(61) What enables the teacher to achieve this moral detachment from the conflict he is describing is the fact that the "family" in question is not his own. Yet Conrad, by making us sympathise with Razumov, is all the time suggesting that what holds true for the Russian "family" may well hold true, on a deeper level, for the West as well. The teacher's claim that "this is a Russian story for western ears, which as I have observed already, are not attuned to certain tones of cynicism and cruelty, of moral negation, and moral distress already silenced at our end of Europe"(180)[235] is a remarkable assertion to make when one bears in mind that it appears in a novel immediately preceded by *The Secret Agent* in the Conradian canon. As H. M. Daleski has pointed out, "Despite the narrator's reiterated assertion that the materials of his narrative are utterly alien to the western world, we thus cannot help noticing that the Russia of his tale is not notably different from the England of *The Secret Agent*."[236] All the teacher's attempts at definition and clarification of the Russian character are thus thinly disguised denials of identification, for the conflict between reason and feeling which assails Razumov is a universal conflict, not limited by geographical or cultural boundaries. The teacher hints as much when he says that his task in *Under Western Eyes* is "not in truth the writing in the narrative form a *precis* of a strange human document but the rendering [...] of the moral conditions ruling over a large portion of this earth's surface"(105). The reader assumes that this "large portion of this earth's

---

[234] As Douglas Hewitt has remarked, "this inability of Western minds fully to understand and sympathize with Russian characteristics and motives is what the language teacher stresses more than anything else. Russia is unlike the West." (Ibid., p80).

[235] Tony Tanner points out that "With unwarranted confidence and impenetrable complacency [the narrator] speaks as though the West has managed to eradicate the irrational and tragic elements out of life once and for all." "Nightmare and Complacency: Razumov and the Western Eye", *The Critical Quarterly* IV 1962, (pp197-214) p199.

[236] *Joseph Conrad: The Way of Dispossession*, p185.

surface" refers to Russia but it could equally well apply to a larger geographical area still, including London and Costaguana, for individual or cultural cynicism, as Conrad has shown before, is not a preserve of Russia. He proudly announces his discovery that "the spirit of Russia is the spirit of cynicism", yet he himself displays a high degree of professional cynicism when he says: "To a teacher of languages there comes a time when the world is but a place of many words and man appears a mere talking animal not much more wonderful than a parrot."(55) The cynicism latent within the teacher's own personality and culture is thus projected onto Russia as a means of disavowal. This comes out clearly in the following oxymoronic statement: "I suppose one must be Russian to understand Russian simplicity, a terrible corroding simplicity in which mystic phrases clothe a naive and hopeless cynicism."(134) For someone who is not Russian, this shows a remarkable understanding of "Russian simplicity".

Like Razumov who, feeling threatened by the fanaticism and irrationality of Haldin, consciously disavows him and his cause, so the English teacher of languages ostensibly denies any similarities between western and Russian realities and modes of thought, keeping the two strictly separate in the narrative. "It is unthinkable", he says, "that any young Englishman should find himself in Razumov's situation. This being so it would be a vain enterprise to imagine what he would think. The only safe surmise is that he would not think as Mr Razumov thought at the crisis of his fate."(72)[237] What Conrad is anticipating here is the western reader's unwillingness to identify with Kyrilo Sidorovitch Razumov. The English teacher can thus be said to stand for Conrad's more unresponsive and unimaginative readers while at the same time asking us to examine our own responses to the "strange human document" on which *Under Western Eyes* is based. "The thoughts themselves were not numerous", he explains, "they were like the thoughts of most human beings, few and simple". We are, thus, both repelled by the particular horrors of Russian life, and moved to look beyond them and sympathize with the simple, ordinary human beings suffering under Russian autocracy and Russian revolt: "By an act of mental extravagance [an Englishman] might imagine himself arbitrarily thrown into prison, but it would not occur to him unless he were delirious (and perhaps not even then) that he could be beaten with whips as a practical measure either of investigation or of

[237] As Jacques Berthoud has noted, "Razumov's situation consists precisely in the fact that in many essential respects he is a young Englishman transported into the middle of Czarist Russia." *The Major Phase*, p170.

punishment." Thus, although Russian and western notions of civil rights might be poles apart and a young Englishman would think and respond quite differently in a given situation from a young Russian, cruelty and suffering are universal facts of life and unite all human beings. It is this understanding which stops *Under Western Eyes*, from being excessively biased as a work of art.[238]

Schopenhauer stressed that objectivity does not fall within the scope of an individual's perception and *Under Western Eyes* shows that true objectivity is impossible to practice when trying to convey an impression of the outside world and other people: all human interpretations remain necessarily fictitious and self-reflexive, like Razumov's diary. By basing his novel on such a source, Conrad is dramatizing a key point in Nietzsche's linguistic philosophy: that there is no *a priori* "logos" or original text - all utterances being interpretations of interpretations. Yet, the English teacher of languages reiterates over and over again that he is not inventing anything in conveying Razumov's story to us, and is keeping strictly to the evidence provided by the diary itself. As he says: "I wish to disclaim the possession of those high gifts of imagination and expression which would have enabled my pen to create for the reader the personality of the man who called himself [...] Kirylo Sidorovitch - Razumov."(55) All he has brought to the original document, he claims, is his knowledge of the Russian language. However, as is typical of the positivist way of thinking, the teacher is leaving himself out of the process of representation not realizing that he is projecting rather than merely reporting what he reads and sees. For example, the word "cynicism" which according to him "persists in creeping under the point of the pen"(105) and is "the mark of Russian autocracy and Russian revolt" does not write itself, as he would have us think. It is a label which he is attaching to the political situation in Russia in an attempt to mark the "monstrous blank page" and linguistically appropriate something which is inherently mysterious. As Schopenhauer wrote, a man "does not know a sun and an earth but only an eye that sees a sun, a hand that feels an earth, that the world around him is there as representation [...] only in reference to another thing namely that which represents [...] that is himself."(WWR I 3)

---

[238] Tony Tanner has argued that "Anybody who reads *Under Western Eyes* as an anti-Russian polemic has not learned to respond to the full range of Conrad's wide-ranging irony and scepticism, nor to the depths of his insight into the human mind." "Nightmare and Complacency: Razumov and the Western Eye", p199.

In his own way, Razumov can also be said to resemble something of a "blank page": "With his younger compatriots he took the attitude of an inscrutable listener, a listener of the kind that hears you out intelligently and then just changes the subject."(57) This procures for him "the reputation of profundity" but it also leaves him open to being misunderstood, for people tend to project onto him those qualities they want to see and expect to be confirmed in their opinions. Seeing him as "an altogether trustworthy man" and "someone worthy of being trusted with forbidden opinions", Haldin deems it advisable to seek asylum in his rooms after assassinating the President of the Repressive Commission with disastrous results - at least for Razumov's future. "He has a strong character this young man", Haldin says to himself, "He does not throw his soul to the winds."(64) But Razumov will metaphorically "throw his soul to the winds" by seeking refuge with the forces of autocracy and betraying Haldin's misplaced trust in him. "Your reserve has always fascinated me, Kyrilo Sidorovitch", says Haldin, and on the basis of this "fascination" he assumes that Razumov is sympathetic to the revolutionary cause he has pledged his life to. He even goes as far as to assume Razumov will condone his assassination of Mr de P- because he has not "met anybody who dared to doubt the generosity of [Razumov's] sentiments". From this misunderstanding onwards, virtually every character in the novel tries to enlist Razumov's sympathies and linguistically appropriate someone who has, as General T- puts it, "the great and useful quality of inspiring confidence"(91).

Natalia Haldin makes the same mistake as her brother and takes Razumov for a "fellow believer [...] someone she could give [her] confidence to in a certain matter"(190). Natalia sees in Razumov only what she wants to see and fictionalizes his responses in accordance with her psychological needs. When she mentions her brother's name to him, she observes that he was "quite overcome [...] He positively reeled. He leaned against the wall of the terrace."(187) From this display of emotion - which is anything but a symptom of mourning - she mistakenly concludes: "their friendship must have been the very brotherhood of souls." Like anyone else in her circumstances, Natalia has made for herself a "representation of that exceptional friend, a mental image of him"(185) and clings to it despite any evidence to the contrary. The teacher of languages in his protective role tries to make her scrutinize her assumptions about Razumov in order to safeguard her against disillusionment: "You were not disappointed", he asks her, "What do you mean? His personal appearance?", she replies, "I perceived she was not listening", remarks the teacher. It is clear that, even if there were good cause to, Natalia doesn't wish to doubt her mental image of Razumov, inspired by her brother's words: "Unstained, lofty and solitary existences"(184). In Geneva, Razumov is branded by these words of Haldin's and cannot avoid being measured up by them. "Without doubt", says the teacher to himself upon meeting Razumov, "he seems a sombre, even a desperate revolutionist; but he is young, he may be unselfish and humane, capable of compassion."(196) The teacher himself is prepared to disregard his first impressions of Razumov and to give him the benefit of the doubt because he senses how invaluable he will be later on as a source of consolation for her lost brother.

The revolutionaries too are keen to put aside the fact that Razumov is highly reserved and mysterious and find in him something that will match the prestige of his supposed collaboration with Haldin in the successful attempt on de P-'s life: "You are clearly a superior nature - that's how I read you", says Peter Ivanovitch, "Quite above the common - h'm - susceptibilities. But the fact is, Kyrilo Sidorovitch, I don't know your susceptibilities. Nobody, out of Russia, knows much of you as yet!"(216) Because Peter Ivanovitch thrives on the power which being the head of the Chateau Borel gives him and doesn't want anyone to escape his domineering influence, he is keen to appropriate Razumov and claim him for the group despite the mystery surrounding this "uncommon" young man: "You are one of us - *un des notres*", he tells Razumov, "I reflect on that with satisfaction."(216) "I don't want anyone to claim me"(215), says Razumov but he cannot avoid being "read" by Peter Ivanovitch and claimed in a fictional way even though, like the "blank page" of Russia, he is difficult to define accurately: "You are close, very close. This taciturnity, this severe brow, this something inflexible and secret in you, inspires hopes and a little wonder as to what you may mean."(214) Madame de S-remarks to him: "You are very reserved. You haven't said twenty words altogether since you came in"(224), yet Razumov hears her murmur under her breath "Later on in the diplomatic service; which could only but refer to the favourable impression he had made." Sophia Antonovna is also struck by his reserve - "One doesn't know what to think, Razumov"(250), she tells him yet her wonder at his having assisted Haldin in killing Mr de P- overcomes any reservations she may have concerning his character: "But you might tell me. One would like to understand you a little more. I was so immensely struck...Have you really done it?"(251) Tekla too sees in Razumov what she wants to see: "Directly I saw you for the first time", she tells him, "I was comforted. You took your hat off to me. You looked as if one could trust you [...] I have been starving for, I won't say kindness, but just for a little civility, for I don't know how long."(234)

Although Razumov has no real sympathy for the autocrats any more than he does for the revolutionaries, his betrayal of Haldin to the authorities, the consequence of fear, will be regarded by the former as an act of great courage and patriotism. "This is an honourable young man whom Providence itself..."(87) says Prince K- to General T- who is quick to label Razumov "a staunch and loyal Russian"(89). Razumov himself will begin to encourage such interpretations merely to remain trusted when in reality he is not committed to either side: "I am a man of deep convictions", he tells General T-, "Crude opinions are in the air. They are not worth combatting. But even the silent contempt of a serious mind may be misunderstood by headlong utopists."(90) Ironically, Razumov harbours just as much "silent contempt" for General T- as for Haldin yet his "serious mind" will be equally "misunderstood" by both "headlong utopists" and blind defenders of autocracy. "A serious young man. *Un esprit superieur*", remarks Prince K-, "I see that, *mon cher Prince,*" replies the General, "Mr Razumov is safe with me. I am interested in him." Another man who is interested in Razumov is Councilor Mikulin who cleverly manipulates Razumov's "imperfect trust in his convictions" and enlists him as a double agent to spy on the revolutionaries in Geneva: "You are a man of great independence", he shrewdly points out, "You are going away as free as air, but you shall end by coming back to us."(283) Thus, as a consequence of being misinterpreted and misunderstood by both revolutionaries and autocrats, Razumov will be linguistically appropriated by both and enlisted to further their causes.

Reason and feeling

Schopenhauer saw the human mind and its capacities as pitifully limited and inherently both subsidiary and subservient to feeling and instinct. One of the ways *Under Western Eyes* dramatizes this idea is by showing how Razumov is unable to live his life according to rational principles when the irrational in the form of Victor Haldin enters his life. Razumov, as his name suggests ('son of reason') is intended to represent the thinking or calculating side of man. "I am reasonable", he tells Councilor Mikulin, "and I take the liberty to call myself thinker"(123). He prudently avoids becoming involved in the political conflict in Russia, his main concern being with "his work, his studies and his own future"(61). But all his attempts to lead a rationally determined existence are undermined when Haldin seeks refuge in his rooms after assassinating the President of the Repressive Commission thus provoking Razumov to reveal the non-rational side to his personality while putting to the test his "dormant instincts, his half-conscious thoughts and almost wholly unconscious ambitions"(281).[239] Haldin appeals to Razumov's feelings rather than to his reason, forcing him to take sides in the "violent family quarrel" which embroils their common land: "You have enough heart to have heard the sound of weeping and gnashing of teeth this man raised in the land", remarks Haldin referring to Mr de P-, "That would be enough to get over any philosophical hopes."65)

Leaving Haldin in search of Ziemianitch, Razumov is impelled not by his "cool superior reason"(80) but by the irrational instinct of survival which Schopenhauer regarded the common denominator between all men: "It was the thought of Haldin locked up in his rooms and the desperate desire to get rid of his presence which drove him forward. No rational determination had any part in his exertions."(73) Confronted by the irrational, Razumov cannot maintain his logical self-possession, and he later asks himself why he had simply not asked Haldin to leave at the first opportunity. When he has to search for Ziemianitch in the low eating house, Razumov is suddenly immersed in the world of base human passions which his detached, stoical existence had insulated him from. The misery and squalor which Razumov encounters there are in stark contrast to the clinical, academic environment he has insulated himself with all his life while the stress on Ziemianitch's Russianness serves to undercut Razumov's intellectual pretensions.[240] The 'man of reason' is now caught between two manifestations of the irrational in man: "Between the drunkenness of the peasant incapable of action and the dream intoxication of the idealist incapable of perceiving the reason of things and the true character of men."(77)[241]

---

239 As Royal Roussel points out, "Haldin's abrupt entrance into Razumov's life destroys Razumov's belief in his ability to choose his identity and brings to hi the dark and unhappy knowledge of the irrationality which lies at the centre of the world of *Under Western Eyes.*" *The Metaphysics of Darkness*, p142.

240 John F. Haugh argues that "The squalor nauseates [Razumov] because he is already tormented by a sense of self-betrayal; this affront to his fastidiousness (which has a moral taint) is a first consequence." *Joseph Conrad: Discovery in Design*, p122.

241 As Wilfred S. Dowden has observed, "Razumov is caught between the two forces which are beyond his control and foreign to his philosophy." *Joseph Conrad: The Imaged Style*, p124.

When he finally locates Ziemianitch and is frustrated to find him unconscious with drink, all Razumov's pent-up fury against Haldin is released in a spontaneous display of feeling that is anything but to be expected from such a normally self-possessed intellectual: "A terrible fury - the blind rage of self-preservation - possessed Razumov, 'Ah! the vile beast' he bellowed out [...] I shall wake you!' [...] He looked round wildly, seized the handle of a stablefork and rushing forward struck at the prostrated body with inarticulate cries."(76) Razumov ironically acts in an instinctive fashion while expressing his indignation at the "beastly" Ziemianitch - something which further emphasizes the deep common bond between them.[242] Later on, "the fearful thrashing he had given Ziemianitch seemed to him a sign of intimate union, a pathetically severe necessity of brotherly love"(80). Razumov also obtains a certain physical relief from beating Ziemianitch which further undermines his pose of intellectual superiority, and ironically clears his mind: "He was glad he had thrashed the brute. The physical exertion had left his body in a comfortable glow. His mental agitation too was clarified as if all the feverishness had gone out of him in a fit of outward violence"(77). Razumov here can be said to be 'beating' the unconscious part of his own character which hasn't yet 'woken up' to the danger posed to his rational world by Haldin's irrationality. At this point he reflects that, "It was like harbouring a pestilential disease that would not perhaps take your life, but would take from you all that made life worth living."(77)

Haldin himself in committing his crime has worked on instinct and feeling, being convinced that he has doing God's will in assassinating Mr de P-: "When the necessity of this heavy work came to me what did I do [...] Did I try to weigh its worth and consequence. No! I was resigned. I thought 'God's will be done!"(71-72) Haldin is aware that Razumov, being a thinker, does not function like this and warns him not to allow his rational impulses to betray the better part of the Russian character which he calls resignation: "When the day of you thinkers comes don't forget what's divine in the Russian soul - and that's resignation. Respect that in your intellectual restlessness and don't let your arrogant wisdom spoil its message to the world."(70) But in betraying Haldin Razumov will betray the feeling part of his own character and symbolically of the Russian soul. He doesn't see the demands which feeling places on man and the higher necessity which Haldin speaks of when he says Mr de P- was "uprooting

242 As John F. Haugh has observed, Razumov "himself, in his brutal treatment of Ziemianitch [...] is acting unwittingly the role of the Russian monster." (*Discovery in Design*, p123).

the tender plant. He had to be stopped"(65). Razumov sees the situation from a purely rational perspective and doesn't heed Haldin's warning that reason should respect the claims of feeling. He is exclusively concerned with the fact that Haldin has broken the law and thereby placed him in great danger by entering his rooms while severely jeopardizing his plans for the future.

Despite any sympathy which Razumov may feel towards Haldin, he tries to keep the legal transgression uppermost in his mind so that a clear-cut condemnation may result, unclouded by any unconscious identification between himself and the outlaw: "For it is a crime', he was saying to himself, 'A murder is a murder."(73) This process of emotional disavowal reaches its peak during Razumov's 'religious conversion' upon which he convinces himself that his entirely emotional betrayal of Haldin is rationally justifiable:

> 'Haldin means disruption,' he thought to himself, beginning to walk again. 'What is he with his indignation, with his talk of bondage - with his talk of God's justice? All that means disruption. Better that thousands should suffer than that a people should become a disintegrated mass, helpless like dust in the wind'. (79)

Razumov is here engaged in the fictionalizing process which will turn Haldin into a pure villain when his status was previously ambiguous in Razumov's mind ("A murder is a murder. Though, of course some sort of liberal institutions...") The "silent soul"(71) of Razumov begins to find the words he had lacked to appropriate Haldin with and betray him while retaining his own self-esteem: "He went on thus heedless of the way, holding a discourse with himself with extraordinary abundance and facility. Some superior power had inspired him with a flow of masterly argument as certain converted sinners become overwhelmingly loquacious."(80) The intellect according to Schopenhauer is not the source of human motivation - merely the self-justifying part, and here Razumov begins to rationalize his act of betrayal into moral significance: "He was persuaded that he was sacrificing his personal longings of liberalism - rejecting the attractive error for the stern Russian truth...'That's patriotism,' he observed mentally [...] and then remarked to himself, 'I am not a coward."(80)[243]

Razumov chooses autocracy to revolt because it seems to promise security and peace - conditions that appeal to his rational character; yet even after his 'conversion' he is plagued by irrational doubts and hasn't completely reconciled himself to the thought of informing on Haldin: "But he felt a suspicious uneasiness, such as we may experience when we enter an unlighted place - the irrational feeling that something may jump upon us in the dark - the absurd dread of the unseen."(80) The feelings of sympathy and identification Razumov has tried to repress re-assert themselves and he only just manages to avoid confessing to Haldin rather than to Prince K-: "A strange softening emotion came over Razumov - made his knees shake a little. He repressed it with a new-born austerity. All that sentiment was pernicious nonsense"(84), he says to himself. The narrative undercuts Razumov's rationalistic exercise of self-justification by showing him in need of moral support even after he has discovered "what he had meant to do all along" with Haldin: he "longed for a word of moral advice, for moral support."(80) Razumov confesses to Prince K-, this being the only man who has shown him any tenderness or affection in his life: Prince K- "once had pressed his hand as no other man had pressed it - a faint and lingering pressure like a secret sign, like a half-unwilling caress."(84) It is at this moment that Razumov's allegiances are decided and, out of a largely subconscious, non-rational impulse, he finds himself drawn to the ranks of the autocrats.[244] The conservative 'credo' which he nails above his bed following his betrayal of Haldin constitutes one last desperate attempt to legitimize what was clearly an act of emotional weakness on his part: "History not Theory/ Patriotism not Internationalism/ Evolution not Revolution/ Direction not Destruction/ Unity not Disruption."(104)[245]

---

243 As Albert Guerard has remarked, Razumov's "egoism and fear create the doctrinal commitment which alone can rationalize the betrayal." *Conrad the Novelist*, p233. Also Tony Tanner has claimed that Razumov's "mental faculties, scattered by the sudden intrusion of Haldin, now marshall themselves behind the emerging notion of an intellectual (not impulsive) renunciation of all that Haldin stands for." "Nightmare and Complacency: Razumov and the Western Eye", p206.

244 Claire Rosenfield has observed that "If at this point [Razumov] chooses the personal father who must deny him rather than the social "brother" he shares with all of revolutionary Russia he does so without speculating upon it, without making deliberate choices, instinctively." *Paradise of Snakes*, p144.

245 As H. M. Daleski observes, "When Razumov writes his manifesto [...] he formulates a mature, intellectual justification of the betrayal, but the 'almost childish' hand it is written

Before General T-, as before Haldin, Razumov feels the force of irrationality, "the stunning force of a great fanaticism"(71) crushing his thinking powers and making him lose "all hope in saving his future which depended on the free use of his intelligence"(118). He wonders why he has been called to the police headquarters and discovers that there was no possible way of telling: "perhaps the superior authorities of police meant to confront him with Haldin in the flesh", he speculates, "But why? For what conceivable reason?"(119) He also realises that he could not appeal to anything reasonable before General T- because "his omnipotence made him inaccessible to reasonable argument." During his interrogation at the hands of Councilor Mikulin, Razumov only has to keep his visit to Ziemianitch out of the answers to be safe, but he finds to his dismay that his responses are beyond his conscious control. This realization is very much in keeping with Schopenhauer's theory about the supremacy of instinct over reason: "It seemed impossible to keep Ziemianitch out. Every question would lead to that because of course, there was nothing else. He made an effort to brace himself up. It was a failure."(123) Throughout the interview, Razumov is constantly tempted to act impulsively and confess to Councilor Mikulin proving that his reactions are not within his control: "I must positively hold my tongue unless I am obliged to speak,' he admonishes himself. And at once against his will the question, 'Hadn't I better tell him everything?' presented itself with such force that he had to bite his lower lip."(124)

After Haldin's entry into his life, Razumov discovers that he has been living on false security by putting his trust in himself and his rational mind in the hope of prudently determining his own future and escaping the dangers of existence: "What is the good of exerting my intelligence, of pursuing the systematic development of my faculties and all my plans of work?' he asked himself. 'I want to guide my conduct by reasonable convictions, but what security have I against [...] some destructive horror walking in upon me as I sit here...?"(113) Not only does his intelligence not help him to keep control of his life but he suspects that it might even be a disadvantage in a world seemingly governed by absurdity: "I can't afford to despise anything. An absurdity may be the starting point of the most dangerous complications", he muses, "How is one to guard against it? It puts to rout one's intelligence. The more intelligent one is the less one suspects an absurdity."(217) He realizes that, contrary to the beliefs he has

---

reveals the emotional immaturity in which the betrayal is rooted."*Joseph Conrad: The Way of Dispossession*, p196.

held prior to the Haldin incident, he is at the mercy of accident and human error:

> 'Three years of good work gone, the course of forty more perhaps jeopardized - turned from hope to terror because events started by human folly link themselves into a sequence which no sagacity can foresee and no courage break through. Fatality enters your rooms while your landlady's back is turned' (118).[246]

As Schopenhauer argued, "the suffering of mankind is produced partly by chance and error and these stand as the rulers of the world personified as Fate."(WWR I 253)

Betrayal and self-knowledge

Talking to Razumov before his death, Haldin stresses the soul - the non-physical side of man which for him presupposes an ethical universe: "look here brother!", he says, "Men like me leave no posterity, but their souls are not lost. No man's soul is ever lost. It works for itself - or else where would be the sense of self-sacrifice, of martyrdom of conviction, of faith - the labours of the soul?"(69) Yet in betraying Haldin, Razumov implicitly denies this side of man and suffers the consequences, being haunted by phantoms and hallucinations of Haldin till the end. As the novel makes clear, the labours of both men's "souls" will indeed not be lost but follow them either posthumously, or while they are still alive: Razumov will be plagued by guilt and remorse for his cowardly betrayal of his fellow man and Haldin will become a martyr for the revolutionary cause and be fondly remembered by his family and comrades. As Razumov later admits, "It's myself whom I have given up to destruction", while "It was [Haldin] who had attained to repose and yet continued to exist in the thoughts of all those people posing for lovers of humanity."(318) Haldin claims that his soul shall not be destroyed along with his body but shall carry on his struggle for 'justice' and 'truth' in another body. What neither men are aware of at this stage is how prophetic these words shall turn out

---

[246] As Royal Roussel argues, "In such a world, there is no certainty and no plans are valid. Reason is useless because the acts from which this chain flows are not rational and therefore predictable." *The Metaphysics of Darkness*, p144.

to be for Razumov himself will be 'possessed' by Haldin's 'spirit' and it will go on warring in him until the truth is revealed (at least as regards Razumov's part in Haldin's death): "What will become of my soul when I die", asks Haldin, "It shall not perish. Don't make a mistake Razumov [...] My spirit shall go on warring in some Russian body till all falsehood is swept out of the world."(69)[247]

Despite wishing to dissociate himself from everything that Haldin believes and stands for, Razumov finds himself subconsciously identifying with the revolutionary from the moment of the betrayal: "His mind hovered on the borders of delirium. He heard himself suddenly saying, 'I confess,' as a person might do on the rack."(103)[248] The morning after the betrayal, Razumov mimics Haldin's last gestures proving that the bond which existed between them is more valid than ever: "Lying on his back, he put his hands under his head and stared upward. After a moment he thought, 'I am lying here like that man. I wonder if he slept while I was struggling with the blizzard in the streets. No he did not sleep. But why should I not sleep?"(107) As he expects Haldin to be tortured and interrogated, so Razumov assumes the role of the suspect: "I am a suspect now there's no use denying the fact."(103) He imagines a pale figure drawn on the rack but can't see the face because it is both Haldin and himself together: "At that moment Razumov beheld his own brain suffering on the rack - a long, pale figure drawn horizontally with terrific force in the darkness of a vault, whose face he failed to see."(121) In general T-'s office Razumov goes as far as to play devil's advocate for Haldin by stressing the revolutionary's willingness to sacrifice even his life for the cause he is fighting for: "They shall be destroyed then", says the general, "They have made a sacrifice of their lives beforehand, said Razumov with malicious pleasure."(92) This pleasure which Razumov feels in defending Haldin's courage is in stark contrast with the hatred he said he felt for him, which suggests a powerful bond has been forged between the two men without Razumov knowing it. Like Marlow with his "choice of nightmares" in *Heart of Darkness,* Razumov finds himself paradoxically taking the side of the outlaw when faced with the impudent self-righteousness of General T- representing the forces of law and order:

---

[247] Claire Rosenfield has observed that "Haldin has made Razumov his second self, his promise of immortality." *Paradise of Snakes*, p142.

[248] "That the man whom Razumov has betrayed," writes Claire Rosenfield, "is the figure whom the student's guilt-ridden imagination summons as an eternal comrade, a constant presence, is obvious. No reassurance but self-torture is, however, the psychic validity for the dream figure who constantly accompanies him." Ibid., pp139-40.

"If Haldin does change his purpose tonight," says Razumov, "you may depend on it that it will not be to save his life by flight or some other means."(92) As though Haldin were indeed in possession of Razumov's body, the latter cannot help defending the former before his enemies. This recalls Marlow's strange compulsion to defend Kurtz's reputation when he returned to Europe: "He felt ready to stand by his opinion of Haldin to the last extremity", we are told.

In betraying Haldin, Razumov can be said to have betrayed two bonds. Firstly there is the bond of hospitality which demands that a guest be offered shelter and protection -regardless of other considerations. Despite his attempts to deny that he bears any responsibility whatsoever for Haldin, Razumov's powerful inner conflict, and the tension it produces, suggests that merely having Haldin in his rooms has placed a moral obligation on him: "And you tell me, Victor Victorovitch, not to be anxious! Why! I am responsible for you.' Razumov almost shrieked."(99)[249] Then, there is the universal bond of human fellowship which Conrad saw as uniting all men together in brotherhood.[250] Regardless of the political or ideological differences which separate Razumov and Haldin, Razumov owes Haldin that allegiance and solidarity which springs from a common mortality; this is further emphasized by the fact that, in death, Haldin is far more attached to Razumov then he ever was alive. That Razumov has indeed transgressed important unwritten laws in betraying Haldin is obvious when Razumov asks himself: "why not simply keep on as before? Study. Advance. Work hard as if nothing had happened [...] It's you crazy fanatic who stands in the way!"(287-88), he admits, yet the man is dead. And when he does try to return to some sort of ordinary routine with his work, he fails dismally: "the work in the library was the mere dumb-show of research. He sat with many volumes open before him trying to make notes and extracts. His new tranquillity was like a flimsy garment and seemed to float at the mercy of a casual word."(108) Knowing that Haldin has been executed and not implicated him in revolutionary activity, Razumov automatically gets up to leave Mikulin's office but although he is free as far as the authorities are concerned, he is not free from the point of view of his own conscience: "the official could have set a lot of bells

---

[249] "In that cry", writes Tony Tanner, "is the horror of recognizing that fatal bond which the mind denies." "Nightmare and Complacency: Razumov and the Western Eye", p206.

[250] As Albert Guerard has remarked, "The energizing conflict derives from the fact that Razumov, this sane conservative scorner of visionaries and servant of law and victim of revolutionary folly, is (when he informs on Haldin) dramatized as committing a crime; he has violated the deepest human bond." (*Conrad the Novelist*, p243).

ringing all over the building without leaving his chair. He let Razumov go quite up to the door before he spoke [...] 'Where to?' asked Councilor Mikulin softly."(130) Clearly, there is nowhere for Razumov to go until he can reconcile himself with his conscience.

The imagery of the novel suggests that, in siding with the autocrats, Razumov has sided with the forces of death:

> The silence of [General T-'s] room was like the silence of the grave; perfect, measureless for even the clock on the mantlepiece made no sound. Filling a corner on a black pedestal stood a quarter-life-size, smooth-limbed bronze of an adolescent figure running. The Prince observed in an undertone - 'Spontini's "Flight of Youth". Exquisite' (86)

Just as the idealistic promptings of youth are symbolically arrested in mid-flight in General T-'s office, Haldin's youth shall be cut down in its prime thanks to Razumov. Also, as the cowardly officers of the Patna betray the bond of human fellowship in *Lord Jim* and those illusions which are most valuable for life when they save their lives, Razumov can be said to have betrayed the illusions of youth and the promptings of the heart which redeem the sordidness of life. Upon leaving Razumov's room, the betrayed Haldin is compared to Spontini's "Flight of Youth" implying that cynicism has displaced idealism in Razumov's life:

> Haldin already at the door, tall and straight as an arrow, with his pale face and hand raised attentively, might have posed for the statue of a daring youth listening to an inner voice. Razumov mechanically glanced down at his watch. When he looked towards the door again, Haldin had vanished [...] He was gone almost as noiseless as a vision. (102)

Just as Haldin is the embodiment of youthful idealism in the novel, General T- is shown to represent cynicism and reflects the reality of Razumov's betrayal which was cynical and cowardly rather than noble and patriotic: "When the general turned to the providential young man, his florid complexion, the blue, unbelieving eyes and the bright flash of an automatic smile had an air of jovial, careless cruelty. He expressed no wonder at the extraordinary story - no pleasure or excitement - no incredulity either. He betrayed no sentiment whatever."(87) General T-employs the image of the bird to represent Haldin and this image is associated in the novel with the human soul: "with a politeness almost differential [he] suggested that 'the bird might have flown while Mr - Mr Razumov was running about the streets."(87) Haldin has spoken of those men "who destroy the souls which aspire to the perfection of human dignity"(98) and it is clear that the general is such a man, yet by locking Haldin in his rooms and helping the autocrats to catch him alive so that he may be interrogated before his death, Razumov allies himself to them. "We want that bird alive", says General T-, "It will be the devil if we can't make him sing a little before we are done with him. The grave-like silence of the room with its mute clock fell on the polite modulations of this terrible phrase."(88) This suggests that Razumov has metaphorically buried himself alive by betraying Haldin just as Jim and the officers of the Patna are said to be "walled up quick in a roomy grave" after betraying their charges. Razumov subconsciously identifies with Haldin via the bird image suggesting that he has been trapped in the same cage by the autocrats, just as he feared he would be: "I am his prey - his helpless prey,' thought Razumov. the fatigues and the disgusts of that afternoon, the need to forget, the fear which he could not keep off re-awakened his hate for Haldin."(91) Haldin represents Razumov's *döppelganger*, the secret sharer of his personality and physical body - the man metaphorically trapped in the same cage as he - which Razumov wishes to deny and cut himself off from. But he cannot escape this 'dark brother' and from this fact springs the hatred he feels for him,

As Spontini 's statue suggests, Razumov's youth is abandoning him as the betrayed Haldin leaves his rooms and, with the departure of this youthful idealist, a cynicism and world-weariness takes hold in Razumov's life. The morning after, "The light coming through [Razumov's] window seemed strangely cheerless, containing no promise as the light of each new day should for a young man - It was the awakening of a man mortally ill, or a man ninety years old."(106) Having symbolically betrayed the spiritual side of life which redeems the baseness and corruption, Razumov is left with the dead body and his room begins to resemble a grave in its deathly silence: "An incredible dullness, a ditch water stagnation was sensible to his perceptions as though life had withdrawn itself from all things and even from his own thoughts. There was not a sound in the house."(106) For the security of autocracy, Razumov has sacrificed the hope and idealism of the revolutionary who, albeit naively, seeks to improve the lot of mankind and relieve the squalor of the poor: As Sophia Antonovna points out, "Life, Razumov, not to be vile must be a revolt - a pitiless protest all the time"(256). Indeed, as

Haldin descends the spiral staircase to be captured by the police, Razumov's life becomes "vile": "a fleeting shadow passed over the glimmer - a wink of the tiny flame. Then stillness. Razumov hung over, breathing the cold air tainted by the evil smells of the unclean staircase."(102)[251]

To use Nietzschean terms, Razumov, in betraying Haldin, has raised the Apollonian veil and is instantly immersed in the Dionysian darkness lying just beneath the surface of life.[252] Like Kurtz, he is trapped in the extraordinary and cannot return to normality: "Extraordinary things do happen," he thinks to himself, "But when they have happened they are done with [...] and the daily concerns, the familiarities of our thoughts swallow it up - and life goes on as before with the mysterious and secret sides out of sight, as they should be"(95). But the mysterious and secret sides of life now rise menacingly to the surface instead of receding for Razumov, while the normality of life is lost: what is imaginary becomes real and what is real becomes illusory. Haldin's "body seemed to have less substance than its own phantom walked over by Razumov in the street with snow. It was more alarming in its shadowy persistent reality than the distinct but vanishing illusion."(96) His contact with Haldin and his response to the challenge of the irrational have given Razumov Dionysian self-knowledge which is knowledge of man's intimate alliance with the amoral forces of nature: "it was as if his soul had gone out in the night to gather the flowers of wrathful wisdom. He got up with a mood of grim determination and as if with a new knowledge of his own nature."(114) Having seen the treacherous or dark side of his own personality, he can imagine its presence everywhere: "Razumov looked apprehensively towards the door of the outer room as if expecting some evil shape to turn the handle and appear before him silently." Moreover, having once practised deceit and subterfuge himself, he begins to suspect it everywhere around him: "That man belonged to one of the revolutionary circles. The same in fact, that I am affiliated to' remarked the student. [Razumov] dared not leave the fellow there. 'He may be affiliated to the

---

[251] H. M. Daleski remarks that "What Razumov breathes into his deepest being is an air which is 'tainted' not so much by 'the evil smells of the unclean staircase' as by the corruption of betrayal." (*Joseph Conrad: The Way of Dispossession*, p195).

[252] As Tony Tanner has written, "Under Western Eyes is the compelling account of a man forced into wide-awakeness, a man unwittingly made intimate with the nightmare which hovers forever just under the complacencies of civilized existence." "Nightmare and Complacency: Razumov and the Western Eye", p214.

police' was the thought that passed through [Razumov's] mind, who could tell?"(109)

Razumov begins to resemble a Schopenhauerian sceptic after his betrayal of Haldin and muses on "the miserable lot of humanity" as well as the nature of happiness: "What was happiness [...] Looking forward was happiness [...] to the gratification of some desire, to the gratification of some passion, love, ambition, hate [...] And to escape the dangers of existence, to live without fear."(107) But Razumov, having lost hope in his silver medal, has neither anything to look forward to any more nor is he able to live without fear. His scepticism and lack of faith after his betrayal know no bounds - so much so that he won't accept a single statement of the teacher's at face value and even raises doubts as to his own fictional status: "Upon my word what is it to me whether women are fools or lunatics? I really don't care what you think of them. I am not interested in them [...] I am not a young man in a novel."(197) Razumov questions everything because he is himself completely questionable. This is the opposite of the resignation which Haldin told him was the sacred part of the Russian character: "You spring up from the ground before me with this talk," he tells the teacher, "Who the devil are you? This is not to be borne! Why! What for? What do you know what is or is not peculiar? What have you got to do with anything that happens in Russia anyway?"(198)

Because of the self-knowledge which his betrayal of Haldin has afforded him, Razumov is in the ideal situation to ask the crucial question in the book: "How can you tell truth from lies"(199) For Razumov, the sustained subterfuge he has had to maintain since Haldin entered his rooms has had the effect of blurring the distinction between truth and falsehood in his mind, and he can see better than anyone else in the novel that identity is a question of role-playing and nothing more:[253] "what are you flinging your heart against?", Sophia Antonovna asks him, "Or perhaps you are only playing a part"(248), to which he replies, "I am doing it no more than the rest of us."(249) But to know this is to be set apart from others and Razumov's Dionysian self-knowledge adds to the isolation which his guilty conscience has placed him in. He can be said to possess Silenus's wisdom which holds that the truth is not worth knowing for man. When asked by the teacher to say something consoling to the

[253] As Royal Roussel has observed, "Razumov in Geneva adopts a role and is able to impose it on the revolutionaries. It is however a hollow victory because it does not allow him to establish a positive identity. Because he must remain always hidden or risk being controlled he is forced to live a series of lies." (*The Metaphysics of Darkness*, p147).

Haldins in the capacity of Victor's closest friend and ally before his death, he replies: "Must I go then and lie to that old woman!' [...] 'Dear me!", says the teacher, somewhat taken aback, "Won't the truth do then? I hoped you could have told them something consoling [...] What if it is not worth telling?"(201), replies Razumov. Later on, in one of his more cynical moods, Razumov imagines the effect that telling the truth would have on the Haldins: "Yes the truth would do! Apparently it would do. Exactly. And receive thanks, he thought formulating the unspoken words cynically. Fall on my neck in gratitude no doubt, he jeered mentally."(208)

But cynicism is not the last word of wisdom in *Under Western Eyes* and Razumov discovers a new self through the mediation of Natalia which enables him to escape the "prison of lies"(334) which his betrayal of Haldin has consigned him to: "you have freed me from the blindness of anger and hate", he tells her, "the truth shining in you drew the truth out of me [...] In giving Victor Haldin up, it was myself after all whom I have betrayed most basely."(333) This realization marks Razumov's recognition of the bond of human fellowship which he had consistently tried to deny in the past and with it the acceptance of Haldin as a spiritual brother. The moral or spiritual claims of life are also implicitly acknowledged by Razumov who admits that "You don't walk with impunity over a phantom's breast."(334) Razumov's confession to the revolutionaries represents the victory of Haldin who had prophesied that his soul shall go on warring in another Russian body until "all falsehood" is defeated. During his confession, Razumov employs the same type of language that Haldin used to describe Ziemianitch signifying the acceptance of the double - it is as though Haldin himself were speaking through his mouth: "In justice to that individual, the much ill-used peasant, Ziemianitch, I now declare solemnly that the conclusions of that letter calumniates a man of the people - a bright Russian soul."(336) Thus Razumov's betrayal of Haldin both makes and breaks him by plunging him in a nightmare world of guilt and despair and then affording him tragic wisdom through the acquisition of moral knowledge.[254]

---

[254] Tony Tanner has argued that "Razumov acquires great stature not only because of what he suffers but because in the depths of that suffering he discovers that no matter what is in the balance, he cannot live a lie." "Nightmare and Complacency: Razumov and the Western Eye", p213.

"Truth", illusion, and fiction

Although illusions are viewed in the novel as life-sustaining and positive, the truth is seen as both redemptive and destructive and is thereby associated both with light and darkness. Firstly, as in *Lord Jim* and *Heart of Darkness,* the truth is here associated with the Dionysian darkness which lies just beneath the Apollonian illusions of life and is destined finally to engulf and destroy them. The English teacher of languages sees the darkness as a cynicism originating in Russia and irresistibly encroaching upon the innocence of the Haldins in Geneva: "I saw the gigantic shadow of Russian life deepening around [Natalia] like the darkness of an advancing night. It would destroy her presently. I inquired after Mrs Haldin - that other victim of the deadly shade."(210) This process reaches its conclusion when Razumov confesses to Natalia his role in the arrest of her brother thereby disillusioning her regarding his own integrity while destroying all her hopes in a union between them. The teacher describes the effect which this severe disillusionment as on her: "Her hands were lying lifelessly, palms upwards, on her lap. She raised her grey eyes slowly. Shadows seemed to come and go in them as if the cross-currents of poisoned air from the corrupted dark immensity claiming her for its own"(329). The light of Natalia's idealism and virtue is thus seen to be temporarily overcome by the darkness that is Russia "where virtues themselves fester into crimes in the cynicism of oppression and revolt." But in Razumov's diary the truth which Natalia represents is seen to be finally victorious over the dark reality of Razumov's cynical deed: "It was as if your pure brow bore a light which fell on me, searched my heart and saved me from ignominy, from ultimate undoing [...] Your light! your truth!", says Razumov associating the truth with light instead of darkness.

Thus, we can detect a double movement in the novel towards darkness and towards light where the two elements compete with one another for the truth. This mirrors the inner struggle of Razumov where Haldin's spirit is vying against his own for mastery over his body. One part of Razumov wants to tell the truth and break out of the "prison of lies"(334) and the other is enjoying the feeling of power and superiority which fooling his interlocutors gives him: "It gave him a feeling of triumphant pleasure to deceive [Sophia Antonovna] out of her own mouth. The epigrammatic saying that speech has been given to us for the purpose of concealing our thoughts came into his mind."(257) Yet, at the same time, Razumov finds it almost impossible to tell a direct lie and in his heart hates having to be dishonest: "Razumov listened without hearing, gnawed by the newborn desire of safety with its independence from that degrading method of direct lying which at times he found it almost impossible to practice."(271) Just as language can be used either to lie or to tell the truth, Razumov's speech can be said to be simultaneously revealing and concealing his thoughts throughout the novel.[255] As soon as he has betrayed Haldin, he feels an irresistible urge to confess but his actions have rendered the truth diabolical so he cannot speak out: "Well and what have you arranged?", Haldin asks him after his return from Ziemianitch, "A diabolical impulse to say, 'I have given you up to the police,' frightened him exceedingly, but he did not say that."(95) Because he cannot speak the truth directly, Razumov is always revealing himself indirectly by disguising his revelations so that only he understands their true meaning: while describing his interview with Ziemianitch to Haldin, "A mocking spirit entered into him and he added, 'It was satisfactory in a sense. I came away from it much relieved."(96) Razumov craves understanding but having betrayed Haldin and visited Ziemianitch he has compromised himself with both revolutionaries and autocrats and cannot fully confide in either. Upon his return from General T-'s office he tries to explain to Haldin the pressure he has put him under by his unexpected visit without actually revealing what he has been driven to do: "What will you have? Consider a man of studious, retired habits - and suddenly like this...I am not practised in talking delicately...But"(101)

Before Councilor Mikulin too, Razumov is strongly moved to confess the truth of his experience and obtain understanding but he cannot do so without implicating himself so he transfigures the truth, making it is unrecognizable. As he tels Mikulin:

> But if a drunken man runs out of a grog shop falls on your neck and kisses you on both cheeks because something about your appearance has taken his fancy, what then kindly tell me? You may break, perhaps a cudgel on his back and yet not succeed in beating him off...(128)

---

[255] For an excellent essay on the uses and abuses of language in Under Western Eyes, see Jeremy Hawthorn, *Joseph Conrad: Language and Fictional Self-Consciousness*, pp102-128. Tony Tanner has also pointed out that Razumov "is driven to blurting out remarks which at once reveal and conceal his guilt. It is as though whatever he starts saying his words coil back to pick at his past." "Nightmare and Complacency: Razumov and the Western Eye", p210.

In this statement which resembles a riddle, Razumov conveys the essence of his experience with Haldin and Ziemianitch. In this version of events Haldin becomes the "drunken man" and Ziemianitch's beating is transferred to him because it was essentially an attempt to "beat off" the revolutionary intoxicated with radical fanaticism and not the relatively harmless drunken peasant. In Geneva, Razumov realizes that although the truth may not be in his interests to divulge, he cannot do away with it altogether because it forms an integral part of ordinary human existence: "All sincerity was an imprudence. Yet one could not renounce truth altogether, he thought with despair."(215) Razumov mocks the revolutionaries with the tainted knowledge that only he possesses but he also finds that the truth is irrepressible and that he can't avoid revealing himself in riddles and innuendos which only he understands: "Ah, Peter Ivanovitch," he says, "If you only knew the force which drew - no which *drove* me towards you. The irresistible force."(230) This force is ostensibly the power of autocracy and not, as Peter Ivanovitch probably assumes, his world-wide reputation as a writer and a revolutionary feminist. Until his final confession proper, Razumov is constantly compelled to speak out about his experience with Haldin despite resolving to keep all discourse to a bare minimum. While in the company of Madame de S- he suddenly blurts out: "I myself have had an experience [...] I've seen a phantom once."(220)

As in most of Conrad 's work, illusion is presented in *Under Western Eyes* as necessary for life because the truth is often too much for human beings to bear. Thus, having been deprived of the few illusions which Razumov possessed, he is placed in a vulnerable position and becomes highly susceptible to the ugliness and cruelty of life. As he says to Natalia: "you have given yourself up to vain imaginings while I have managed to remain amongst the truth of things and the realities of life - our Russian life - such as they are.' 'They are cruel,' she murmured. 'And ugly", he replies. "One must look beyond the present", she tells him. "The blind can do that best", he replies, "I have had the misfortune to be born clear-eyed."(321) Everyone in the novel is allowed to have some sustaining faith or "saving illusion" except for Razumov: In Peter Ivanovitch's book there are "whole pages of self-analysis whence emerges like a white figure from a dark confused sea the conviction of women's spiritual superiority - his new faith confessed since in several volumes."(148) Haldin's revolutionary faith also clearly differentiates him from Razumov: "Your brother believed in the power of a people's will to achieve anything?", asks the teacher, "It was his religion,' declared Miss Haldin."(157) Natalia herself is sustained by her faith in love and forgiveness and looks forward to the era of concord and justice: "Let the tyrants and the slayers be forgotten together, and only the reconstructors be remembered", she tells Sophia Antonovna who replies, "It is good for you to believe in love."(310)

Tekla suggests to Razumov that illusion may be more valuable than life itself and she and the teacher take it upon themselves to protect Natalia's illusions as she can be said to represent innocence in the novel. Tekla tells Razumov to keep Natalia away from Peter Ivanovitch and the Chateau Borel: "you had better tie a stone round her neck and throw her into the lake [...] That's the best you can do unless you want her to become like me - disillusioned!"(234) She herself has reached that state as a result of taking down the books of Peter Ivanovitch from dictation and discovering that he had to "grope for words as if he were in the dark as to what he meant to say"(168): "it seemed to freeze my beliefs in me"(169), she exclaims. The teacher is also aware of the importance of illusion for the psychological well-being of individuals and so warns Razumov that Natalia "is a frank and generous creature, having the noblest - well - illusions. You will tell her everything or you will tell her nothing."(202) Razumov himself may be lacking any life-sustaining faith comparable to Peter Ivanovitch's belief in the spiritual superiority of women but, as the latter points out, it is impossible for human beings to harbour no illusions whatsoever - to be alive is to be deceived to some degree: "it's just as well to have no illusions", says Razumov, to which Peter Ivanovitch replies, "The man who says that he has no illusions has at least that one."(214)

Whether an opinion is true or false is viewed in the novel as less important than the psychological needs of the characters which determine their perspective on things. Because Natalia desperately needs to see in Razumov a substitute for her late brother, he will appear to her as exactly that: "Do you know what my last hope is?", she asks the teacher, "Perhaps the next thing we know, we shall see [Haldin] walking into our rooms."(139) Although it is not Haldin but Razumov - in whom the spirit of Haldin resides - who walks into their rooms, Natalia will receive him as though he were her late brother: "I don't want to abuse your sympathy", she tells Razumov, "but you must understand that it is in you that we can find all that is left of his generous soul."(321) Just as Natalia "would take liberty from any hand as a hungry man would snatch a piece of bread"(158), so she will try to find consolation for the death of her brother from anywhere she can: "Only think", she tells the teacher, "such a friend. The only man mentioned in his letters. He would have something to give me if nothing more than a few poor words."(159) Thus, anything about

Razumov which does not fit in with her brother's estimation of him as one of those "Unstained, lofty, and solitary existences" is disregarded by Natalia who saw that "he was not an ordinary person, and perhaps she did not want him to be other than he appeared to her trustful eyes."(321) Reality in the novel is seen to be psychologically determined and what is strongly enough imagined finally becomes real: Mrs Haldin "now expects to see *him*!" [Haldin], Natalia exclaims, "the veil dropped from her fingers and she clasped her hands in anguish. 'It shall end by her seeing him,' she cried."(323)

The teacher of languages claims to believe in "the psychological value of facts"(281). Talking to Razumov about the truth or otherwise of the newspaper report on Haldin's arrest and execution, he stresses that what's important for him is the effect which the article had on the emotional state of the Haldins: "I pointed out that whether the journalist was well or ill informed, the concern of the friends of these ladies was with the effect the few lines of print in question had produced - the effect alone."(200) This echoes Nietzsche's theory that the "falseness of a judgement is not necessarily a objection to a judgement [...] The question is to what extent it is [...] life-preserving"(BGE 4). Razumov is placed in the same position as Marlow was before the Intended, for it is in his power to preserve or destroy the life-sustaining illusions of a fellow human being by revealing or withholding the truth. The teacher asks him to consider the state which Mrs Haldin is in and come up with some vital fiction: "Perhaps something could be invented under your authority as a cure for a distracted and suffering soul"(202). But Razumov doesn't possess Marlow's faith in "saving illusions" nor his compassionate nature and exclaims resentfully, "Must I go then and lie to that old woman!"(201) Although the teacher doesn't always share the illusions of others he is often careful to preserve them, realizing their psychological value for those harbouring them: "I am confident that we shall meet again", says Natalia referring to Razumov, "Because I've told him that I was in great need of someone, a fellow countryman, a fellow believer, to whom I could give my confidence in a certain matter", to which the teacher replies, "I confess that this is good ground for your belief in Mr Razumov's reappearance here before long"(190). The teacher knows that Razumov being a "fellow countryman" does not presuppose his being a "fellow believer" as Natalia innocently assumes, yet he is careful not to reveal this to her.

Although Razumov may be deprived of illusions and possess no sustaining faith in contrast with the other characters in the novel, he finds the strength to carry on by writing in his secret diary: "He had regained a certain measure of composure by writing in his secret diary. He was aware of the danger of that strange self-indulgence [...] but he could not refrain. It calmed him - it reconciled him to existence."(316) Like illusion, fiction is seen in Conrad as a life-sustainer because it has the power to cover over the imperfections and contradictions of life. That *Under Western Eyes* regards life as inherently flawed is suggested by Peter Ivanovitch when he introduces Madame de S- to Razumov: "No one is perfect", he says, "Thus the possessor of a rare jewel might before opening the casket warn the profane that no gem perhaps is flawless."(218) Razumov is reconciled to the 'flawed jewel' that is life by reflecting upon it and finding in the reflection some redeeming feature or excuse for the way things are:

> Mr Razumov looked at [the diary] as a man looks at himself in a mirror, with wonder, perhaps with anguish, with anger or despair. Yes, as threatened man may look fearfully at his own face in the glass formulating to himself reassuring excuses for his appearance marked by the taint of some insidious hereditary disease. (220)

This "insidious hereditary disease" which Razumov has inherited from his Russian parentage is a cynicism and a mistrust of life in general. Writing can also be said to reconcile Razumov to existence because it distances him from himself so that he is both actor and spectator of the play in which he seems to be playing such an ignominious part. As Nietzsche claimed, "Only as an aesthetic phenomenon can the world be justified to all eternity"(BT 42) and by transforming his experience into writing, Razumov can be said to be turning his life into a redeeming aesthetic phenomenon. His gesture of wrapping up the completed work in Natalia's veil before sending it to her can be seen as a symbol for Conrad's aesthetic philosophy as a whole which is that art has the power to restore the veil of illusion and reconcile man to existence.

The tragedy of Razumov

There are many aspects of Razumov's story which suggest that Conrad had a tragic framework in mind when writing the novel.[256] Razumov is set

[256] My assumptions on tragedy and the tragic hero are derived from A. C. Bradley's *ShakespeareanTragedy: Lectures on Hamlet, Othelo, King Lear, Macbeth*, pp5-39.

up as a species of tragic hero who, having to face a crucial test, fails to foresee the full consequences of his actions, and is tormented by guilt until the end of the novel whereupon he is redeemed by an act of atonement. As J. I. M. Stewart has claimed, "*Under Western Eyes* exhibits the spectacle of an authentic purification through suffering and is a book in the great tragic tradition."[257] As in *Lord Jim*, the protagonist is an ordinary young man placed in an extraordinary position which he cannot cope with due to his inexperience and emotional immaturity. In his Author's Note Conrad observes that Razumov has a "healthy capacity for work and sane ambitions. He has an average conscience. If he is slightly abnormal it is in his sensitiveness to his position"(50). This "sensitiveness to his position is exactly what set Jim apart from his fellow officers on the Patna and lead to his facing the official inquiry which first breaks him by depriving him of his seaman's certificate and then makes him by leading to his tragic redemption in Patusan. Razumov is also rendered extraordinary and attains tragic stature through the self-knowledge and acute suffering which his betrayal of Haldin affords him.[258]

As befits a tragic hero, Razumov is singled out from the start by his illegitimacy and lack of family ties: "He was as lonely as a man swimming in the deep sea", we are told, "The word Razumov was the mere label of a solitary individuality. There were no Razumov's belonging to him anywhere. His closest parentage was defined in the statement that he was Russian."(61) Razumov's solitary condition is significant because it means that when he is forced to undergo his crucial test, he is lacking the emotional and moral support necessary to withstand it and fails to act with courage or foresight: "Other men had somewhere, a corner of the earth - some little house in the provinces where they had a right to take their troubles. A material refuge. He had nothing. He had not even a moral refuge - the refuge of confidence. To whom could he go with this tale - in all this great, great land!"(78) Razumov finds support in his tragic dilemma in the idea of autocracy - "the one great historical fact of the land"(79) - and in the feeling of patriotism because Russia is his sole inheritance and the only family he possesses. Returning from his unsuccessful errand to contact Ziemianitch, he "turned to autocracy for the peace of his patriotic conscience as a weary unbeliever, touched by

---

257 *Joseph Conrad*, p208.

258 As Albert Guerard has observed, "Once again we have the story of a not un-common man whom chance and suffering render extraordinary; who suddenly has to face a boundary situation and most difficult choice; whose crime both makes and breaks him." (*Conrad the Novelist*, p231).

grace, turns to the faith of his fathers for the blessing of spiritual rest. Like other Russians before him, Razumov, in conflict with himself, felt the touch of grace upon his forehead." One could say that Razumov's predicament is doubly tragic because Haldin chooses to confide in him for the very same reason that he was isolated in the first place: "Speaking to a superior mind like yours", says Haldin, "I can well say all the truth. It occurred to me that you - you have no one belonging to you - no ties, no one to suffer for it if this came out by some means."(67)

Razumov's isolation throughout the novel is a characteristic feature of his tragedy and one of the main causes of the pity which his story inspires. The teacher reminds us at regular intervals in the narrative that "Mr Razumov's youth had no one in the world, as literally no one as it can honestly be affirmed of any human being"(281). After he has decided to betray Haldin he still "felt the need of some other mind's sanction"(83) and is seen to have reached a point of moral solitude which few human beings ever experience in their lives and none could withstand for long:

> Razumov longed desperately for a word of advice, for moral support. Who knows what true loneliness is - not the conventional word but the naked terror? [...] Now and then a fatal conjunction of events may lift the veil for an instant [...] only. No human being could bear a steady view of moral solitude without going mad. Razumov had reached that point of vision. (83)

Razumov's first impulse is to confess to Haldin, but because of the latter's crime, this potential friend and spiritual brother is lost for Razumov - something which stresses all the more his moral and emotional isolation: "he embraced for a whole minute he delirious purpose of rushing to his lodgings and flinging himself on his knees by the side of the bed with the dark figure stretched on it; to pour out a full confession in passionate words that would end in embraces and tears; in an incredible fellowship of souls - such as the world had never seen."(83) His subsequent betrayal of Haldin, instead of safeguarding his future by protecting his independence as it was intended to do, only serves to confirm Razumov's total isolation in a land where everyone is his 'brother' but no one his confidant: "Several times that night he woke up shivering from a dream of walking through drifts of snow in a Russia where he was completely alone as any betrayed autocrat could be"(104).[259]

The need to talk with someone, to obtain moral support for his personality, the "universal aspiration"(83) to be understood in his predicament, all these factors conspire tragically to push Razumov into the hands of the autocrats: "he went to [Councilor Mikulin] with a certain eagerness", relates the teacher, "which may appear incredible till it is remembered that Councilor Mikulin was the only person on earth with whom Razumov could talk, taking the Haldin adventure for granted"(289).[260] Razumov's isolation is compounded when he consents to act as a secret agent for Mikulin in Geneva whereupon, in the midst of Haldin's family and comrades, he is forced to carry inside himself the tainted knowledge of his deed and practice subterfuge as a way of life.[261] At one point he asks himself, "How am I to go on day after day if I have no more power of resistance - moral resistance?"(232) When he sees Haldin's mother and the way she grieves for her lost son, it serves to remind him that he has been singled out by fate to go through life without the basic human bonds that other people take for granted: "The old anger against Haldin reawakened by the contemplation of Haldin's mother. And was it not something like enviousness which gripped his heart, as if a privilege denied to him alone of all the men that ever passed through this world?"(317) Natalia asks him to say something consoling to her distracted mother about Victor to which Razumov pathetically replies: "In order to speak fittingly to a mother of her lost son one must have had some experience of the filial relation. It is not the case with me - if you must know the whole truth. Your hopes have to deal here with 'a breast unwarmed by any affection', as the poet says."(320) Yet Conrad is careful to stress the human aspect of Razumov's predicament and to enlist our sympathy for his tragic isolation by making it appear as something not altogether unnatural: "And it must be admitted," says the teacher, "that in Mr Razumov's case the bitterness of solitude from which he suffered was not an altogether morbid phenomenon."(289)

As the consequences of his decision to inform on Haldin suggest, there was no safe choice or simple solution to Razumov's tragic dilemma -

---

[259] As H. M. Daleski points out, "If betrayal is a denial of the bonds of fellowship its logical consequence is complete isolation." (*Joseph Conrad: The Way of Dispossession*, p198).

[260] H. M. Daleski observes that "it is the intensity of his need for human contact that accounts for the irrationality of Razumov's urge to return to Mikulin and confess to him." (Ibid., p201).

[261] As Jeremy Hawthorn points out, "If Razumov is an isolate at the start of the novel, he is isolated yet more by lying."(*Joseph Conrad: Language and Fictional Self-Consciousness*, p117).

whichever way he chose he was doomed.[262] When Ziemianitch fails to respond to Razumov's beating, the latter realizes that he is trapped between "the drunkenness of the peasant incapable of action and the dream intoxication of the idealist incapable of perceiving the reason of things, and the true character of men"(77).[263] Between the two "he was done for", claims the teacher. The terms which Conrad uses to convey Razumov's predicament at this point - being caught between "drunkenness" and "dream-intoxication" - are the same which Nietzsche employed in *The Birth of Tragedy* to symbolize the twin deities of Dionysos and Apollo whose universal conflict is deemed responsible for the tragic genre. Razumov's conflict is thus presented as an explicitly tragic conflict, comparable to the universal opposition between reason and feeling in man - the irreconcilable antagonism between Apollo and Dionysos. Like Hamlet who feels resentment at having to be the one to "set aright" the time which "out of joint" in Denmark, Razumov rails inwardly against his fate which has trapped him in a situation that offers no escape and no solution save suicide:

> in his abhorrence [Razumov] said to himself, 'I'll kill him when I get home.' But he knew very well that was no use. The corpse hanging round his neck would be nearly as fatal as the living man. Nothing short of complete annihilation would do. And that was impossible. What then", he asks himself, "Must one kill oneself to escape this visitation? (77)

Razumov had wanted to remain impartial in the political conflict which his homeland was involved in but fate forces him to take sides in a quarrel not of his making and he is tragically drawn into the fray against his will.[264] We are reminded of Heyst who had wanted to practice stoic detachment, but, as both novels demonstrate, life will inevitably put to the

---

262 John F. Haugh has observed that "by his own attempts to escape he subjects himself to the iron imperatives of the czarist state. Whichever way he turns, left or right, he is doomed to the same end." (*Discovery in Design*, p124).

263 Wilfred S. Dowden has argued that "The conflict which provides the principal theme is explicit in the extremes presented in various scenes and images. Razumov is caught between the two forces which are beyond his control and foreign to his philosophy." (*The Imaged Style*, p124).

264 As H. M. Daleski remarks, "The plot of the novel [...] at once makes it clear that in Russia it is impossible to maintain such detachment: slipping into Razumov's rooms after the assassination, Haldin silently demonstrates that one cannot close one's door on dissensions in the street." (*Joseph Conrad: The Way of Dispossession*, pp186-87).

test all man's half-formed plans and vague intentions, making it impossible for him to stand idly by as its flowing current rushes incessantly on. First the revolution seeks Razumov out "to put to a sudden test his dormant instincts, his half-conscious thoughts and almost wholly unconscious ambitions"(281) and then his conversations with Mikulin bring "Mr Razumov as we know him to the test of another faith"(282) - that of autocracy. Tragedy presupposes a reversal of fortunes and accordingly the natural flow of Razumov's life is destroyed by Haldin who, like the Ghost in *Hamlet*, appears in his rooms "lithe and martial"(64) and imparts tainted knowledge which, as Razumov immediately realizes , will irrevocably change his life for the worse, making it impossible for him to carry on as before: "The sentiment of [Razumov's] life being utterly ruined by this contact with such a crime expressed itself quaintly by a sort of half-derisive mental exclamation, 'There goes my silver medal."(65)[265] Thus Razumov is unwittingly caught in the political conflict like the innocent bystanders are caught in the blast of Haldin's bomb, while his prospects for the future are tragically cut short. He had good chances of winning the silver medal and "putting a claim to an administrative appointment of the better sort after he had taken his degree"(61) but suddenly he finds "three years of good work gone, the course of forty more perhaps jeopardized - turned from hope to terror, because events started by human folly link themselves into a sequence which no sagacity can foresee and no courage can break through."(118) This, Razumov muses, is "Fatality".

Razumov acts freely when he betrays Haldin to the authorities, yet this action only serves to bind him hand and foot for the rest of the novel. After the betrayal he perceives that he has completely lost his self-determination and, like Hamlet bound to the service of his dead father, he wonders whether it were better that he weren't alive at all:

> The feeling that his moral personality was at the mercy of these lawless forces was so strong that he asked himself [...] if it were worth while to go on accomplishing the mental functions of that existence which seemed no longer his own.(113)

When he realizes that he will never be left alone by either the forces of autocracy or revolution, he asks the crucial existential question: "Was it

[265] H. M. Daleski has observed that "Razumov's imagination like that of Jim or Jukes, is readily susceptible to intimations of disaster: he at once accepts that 'the sentiment of his life is utterly ruined' and that his silver medal is lost." (Ibid., p190).

possible that he no longer belonged to himself?"(287)[266] Partly as a means of proving that the moral bond he has broken in betraying Haldin had no validity and that he acted out of deeply felt political convictions, Razumov joins the ranks of the autocrats. He fools the simple minded Kostia into stealing his father's money with the notion that it would help him to escape the authorities and then goes to spy on the revolutionaries instead - and all this so as to appear consistent in his own eyes to his initial "act of conscience"(82), as he calls the betrayal: "I had to confirm myself in my contempt and hate for what I betrayed"(331), he writes in his diary.

Thus, Razumov's initial deed is attended by tragic necessity - the necessary connection between a tragic action and its consequences - and this starts a sequence of events which leads to catastrophe. The rushing water image with which the Second Part of the novel ends can be seen as an image of Razumov's inevitable movement towards destruction, like a helpless creature borne on an irresistible flood.[267] As the teacher remarks:

> [Razumov] hung well over the parapet, as if captivated by the smooth rush of the blue water under the arch. The current there is swift, extremely swift, [...] it makes some people dizzy; I myself can never look at it for any length of time without experiencing a dread of being suddenly snatched away by its destructive force. Some brains cannot resist the suggestion of irresistible power and of headlong motion. (206)

Speaking to the revolutionaries who will finally burst his ear-drums and precipitate his fatal accident, Razumov says "What else has drawn me near you, do you think? [...] I was irresistibly drawn, let us say impelled, yes, impelled: or rather, compelled, driven - driven."(230)[268] Razumov's catastrophe is set into motion when he is impelled by Haldin's description of Natalia as the girl with the "most trusting eyes in the world"(330) to

---

[266] As Royal Roussel argues, "Razumov's sense of not belonging to himself is a revelation of the way in which we are at the mercy of the irrationality which governs others." (*The Metaphysics of Darkness*, p143).

[267] Tony Tanner has observed that "the written confession, the confession to Miss Haldin [...] his confession to the revolutionaries as he stands fully exposed dripping with the rain which 'washes him clean' [...] all this follows with a precipitous down-hill inevitability." "Nightmare and Complacency: Razumov and the Western Eye", p212.

[268] Albert Guerard argues that the force which irresistibly drives Razumov towards the revolutionaries is the desire to destroy himself: "Ah, Peter Ivanovitch, if you only knew the force which drew - no which *drove* me towards you! The irresistible force.", he quotes. "but the reader is likely to think of a generalized self-destructiveness [...] That is the hidden motive, hidden even from him." (*Conrad the Novelist*, p235).

seek her out in Geneva, fall in love with her, and confess to her his betrayal of her brother: "I felt I must tell you that I had ended by loving you. And to tell you that I must first confess. Confess, go out - and perish."(330)

As in *Lord Jim*, there is a sense in *Under Western Eyes* that human beings are the helpless pawns of chance which almost appears as an active and malign providence - "a joke hatched in hell": "But there was no tragedy there", says Razumov, "This was a comedy of errors. It was as if the devil himself were playing a game with all of them in turn. First with him, then Ziemianitch then with those revolutionists."(274) This element of the story is not tragic in the classical sense because the notion of 'tragic justice' is missing. According to this concept, the tragic hero's critical deed must be seen to be wrong or bad in some sense so that there is a connection between it and the catastrophe which befalls him. In fact, *Under Western Eyes* implies both a moral order which Razumov has contravened so that his betrayal of Haldin justly returns to plague him and the notion of a man as a blind and helpless play thing of an inscrutable power such as Fate. Chance or accident also play a considerable part in Razumov's tragedy showing that man may begin a sequence of events but not calculate or control it. Thus it is chance which dispatches the idealistic but rather naive Haldin to seek shelter in Razumov's room and it is by chance that Ziemianitch lies unconsciously drunk on the night that Razumov visits him to get rid of Haldin. Both these chance events play a crucial part in precipitating the tragedy. On the other hand, it is also chance that renders Razumov safe in Geneva without him having to exert himself because the revolutionaries come to believe that Ziemianitch was the one responsible for Haldin's arrest and so it "was as if Ziemianitch had hanged himself to help [Razumov] on to further crime."(332) But chance or accident alone cannot bring about tragedy and so Razumov is moved to confess despite being placed beyond suspicion by Sophia Antonovna's letter, thereby proving that a moral order is in place and permeates the world of the novel.[269]

Razumov is essentially good and so wins sympathy in his tragic error. When Tekla tells him that he looked trustworthy the first time she saw him he replies, "I am very glad you trust me. It's possible that later on I may..."(235) Later on Razumov does indeed vindicate Tekla's trust in him and, by confessing, proves his essential goodness. There is something else

---

[269] As Albert Guerard has pointed out, "When [Razumov] has finally won outward impunity he must, because of that other rack of guilt, confess what no one would have ever discovered."(*Conrad the Novelist*, p235).

which suggests that the tragic hero in *Under Western Eyes* is essentially good: at one point he is tempted to marry Natalia without confessing to her, which would amount to abusing both her trust and love - what he calls "stealing her soul" - but he resists this temptation.[270] It was something "like a believer who had been tempted to an atrocious sacrilege"(332), observes the narrator. Razumov also meant well in committing his crime and remarks during his confession to the revolutionaries that Haldin's betrayer "had certain honest ideals in view"(337) but his good intentions prove to have been to no avail. There is also a sense that Razumov's punishment exceeds his crime so that he seems to be atoning for original sin or the 'guilt of existence' as well as for his own particular crime. The tragedy is thus seen to spring from a deeper source of evil than that of Razumov's deed - it springs from the evil that is Russia "where virtues themselves fester into crimes in the cynicism of oppression and revolt."(329) What Razumov stands for and exemplifies is thus the equal potential for good and evil in the human soul. As he admits himself, "I had neither the simplicity nor the courage nor the self-possession to be a scoundrel or an exceptionally able man."(334)

[270] H. M. Daleski notes that "In refusing to take advantage of [Natalia's] love and in deliberately and selflessly renouncing her Razumov not only affirms that need for integrity in personal relations which he has denied in his betrayal of Haldin but demonstrates his newly acquired wholeness, an integrity of being." (*Joseph Conrad: The Way of Dispossession*, p207).

5

Victory: The Functional and the Ornamental

Heyst and the "scientific age"

The first time we encounter the protagonist of *Victory*, Baron Axel Heyst, he is displaying a "persistent inertia"(19)[271] on Samburan, the exact reasons for which are not immediately apparent. The Tropical Belt Coal Company, following the "evaporation" of its capital, has recently gone into "liquidation" but Axel Heyst, "Manager in the East"(38), is "keeping hold". Given the "fascination"(19) of coal as the "supreme commodity" of the "scientific age" and the "deplorable fact" that "a coal-mine can't be put into one's waistcoat pocket", the narrator speculates that "practical and mystical" reasons are preventing Heyst from leaving Samburan. But after reflecting on the paradox of the TBCC's "forced"(20) yet "languid" liquidation, he concludes that "unnatural physics"(19) must lie behind Heyst's "persistent inertia". Like the "mysterious world of finance" in which "evaporation" precedes "liquidation", Heyst's behaviour appears to defy rational explanation. "From the first there was some difficulty in making him out"(21), observes the narrator.

The opening of *Victory* reflects both the pervasiveness of the scientific discourse and its inability[272] to offer more than surface descriptions of an "imponderable"(19) and "mysterious world". As Nietzsche claimed, "We call it 'explanation' but it is 'description' which distinguishes us from earlier stages of knowledge and science. We describe better - we explain just as little as any who came before us."(GS 112) This relates to the fundamental problem of surface and depth and whether it is possible to obtain knowledge of the latter by observing the former, as science attempts to do. Schopenhauer[273] thought not and argued that "we can

271 All quotations are from *Victory*, Penguin Modern Classics.

272 Robert Secor wrongly attributes this inadequacy to Conrad's prose. He writes: "As an introduction to Heyst and his characteristic attitudes and concerns, as an introduction of his relationship to the external world, this opening paragraph seems to fail badly." "The Rhetoric of Shifting Perspectives: Conrad's *Victory*", *The Pennsylvania State University Studies*, No 32 (University Park, 1971), p12.

273 For a general introduction to Schopenhauer's influence on the literature of the period and on Conrad in particular *Joseph Conrad: The Theme of the Outcast*, p6-42.

never get at the inner nature of things *from without*": "However much we may investigate, we obtain nothing but images and names. We are like a man who goes round a castle, looking for an entrance, and sometimes sketching the facades."(WWR I 98-9)

Everyone who wants to understand Heyst at the beginning of the novel is content to give him a name but this merely adds to the general confusion surrounding this "Queer chap"(20).[274] He is called, among other things, "Enchanted Heyst"(22), "Hard Facts", "a u-uto-utopist"(23), "Heyst the Spider"(32), "Naive Heyst"(33) and Heyst the Enemy"(35). The first appellation which is applied to him is "inert body"(19), but this term borrowed from the natural sciences fails to define Heyst adequately. First, there is the inherent ambiguity of language with "inert" meaning stasis in physics and low or non-reactivity in chemistry. Then, strictly speaking, Heyst eludes both meanings as he is neither physically immobile nor his body chemically inert. Finally, taking the term in its metaphorical sense, he has only recently 'reacted' to and been 'moved' by Morrison's misfortunes. Also, Lena's predicament in Zangiacomo's Ladies Orchestra is about to elicit a similar response, although leading to "a very different kind of partnership"(76). As we shall later see, it is only ironically that one can apply such a term to Heyst.

Part of the problem with the scientific discourse is that it can describe *how* a body moves and *how* its particles react, but it cannot account for *why* such phenomena occur so that after every scientific 'explanation' a crucial question remains un-answered. As Nietzsche states:

> Quality, in any chemical change [...] appears as it has always done as a 'miracle'; likewise all locomotion; no one has explained 'thrust'. How could we explain them! We operate with nothing but things which do not exist, with lines, planes, bodies, atoms (GS 112).

The difficulties attending the scientific approach are compounded when the "body" in question is human and possesses its own inner volition as well as a physical substance which can be acted upon from without. To 'explain' why such a "body" moves or, as in Heyst's case, why it fails to move when there appears to be every reason for it to do so, one has to resort to "unnatural physics"(19), as it were.

---

[274] Donald A. Dike writes, "the names for identifying the noumenal Heyst [...] cast eccentric patches of light upon their obscure object."(p102), "The Tempest of Axel Heyst," *Nineteenth-Century Fiction*, 17 (September, 1962), p95-113.

Victory reminds us that, although "every schoolboy"(19) in the "scientific age" can possess precise knowledge of the "chemical relation" between such apparently dissimilar substances as coal and diamonds, such precise knowledge of the physical world does not carry over into the human world despite the attempts of science to reduce all observable phenomena to immutable laws. As Henry J. Laskowsky points out, "Science has made it easy for us to understand that the blackness of coal and the brilliance of diamonds is related by a single 'invisible substance' (the carbon atom) common to both. It is incredibly more difficult to establish the common substance of human relationships or even to define the nuclear essence of a single human being by observing such secondary characteristics as his appearance, his behaviour or his words."[275]

In approaching the last question rationally we are not only faced with the difficulty of understanding things from without and the problem of human volition but also the fact that subject and object are, in this case, one and the same: human nature. Thus, even if we were to look within ourselves in order to overcome the first two difficulties, our investigations would still be frustrated by an inevitable subjectivity arising from the third. As Nietzsche wrote, "The sad truth is that we remain necessarily strangers to ourselves, we don't understand our own substance. We *must* mistake ourselves;"(GM 149) and Schopenhauer presents the same problem in the following way: we simply cannot "be conscious of ourselves [...] independently of the objects of knowing and willing" but "as soon as we enter into ourselves in order to attempt it [...] we lose ourselves in a bottomless void: [...] we grasp with a shudder nothing but a wavering and unstable phantom"(WWR I 278). Conrad himself, in a slightly less philosophical vein, claimed that "one's personality is only a ridiculous and aimless masquerade of something hopelessly unknown."[276]

How then are we to comprehend the protagonist of *Victory*? Is there an essential, unchanging character behind Heyst's external appearance which might enable us to define him and pin him down? This question tells us more about Heyst's condition throughout the novel and its bearing on the "scientific age" than any answer we could possibly obtain to it. In seeking the objective truth behind phenomena while simultaneously denying any metaphysical reality, it is the scientific impulse itself which threatens to turn man into an "inert body" by banishing those "illusions" which had

---

275 "Esse est Percepi: Epistemology and Narrative Method in *Victory*", *Conradiana* IX, 3 (1977), p275-286. p277

276 *The Collected Letters of Joseph Conrad, Vol. I,* 1861-97, Edited by Frederick R. Karl and Lawrence Davies (Cambridge University Press, 1983) to Edward Garnett, 23-24/3/1896, p267.

previously rendered his actions meaningful and participation in life worthwhile. Heyst cannot face life without "the warm mental fog, which the pitiless cold blasts of the father's analysis had blown away from the son"(87) and, at the beginning of the novel, we find him detached.[277] This is the image that emerges from the narrator's observation that an "inert body can do no harm to anyone, provokes no hostility, is scarcely worth derision. It may indeed, be in the way sometimes; but this could not be said of Axel Heyst. He was out of "everybody's way"(19). On Samburan Heyst may be trying to elude the Furies of his guilt following the Morrison episode or that "bad dog" the world that will "bite you if you give it a chance"(59), or even the "fates"; the text allows for various interpretations but not for a final exegesis regarding Heyst's inertia. As Conrad claimed, "The laws [that science] discovers remain certain and immovable for the time of several generations. But in the sphere of an art dealing with a subject matter whose origin and end are alike unknown there is no possible conclusion."[278]

Science has also literally debased man and brought him down to earth by suggesting his origins may be far less than divine. In particular, Darwin's *The Origin of Species* (1859) severely undermined the literal interpretation of the Book of Genesis by proposing a direct evolutionary link between Homo Sapiens and apes. Nietzsche argued that, "all science [...] is now determined to talk man out of his former respect for himself, as though that respect had been nothing but a bizarre presumption. [...] his belief that he was unique and irreplaceable in the hierarchy of beings has been shattered for good: he ha[s] become an animal [...] he who according to his earlier belief was almost a God ("Child of God", "God's own image")."(GM 291) Yet Heyst appears to have fallen even further in the "hierarchy of beings" by resembling a piece of inanimate nature. In keeping with this new status, his most "frequent visitors"(19) are "clouds" and his "nearest neighbour" a volcano "which smoked faintly all day with its head just above the northern horizon". Axel Heyst "was also a smoker", we are told, "he made in the night the same sort of glow and of the same size as that other one so many miles away."(20) Ironically, it is Heyst who mirrors the volcano and not the volcano Heyst. Instead of man defining everything in his own image, like "that first ancestor who, as

277 G. Geddes notes that, "Detachment, as Conrad so clearly understood, was very much a European malaise, a romantic sickness unto death, that would sooner or later take by the throat the whole of Western civilization."(p58) *Conrad's Later Novels*, "*Victory*: The Aesthetics of Rejection".

278 *New York Times*, Saturday Review, quoted in *Collected Letters, Vol. I.*

soon as he could uplift his muddy frame from the celestial mould, started inspecting and naming the animals"(149), everything now begins to define him. The less than flattering names that are applied to Heyst by people who are socially and geographically below this Swedish baron "perched"(19) on "top of a mountain" form an important part of this pathetic reversal. As Tony Tanner points out, "Schomberg's gossip is a kind of verbal mud which sticks to Heyst and drags him back to the old earth of our common origin."[279]

The fact that Heyst seems to have more in common with an "indolent volcano"(19) and "the brooding sunshine of the tropics" than with his own kind also reflects modern man's nausea and alienation. More than any other character Conrad created, Heyst can be said to embody the contradiction arising when man's reflective faculties evolve beyond what is useful from a biological or social point of view.[280] Conrad singles out this aspect of his protagonist in the Author's Note where he writes: "Thinking is the great enemy of perfection. The habit of profound reflection, I am compelled to say, is the most pernicious[281] of all the habits formed by civilized man."(12) Nietzsche also viewed "increasing consciousness" with apprehension, claiming it is "a danger and he who lives among the most conscious Europeans knows that it is even an illness."(GS 354) In order to understand this problem better, it is useful to refer to *The World as Will and Representation* where Schopenhauer makes the important distinction between animal-like perception and human reflection. "As long as our attitude is one of pure perception," he writes, "all is clear, firm and certain. For there are neither doubts nor errors [...] with the appearance of reason, this certainty and infallibility of the will's manifestation [...] are almost entirely lost. Instinct withdraws altogether, deliberation now supposed to take the place of everything begets [...] irresolution and uncertainty. Error becomes possible and in many cases obstructs the adequate objectification of the will through actions."(35, 151-52) Heyst's "inertia" on Samburan can be viewed as one of these "many cases". In reflecting too much on the death of Morrison, he "deemed

---

279 "Joseph Conrad and the Last Gentleman", *Critical Quarterly*, Vol.. 28, nos. 1 & 2, (Spring/Summer 1986) p109-142. p111

280 As G. Geddes points out, *Victory* is "about the dangers of the fragmentation of human nature, where the rational side of man is developed to the exclusion of the others and to the destruction or disintegration of the whole individual."(p66)

281 Frederick R. Karl claims that Heyst's "penchant for reflection" is "an 'imbalance' which, as in Greek tragedy, must lead to his undoing." p247, *A Reader's Guide to Joseph Conrad*. One of the ways in which Heyst's story can be viewed is as the tragedy of civilized man while his "penchant for reflection" links him to Hamlet.

himself guilty"(67). "A rather absurd feeling," according to the narrator, "since no one could have foreseen the horrors of the cold, wet summer lying in wait for poor Morrison at home."(67) This "error" though, nauseates Heyst and inhibits further involvement in life thereby "obstruct[ing] the adequate objectification of the will through actions". Thus we arrive at the strange paradox of a man, "the highest objectification of the will", to use Schopenhauer's terms, resembling a piece of inanimate nature, "the lowest objectification".

In contrast to this debilitating self-reflection is the "purposeful energy"(35) which Heyst displayed while he was managing and promoting the TBCC: "He was running all over the archipelago, jumping in and out of local mail-packets as if they had been tram-cars, here, there and everywhere - organising with all his might."(35) Here we see the real value of coal and other such buried "facts" for Heyst and his "scientific age". Although knowledge and progress, once attained, can lead to disillusionment and regret, their pursuit often constitutes a powerful animating illusion. Heyst originally meets Morrison while wandering around Delli, "possibly in search of some undiscovered facts"(23), according to the narrator. Another trader claims that Heyst "has been no better than a loafer around here as far back as any of us can remember [...] he said he was 'looking for facts'."(34) As long as Heyst is on the move, "looking for facts", he is safe from the dangers attending human consciousness. The scientific 'fetish' even appears to protect him physically, as when he rubs shoulders with New Guinea cannibals and "Goram vagabonds"(22-3) on his travels. But as soon as he 'arrives', as it were - that is makes tangible progress of some sort and discovers some real "facts" - the charm is lost. As a result of his encounter with Morrison, the latter will insist on "Heyst's partnership in the *great discovery*"(33) of the coal outcrops (my italics). Thus, Heyst "gets hold of [a fact] which will do for all of us"(34), claims one trader of the region; "that's what they call development", comments another.

Victory suggests that the mystical belief in material progress, as in Heyst's vision of "tropical distances being impelled onwards"(21), represents one of the most precious illusions of the "scientific age" and is certainly more valuable than the fruits of such progress: "For every age is fed on illusions lest men should renounce life early and the human race come to an end."(89) Thus, in managing the TBCC, Heyst is not motivated by personal profit, "What he seemed mostly concerned for was the 'stride forward', as he expressed it, in the general organisation of the universe."(21) Like religious faith which redeems the physical facts of human existence, Heyst's belief in the great stride forward"(34) reconciles him to the baser aspects of entrepreneurial capitalism. The relatively small amounts of coal extracted in comparison to the great energy and interest generated by the project suggest that the "dream of tropical coal"(21) is more important than its reality: "Engineers came out, coolies were imported, bungalows were put up on Samburan, a gallery driven into the hillside, and actually some coal got out."(34) Even after the company has expired and Heyst is "done with facts"(38), there is still something of a non-physical nature binding him to Samburan. As Schomberg points out, "The company is gone, the engineers are gone but there he sticks."(36-7) Heyst claims to "remain in possession"(37) but it would be more to the point to say that he remains possessed.

Heyst's disillusionment with "facts" and the early demise of the TBCC reflect the inability of science and materialism to satisfy man's spiritual yearnings. What will keep Heyst captivated by and desiring life after the "illusion of progress" has vanished is not what's buried inside the islands, or even the dream of extracting it, but the "lasting fascination"(67) of the Archipelago. This makes Heyst's enchantment an "unbreakable one"(22) for, as the narrator claims, "it is not easy to shake off the spell of island life"(67). Indeed, "the very voices of their people are soft and subdued as if afraid to break some protecting spell", observes the narrator. Samburan is also known as "Round Island"(34) and this shape, associated in *Victory* with natural charm, contrasts with the linear progress envisaged by scientific man on "the march[282] of civilization"(277). In the company prospectus, "Heavy lines radiated from it in all directions [...] lines of influence or lines of distance, or something of that sort"(34) but these lines are merely imaginary as is the influence they betoken for Samburan in the region. Also, "the advanced foot" of Heyst's "great stride forward" will be "drawn back"(277) but he himself will never leave the "magic circle"(22) of islands around North Borneo; natural beauty, it seems, has much more power over man than the modern fetish of science. As the novel progresses, the remains of the TBCC, including Heyst himself, are also following a cyclical course and being gradually repossessed by nature: "Ants have been at work [...] after the men"(283) undermining the supports of the coal-mine, and the "abandoned settlement" is said to be "invaded by the jungle"(20). Also, when Heyst refuses at first to be taken off Samburan, "He marched into the long grass and vanished [...] the

282 Tony Tanner writes that "evolutionary progress" in *Victory* also "seems to be less of a march than a circle - or an oscillating reversibility."(p123)

tropical vegetation [...] was about to close over the last vestiges of the liquidated Tropical Belt Coal Company - A. Heyst, manager in the East."(38)

Victory suggests that not only does science fail to offer man any metaphysical certainty or a satisfactory *raison d'être,* but the will to truth it promotes threatens his very survival by undermining the charm and mystery of life which has kept him enthraled since. As the narrator observes, "There are more spells than your commonplace magicians ever dreamed of."(21) With the failure of his "dream of tropical coal", Heyst becomes invisible, as in those early days when he used to make a "bolt clear out of sight" either in the direction of New Guinea or to Saigon - "to cannibals or to cafes". "The enchanted Heyst! Had he at last broken the spell?", asks the narrator, "Had he died?"(35-36) To "break the spell" here is equivalent to dying or disappearing out of life. Like Jim after the Patna incident and the loss of his heroic illusions, Heyst is dangerously lacking moral confidence at this point and could veer either towards "cannibals or to cafes". The novel suggests that the great stride forward", when it fails to reach its intended goal, could easily become a step backwards to the savagery lying just beneath the veneer of civilization; there is not a great distance from "cannibals" to "cafes" in Conrad's world. But for Samburan and the "magic circle of islands" which keep Heyst in check, he could easily kick himself loose of the earth"(HD 107) just as Kurtz does, away from the civilizing influence of Europe. The "absolute moral and intellectual liberty"(87), which Heyst Senior's extreme rationalism envisages, would 'liberate' man out of life altogether, if ever realised.

Art and "the good will to appearance"

Conrad suggests in the Author's Note that Heyst's predicament is "representative"(11) of "civilized man"(12) but also of the "unchanging man of history". In both cases, "the play of his destiny is too great for his fears and too mysterious for his understanding"(11). Thus, when man's perennial thirst for knowledge has all but dispelled the "enchantment" of life's great spectacle, he needs to call upon that "pagan residuum of awe and wonder which lurks still at the bottom of our old humanity"[283] and

---

283 See Conrad's 'Note to the First Edition'.

regain his aesthetic detachment. By regarding life as a work of art, a "play of destiny" of which he is merely a spectator, man escapes the pain and guilt of conscious existence and returns to a state of innocence once more. As Schopenhauer claimed:

> "the world as representation, if we consider it in isolation by tearing ourselves from willing and letting it alone take possession of our consciousness, is the most delightful, and the only innocent, side of life. We have to regard art as the greater enhancement, the more perfect development, of all this, for essentially it achieves just the same thing as is achieved by the visible world"(WWR I 266).

Nietzsche too claimed that "our ultimate reason for gratitude towards art lies" in the fact that it restores "the *good* will to appearance"(GS 107).

Through metaphors and comparisons art also points to an essential unity behind phenomena[284] which science fails to establish using rational positivism alone. In the case of *Victory* this essential unity corresponds to Schopenhauer's "will" and the phenomenal diversity to its "representation". Thus, the comparison made between Heyst and the volcano, besides suggesting man's fall through heightened consciousness, can also be read as supporting the main thesis of *The World as Will and Representation*: that all physical phenomena are 'representations' of the same metaphysical "will to live". This speculative interpretation based on superficial similarities and entirely untenable from a positivist point of view, is nevertheless considerably more reassuring than a scientific explanation which would dismiss all such similarities as purely coincidental. Not only does the idea of the "will", conveyed through art, suggest a metaphysical basis for the physical world but it also reconciles man to nature so that a transcendent order - albeit a secular one - is re-affirmed once more and existence regains its coherence. Art alone, claimed Nietzsche, "is able to turn [...] nauseating reflections on the awfulness or absurdity of life into representations wherewith it is possible to live"(BT 53-54) and the Heyst/volcano comparison is a case in point.

Artistic comparisons also illuminate both things being compared. Thus, behind the calm exterior of the "inert" Heyst complex and violent

---

[284] As Sharon Kaehele and Howard German observe in their excellent essay on the novel, "the significance of so many of the characters and actions can be judged only when they are viewed in juxtaposition with other related characters and actions."(p56) "Conrad's *Victory*: A Reassessment," *Modern Fiction Studies*, 10 (Spring, 1964) p55-72.

'reactions' are taking place which, as in the case of the volcano, are only hinted at by surface appearances:

> though he had made up his mind to retire from the world in hermit fashion, yet he was irrationally moved by this sense of loneliness which had come to him in the hour of renunciation. It hurt him. Nothing is more painful than the shock of sharp contradictions that lacerate our intelligence and our feelings. (68)

Seen from the opposite perspective, the "indolent" volcano can be said to be full of frustrated passions, like the man. As the novel progresses, it will also become apparent that Heyst possesses a volcano-like unpredictability which makes him dangerous to associate with. After being less than honest with Morrison regarding their friendship,[285] he assumes responsibility for Lena's welfare and then does nothing to oppose the desperadoes who invade their island.[286] Many other aspects of inanimate nature can be said to reflect Heyst's predicament. There is the pathetic fallacy of the thunder-storm which subsides when all the violence on Samburan has come to an end. Similarly, the "shadows of clouds" and "brooding sunshine" reflect his melancholic state following the death of Morrison while the "tepid, shallow sea"(19) surrounding the island mirrors the lack of commitment on Heyst's part to the ascetic ideals of his father.

Art further unites the world of science by suggesting an inter-dependence between object and subject which the latter, in order to maintain its fundamental objectivity, is obliged to overlook. As Schopenhauer states, "materialism is the philosophy of the subject who forgets to take account of himself."(WWR II 13) Art is also more honest about its objectives than science, claiming only to describe phenomena rather than explain them for, as Conrad pointed out, "Most things and most natures have only a surface".[287] This idea corresponds exactly to Schopenhauer's argument that "the world is entirely representation"

---

[285] Helen F. Reiselbach claims that "Heyst drifts along with Morrison out of inertia and, perhaps most worthy of blame he allows Morrison to assume a degree of friendship Heyst does not really feel."(p116) *Conrad's Rebels*, Studies in Modern Literature, no. 42.

[286] Schomberg's malicious warnings about Heyst - "don't you ever get mixed up with that Swede. Don't you ever get caught in his web"(32) - would therefore appear to contain some truth but, as Heyst suspects, "that sort of thing is so universally human that it might be said of anybody"(176).

[287] *The Collected Letters of Joseph Conrad, Vol. II*, 1898-1902, to John Galsworthy, 16/1/98.

(WWR I 30) and is echoed by Heyst himself who says: "Appearances - what more, what better can you ask for? In fact you can't have better. You can't have anything else."(177) But the essential difference between the artistic and scientific approaches according to Schopenhauer is that the latter, being confined to rational deduction based on physical evidence, cannot speculate metaphysically as the former can do. Thus, since the decline in religious faith, it remains for art to point to such transcendent concepts as the "will" which, according to Schopenhauer, "lies outside the principle of sufficient reason and is consequently completely groundless"(WWR I 113). Yet, without recourse to such concepts, existence, particularly the human variety, would not form a coherent and meaningful whole - it could neither be explained, in the strict sense of the word, nor understood. We can therefore define [art] accurately", says Schopenhauer, "as the way of considering things outside of the principle of sufficient reason."(WWR I 185)

Conrad claimed that "science [...] whatever authority it may claim is not concerned with truth at all, but with the exact order of such phenomena as fall under the perception of the senses".[288] In contrast, art is free to represent phenomena in any order it feels is most suitable for its aims. *Victory* begins with a series of temporal indirections which reflect the way past events are reconstructed in the mind[289] either at random, or in accordance with psychological determinants which are ultimately unknowable. This narrative technique also conveys the subjective nature of human perception in which, contrary to the principles of science, an 'effect' can precede its 'cause'[290] just as the "evaporation" of the TBCC's capital preceded its "liquidation". There is also a repetitive quality about the narrative which corresponds to the cyclical patterns[291] of nature as opposed to the linear patterns of logic. The novel begins and ends with Heyst's inactivity - nothing is being done at the beginning and "Nothing"(328) could have been done at the end. Heyst has come full circle and his burning himself at the end of the novel is merely an accelerated and self-induced form of the decomposition and return to

---

288 *The Collected Letters of Joseph Conrad, Vol. II*, to *New York Times*, Saturday Review, p348.

289 Henry J. Laskowsky aptly describes the narrator as "a memory in action" and quotes Hume who writes: "As memory alone acquaints us with the contrivance and extent of this succession of perceptions, 'tis to be considered, on that account chiefly as the source of personal identity."(p278)

290 This relates to Conrad's technique of "delayed decoding" examined in Ian Watt, *Conrad in the Nineteenth Century*, pp175-80.

291 Frederick R. Karl notes that the "circling method [of narration] suits Heyst, for in his incapacity for attachment he himself literally circles"(p250).

origins which death brings about naturally. He will then be 'smoking', just as at the beginning of the novel but now released from his crippling self-consciousness because reduced to inanimate matter. New 'representations' will then be able to emerge from the ashes of the old so that the "play" of life may recommence.

Coal and diamonds: *Victory*'s extended metaphor

The coal and diamond dichotomy introduced at the onset of *Victory* can be seen as the central metaphor[292] of the novel and a model for the many different types of relationship, both abstract and human, which are examined therein. "Coal and diamonds", the most ornamentally and functionally valuable substances respectively, appear to be poles apart yet they are in fact derived from the same element with diamonds taking far longer to form. Similarly, "Hard Facts" and "Enchanted Heyst"[293] are two aspects of the same phenomenon - the same person seen at different times. Similarly, our first image of Heyst is that of a hermit "perched"(19) on top of a "mountain", but shortly afterwards we discover that this modern-day hermit has been excavating his "mountain" for coal.

Heyst had intended to resemble "a masterpiece of aloofness"(149), but there is a 'flaw'[294] somewhere in the work: his reappearance on

---

[292] For other critics who have explored the coal and diamond dichotomy in any depth, see Sharon Kaehele and Howard German (p55-72), also Henry J. Laskowsky (p276-7). The whole idea also crops up rather unexpectedly in a letter of D. H. Lawrence's to Edward Garnett dated 5/6/1914: "You mustn't look in my novel for the old stable ego of the character. There is another *ego*, according to whose action the individual is unrecognisable, and passes through, as it were, allotropic states [...] of the same radically unchanged element. Like as diamond and coal are the same pure single element of carbon. (The ordinary novel would trace the history of the diamond - but I say, 'Diamond, what! This is carbon.' And my diamond might be coal or soot, and my theme is carbon.)" *The Letters of D. H. Lawrence*, p197. Although this letter was written a week after *Victory* was completed, it seems too much of a coincidence to be unconnected. One possible explanation is that Conrad discussed his recently completed novel with Garnett who then mentioned the coal and diamond idea to Lawrence and the above letter continued the discussion.

[293] Leo Gurko has also noted this parallel : "both [coal and diamonds] are contained in Heyst. Appropriately, he has two nicknames "Hard Facts" and "Enchanted Heyst".(p239) *Joseph Conrad: Giant in Exile*, (New York: Macmillan, 1962). Of course, Heyst has more than two nicknames but this correspondence between coal and "Hard Facts" and diamonds and "Enchanted Heyst" holds.

[294] Adam Gillon has observed that, "there is that same infernal alloy in [Heyst's] metal" as in Jim's."(p148) *The Eternal Solitary*.

Sourabaya "shows that his detachment from the world was not complete", and "incompleteness of any sort leads to trouble"(40). Like the "close chemical relation between coal and diamonds", there is an essential affinity between Heyst and his kind which he cannot ignore and which brings him down from his hermit's "mountain" both literally and metaphorically. "Perhaps it was only to see whether there were any letters for him at the Tesmans"(40), speculates the narrator, but he later admits that the "incongruity of a hermit having agents did not strike us, nor yet the absurdity of a forgotten cast-off, derelict manager of a recked, collapsed, vanished enterprise having business to attend to."(42)

And the incongruities don't stop there. When Heyst offers Morrison a small loan to save his brig from auction, the latter is completely taken aback: "To him as to all of us in the islands, this wandering Heyst, who didn't toil or spin visibly, seemed the very last person to be the agent of Providence in an affair concerned with money."(28) Not only does Heyst possess money though, it emerges from his "confessions"(40) that he owns "belongings" too. "Do you mean chairs and tables?", Davidson asks him with unconcealed astonishment". "To Davidson as to any of us," explains the narrator, "the idea of Heyst [...] having any belongings that can furnish a house was startlingly novel. It was grotesquely fantastic. It was like a bird owning real property". After the death of his father, Heyst arranged for his effects to be sent to Samburan, "just as any ordinary, credulous person would have done."(152) "He had entered by then the broad, human path of inconsistencies", we are told.

Just like other people, Heyst also appears to have sexual needs. When Davidson hears of his elopement with Lena, a "mist seemed to roll away from before [his] eyes"(48) suggesting the momentary apprehension of the "thing in itself" as opposed to its deceptive "representation". "'Heyst! Such a perfect Gentleman!' he exclaimed weakly. [...] This startling fact did not tally somehow with the idea Davidson had of Heyst. He never talked of women, he never seemed to think of them, or to remember that they existed; and then all at once - like this! Running off with a casual orchestra girl!"(48) And when Jones discovers the existence of Lena on Samburan his shock is even greater: "I have a good mind to shoot you," he tells Heyst, "you woman-ridden hermit, you man in the moon, that can't exist without - "(310) A pattern emerges from Heyst's diverse worldly involvements which suggests that the only consistent thing about this hermit is his very un-hermit-like behaviour:

> First, it was the Morrison partnership of mystery; then came the great sensation of the Tropical Belt Coal where indeed varied interests were involved: a real business matter. And then came this elopement, this incongruous phenomenon of self-assertion, the greatest wonder of all, astonishing and amusing. (61)[295]

Heyst's innate physicality is constantly reasserting itself. The earthly quality of men, *Victory* suggests, is primarily revealed by the oral activities of speaking and eating with society claiming them through language just as nature does through their physical needs.[296] Thus, although Heyst wants to live a-socially, he cannot avoid human contact altogether and is linguistically appropriated as a result : Davidson brings back news of him after every trip which is then disseminated by Schomberg among his customers. Similarly, Heyst can escape Schomberg's famous "tables d'hote" but cannot do without some form of nourishment on Samburan. "What I want to know", says Schomberg, "is what he gets to eat there. A piece of dried fish now and then - what? That's coming down pretty low for a man who turned up his nose at my tables d'hote!"(37) Of course, "a piece of dried fish now and then" would constitute a fitting meal for a hermit but it turns out that Heyst has a plentiful supply of food from the TBCC's stores and even a cook who grows his own vegetables. The narrator informs us that Davidson's concern in regularly passing by Samburan was "the danger of spiritual nourishment and was sustaining itself proudly on its own contempt of the usual coarse ailments which life offers the common appetites of men"(152). The protracted use of the eating metaphor here and the emphasis on Heyst's peculiar appetite belies the spirituality of his hermitage while ironically mirroring the way Schomberg talks about him in the basest possible terms: "neither was Heyst's body in danger of starvation, as Schomberg had so confidently asserted", comments the narrator ironically.

It appears that communication with his kind is also indispensable to this would-be hermit. The first thing that Heyst does upon being taken off Samburan by Davidson is to start relating his life-story as though speech

---

[295] F. R. Leavis picks up on this idea: "Heyst is a creature of his habit, and his efforts to escape constitute a poignant comedy."(p227) *The Great Tradition*. By "habit" Leavis refers to Heyst's propensity to involve himself in life.

[296] As Tony Tanner points out, Heyst "thinks he can renounce the world mentally: but as long as he is, has, a body, he cannot renounce participation in the world's physicality, and it will not renounce him."(p117)

constituted a primary need for him, like eating, which had long been repressed in isolation. This results in "The confessions of Heyst. Not one of us had ever heard so much of his history. It looks as if the experience of hermit life had the power to loosen one's tongue"(41), observes the narrator. Heyst's language undermines his detachment from the world. Heyst had made no signs on the first occasion and was not known to be "a signalling sort of man"(56) yet he flags Davidson ashore shortly after the elopement and asks him to return Mrs Schomberg's shawl. Also, his ostensible purpose for visiting Sourabaya in the first place is to collect his "letters"(40) from the Tesmans but if Heyst needs "letters", he also needs words and the whole social construct which goes with them. "Axel Heyst ought not to have cared for his letters", suggests the narrator, "But it was of no use. He had not the hermit's vocation! That was the trouble, it seems."(40)

Another way in which the coal and diamond metaphor can be profitably applied to *Victory* is with regard to characterization. Diamonds[297] are almost pure carbon but in its most refined form. Although very valuable, they have few practical applications and don't readily react with other substances. Heyst too is as far removed from his origins as it is possible to imagine: an expatriate Swede of aristocratic birth living on a tropical island in the Malay Archipelago. Like diamonds he also appears completely divorced from functional considerations: "This observer of facts seemed to have no connection with earthly affairs and passions. [...] He was like a feather floating lightly in the workaday atmosphere which was the breath of our nostrils. For this reason whenever this looker-on took contact with things he attracted attention."(61) When Heyst does react with his environment, it is definitely a departure from the norm and he only does so on three definite occasions throughout the novel: with Morrison, with Lena, and in setting up the TBCC. But none of these 'reactions' has a happy conclusion because, as Heyst himself will later admit, "It's pretty clear that I am not fitted for the affairs of this world."(260) It's so clear, in fact, that even old McNab, the local drunkard can observe that "Heyst's a puffect g'n'lman. Puffect! But he's a ut-uto-utopist."(23) Despite the early successes of the TBCC, Schomberg can see through Heyst's entrepreneurial pretensions: "A fellow like that for manager? Phoo!"(35) But the most unrealistic of Heyst's involvements by far is his elopement with Lena. Davidson remarks: "I see a thing all round,

[297] Henry J. Laskowsky claims that "Conrad's novel is not concerned with diamonds but with coal"(p277), but this misses the point of Heyst's dual nature as "Hard Facts" and "Enchanted Heyst".

as it were; but Heyst doesn't, or else he would have been scared. You don't take a woman into the desert jungle without being made sorry for it sooner or later"(55). As Lena suggests, Heyst seems "too good for such contacts [with the world] and not sufficiently equipped"(258).

Not being well-suited to the practical side of life, Heyst "drifts"(167) for the most part, determined "to look on and never make a sound"(151). When deliberate action of a particularly base nature is called for at the end of the novel, he finds that, having "refined everything away"(281), there is neither force nor conviction"(282) left in him, only a feeling of "complete uselessness". He asks himself whether he could murder the desperadoes in cold blood for Lena's sake and has to admit that, "No, it is not in me. I date too late"(290). Heyst is a very "late" manifestation of the will, in other words, and its essential animality is so "refined" in him that it is hardly to be perceived. Also, despite possessing human consciousness, he has pre-determined qualities (one is almost tempted to call them properties) very much as fixed as those of a diamond and being violent is not among them. "It would have been against the grain"(258), he says. Schopenhauer explained the illusion of free-will in the following way:

> because in self-consciousness the will is known directly and in itself, there also lies in this [...] the consciousness of freedom. But the individual [...] is not will as thing-in-itself but is *phenomenon* of the will, is as such determined, and has entered the form of the phenomenon, The principle of sufficient reason. Hence [...] through experience, he finds to his astonishment that he is not free, but liable to necessity (WWR I 113).

Man's practical pre-determination as opposed to a theoretical free-will is exactly what Heyst discovers on Samburan.

Another aspect of Heyst's over-refinement is his "finished courtesy of manner"(21) which makes it difficult for him to communicate emotion. At the climax of Morrison's account of the "villainous plot"(26) to put him out of business, the "lantern-jawed"(24) trader hyperbolically announces: "I am to have my throat cut the day after tomorrow. In the face of this passion Heyst made with his eyebrows, a slight motion of surprise which would not have been misplaced in a drawing room."(26) It is not that Heyst fails to be moved by Morrison's misfortunes at this point, "he understood the other's feelings perfectly", remarks the narrator, "But he was incapable of outward cordiality of manner and felt acutely his defect."(30) This "defect" becomes even more pronounced during Heyst's exchanges with Lena on Samburan. After much verbal misunderstanding between the two lovers, Lena exclaims: "'You should try to love me!' [...] 'Try,' he muttered. But it seems to me -' He broke of, saying to himself that if he loved her, he had never told her so in so many words. Simple words! They died on his lips."(185) Again, it is not that Heyst doesn't love Lena, he is still trying to "look on and never make a sound"(151), as his father had cammanded. When the dying Lena asks him to take her in his arms, Heyst "bent low over her, cursing his fastidious soul, which even at that moment kept the true cry of love from his lips"(324).

Just as in the idea of allotropy[298] we find different forms of the same element but no essential manifestation, so Heyst can be said to possess a wide variety of appearances but no essence. He reflects, at one time or another, every other character[299] and the entire range of human qualities encountered in the novel, running the gamut from "Naive Heyst"(33) to "Heyst the Enemy"(35). But these are only borrowed colours for, in the process of naming him, people project their own qualities onto him. Jones calls Heyst a successful swindler"(307) and Ricardo "had expected Heyst to spring on him or draw a revolver, because he created for himself a vision of him in his own image."(295) Also, it is the narrator who calls Heyst "Naive" and Schomberg who invents the term "Heyst the Spider"(32) for "that - Swede.' He put a stress on the word Swede as if it meant "scoundrel."(36) Of course, there is no bigger "scoundrel" in *Victory* than Schomberg himself. Morrison, who regards Heyst as an "agent of Providence"(28) is himself "a true humanitarian"(25) and would often sail through awfully dangerous channels up to some miserable settlement"(24) only to provide them with what is, in effect, free rice. Whenever one of these villages sight Morrison approaching, it would give him a warm welcome and Morrison "would beam and glitter", which anticipates the way he expects Heyst to change into an angel with a "shining garment"(28) and "dazzling wings". Heyst can also be said to reflect the entire history of human evolution as the Victorians saw it: he moves from

---

298 For a discussion of allotropy and character see R. G. Hampson, *Joseph Conrad: Betrayal and Identity*.

299 "It is a central irony in the novel", writes Daniel R. Schwarz, "that virtually every character parallels in some important way Heyst, the man who would set himself apart from humanity, the man who thinks he is different from his fellows."(p70) *Joseph Conrad: The Later Fiction*. And Frederick R. Karl states that through "this technique [of doubling], the principal character hovers over the scene as a spiritual or psychological presence even when physically absent."(p256)

being an "inert body"(19) to a "perfect gentleman"(48)[300] and (viewing the same movement mythologically) from "the original Adam"(149) to "a man of the last hour"(289). Yet ironically, it doesn't matter to him "what anybody has ever said or believed, from the beginning of the world till the crack of doom!"(177)

In possessing many different appearances but no underlying essence[301] Heyst can be viewed as the perfect symbol for the world as representation. Appropriately, he himself loses "all belief in realities"(282) and comes to view the world as insubstantial: "Here I am on a Shadow inhabited by Shades", he tells Lena. At one point, the narrator compares Heyst to a work of art :[302] "in the fullness of his physical development, of a broad, martial presence, he resembled the portraits of Charles XII, of adventurous memory. However, there was no reason to think that Heyst was in any way a fighting man."(23) Like light being diffused through reflection, Heyst is many times removed from the "martial" prototype he appears to represent and merely "resembled portraits" of a man who is associated with adventure in the public mind. The same physical phenomenon would account for Heyst's rather tenuous resemblance to a hermit as the following observation by Conrad suggests: "Like a natural force which is obscured as much as illuminated by the multiplicity of phenomena,[303] the power of renunciation is obscured by the mass of weaknesses, vacillations, secondary motives and false steps and compromises which make up the sum of our activity."(NLL 16) Ironically, Heyst's desire to renounce all willing bears all the charectiristcs of the will which according to Schopenhauer was naturally weakened as a result of appearing in nature - even will-renunciation requires a great effort of will to achieve, it seems.

Unlike Heyst who has "said to the earth that bore [him]: "I am I and you are a shadow"(281), Schomberg is firmly rooted to his base origins. His essential creatureliness is repeatedly borne out by the narrative: he is described as "a bearded creature"(31), an "ass"(31), a "Teutonic creature"(36), "a brute"(82), a "stupid animal"(178) and his hand is likened

---

300 For a thorough examination of the theme of the gentleman in *Victory* see Tony Tanner (op. cit. note 10) and, by the same, "Gentlemen and Gossip: Aspects of Evolution and Language in Conrad's *Victory*", *L'Epoque Conradienne* (May 1981) p1-56.

301 This elusive quality of Heyst has foxed even some distinguished critics. Thomas Moser claims that "Conrad does not know what he wants to make of Heyst" because "he emerges as neither a romantic nor a sceptic."(p156) *Joseph Conrad: Achievement and Decline*.

302 It will be remembered that Schopenhauer regarded art as the perfect symbol for the world as representation.

303 Conrad's idea here of a "natural force" appearing as a "multiplicity of phenomena" is closely allied to Schopenhauer's philosophy.

to a "thick paw"(32). Also, if the "scientific age" is "a garish, unrestful hotel"(19)[304] for some, Schomberg can be viewed as the proprietor of this hotel and is in his element in its iconoclastic, materialistic climate. "His ambition was to feed [mankind] at a profitable price, and his delight was to talk of it behind its back."(37) He provides his customers with food and gossip, for which, unlike the 'chimera' of tropical coal, there is not likely to be any shortage of demand: "I don't know why so many of us patronized his various establishments", remarks the narrator, "He was a noxious ass and he satisfied his lust for silly gossip at the cost of his customers."(31) The novel implies that it may be because of such coarse qualities rather than in spite of them that one is a worldly success, for as Morrison's case proves, "too much altruism" can be a drawback"(24) and, after all, "people liked to discuss that sort of scandal"(54). Morrison may be "the dearly beloved friend of a quantity of God-forsaken villages"(24), but it is the base Schomberg who is the successful entrepreneur. He was "master [...] of the art of hotel-keeping"(100), notes the narrator.

In contrast to the "delicate, polished"(75) Heyst, Schomberg is full of intense and immediate passions which, rather than being lost through transmission, are magnified still further. His melodramatic response to Heyst's elopement is typical: "Was that a thing to do in a respectable hotel? The cheek, the indecency, the impudence, the atrocity! Vagabond, imposter, swindler, ruffian, *schweinhund*!"(52) Schomberg's reactions are so exaggerated in general as to seem totally out of proportion with that which causes them. The "immense malice"(37) he bears Heyst, for example, is originally provoked by the Swede not having paid "perhaps three visits" to his 'establishment'. This was Heyst's "crime", for which Schomberg "wished him nothing less than a long and tormented existence"(36). Schomberg's customers do not care much for the gossip he regularly dishes out concerning Heyst, "but Schomberg of course could not understand that. He was grotesquely dense."(36) Like an opaque and unreflective lump of coal, Schomberg is "dense" and "unfathomable"(36). His intellect is so clouded by willing, that everything he perceives and communicates becomes grotesquely distorted. This is because, to use Schopenhauer's terms, "Every passion, in fact every inclination or disinclination, tinges the objects of objects of knowledge with its colour."(WWR II 141) Schomberg "was asking everybody about everything, and arranging the information into the most scandalous shape

[304] As Daniel R. Schwarz observes, "Schomberg's hotel becomes a mnemonic device to recall that image [of the scientific age]"(p60).

his imagination could invent"(39), remarks the narrator. When "all concluded that Heyst was boarding with the good-natured"(31) Morrison, Schomberg's version is that Heyst was "sponging on the imbecile"(31). Morrison and Heyst walk past his hotel one evening and Schomberg relates this important piece of news to his customers as "the spider and the fly just gone by gentlemen."(32)[305] Seen through the 'medium' of Schomberg's intellect, Heyst's philanthropic assistance of and attachment to Morrison, becomes something far less noble: "He was saying that Morrison's partner first got all there was to get out of him and then [...] as good as murdered him - sent him out to die."(175)

But there are also advantages attached to being unreflective and "dense". As the narrator is forced to admit, "Most of us can remember instances of triumphant folly; and that ass Schomberg triumphed."(35) Like Captain Macwhirr of *Typhoon* who gets out of his disaster "so well for such a stupid man", Schomberg's "denseness', his impenetrable exterior, appears to protect him from the dangers of life. For one thing, it enables him to hide his weaknesses when dealing with the desperadoes: "It must be said in justice to Schomberg that he concealed his funk creditably," observes the narrator. The habit of throwing out his chest and speaking in a severe voice stood him in good stead."(111) Heyst's "martial" semblance, on the other hand, doesn't fool anyone and his diamond-like transparency ("the fellows life had been open to us for years"p61, claims the narrator) makes him the object of much malicious gossip, finally resulting in the invasion of his island by Jones, Ricardo and Pedro. In the confrontation which ensues Heyst finds that, "never [having] been diplomatic in his relations with mankind"(264), he cannot employ subterfuge against the desperadoes, as Schomberg has done so successfully.

When facts conflict with Schomberg's illusions, as when Lena rejects him in favour of Heyst, he doesn't become disillusioned; the offending fact is first disputed and then a fiction is erected in its place:

---

[305] The narrator will later re-iterate this view of Morrison as "victim of gratitude"(33), but Heyst can hardly be considered his victimizer as he suffers far more through their association than Morrison who dies early and is thus removed from the world of hazard and adventure."(33) Heyst himself can be viewed as the victim of his own compassion: "One gets attached in a way to people one has done something for"(169), he tells Lena. As Nietzsche wrote, "If you possess a virtue, a real whole virtue [...] - you are its victim"(GS 21) and Heyst echoes this idea when he says, "The sacred virtue of hospitality! But it leads to trouble as well as any other."(288)

> the girl who had for weeks resisted his attacks, his fiercest protestations, had been snatched from under his nose by 'that Swede', apparently without any trouble worth speaking of. He refused to believe the fact. [...] His wounded vanity wondered ceaselessly at the means 'that Swede' had employed to seduce her away from a man like him (89-90).

But when the same conflict arises in Heyst's affairs, his "scornful temperament suffered from failure in a way unknown to men accustomed to grapple with the realities of common human enterprise."(67) Schomberg's tendency of seeing only what he wants to see would place him in the same category for Schopenhauer as "all animals and most men", in whom "Knowledge, destined originally to serve the will for the achievement of its aims, [...] remains almost throughout entirely subordinate to its service"(WWR I 152). An "undisciplined imagination"(76) like Heyst's can hit upon things that are not in the will's interest to know, but Schomberg's intellect, like Macwhirr's, is strictly "subordinate" to the service of his will and admits no such information. Having created a fiction which supports his existence, Schomberg embraces it wholeheartedly and unreservedly as the truth whereas Heyst, "seeing clearly the plot of plots"(181) becomes "disenchanted with life as a whole"(67) and "disarmed" before its dangers. As the narrator points out,

> Schomberg believed so firmly in the reality of Heyst as created by his own power of false inferences, of his hate, of his love of scandal, that he could not contain a stifled cry of conviction as sincere as most of our convictions, the disguised servants of our passions, can appear at a supreme moment. (139)

Schomberg is the exact opposite of what Schopenhauer called the "genius": an individual in whom knowledge has "throw[n] off its yoke, and, free from all the aims of the will, exist[s] purely for itself, simply as the clear mirror of the world"(WWR I 152). It is Heyst, one of the "spectators of the world's agitation"(76), a man "used to think[ing] clearly and sometimes even profoundly"(80), that bears all the hall-marks of this type. Like Heyst, "the genius lives essentially alone. He is too rare to be capable of easily coming across his like and too different from the rest to be their companion, with them it is willing, with him it is knowing that prevails"(WWR II 390). The "portfolio of sketches"(22) which Heyst brings back with him from New Guinea and "the Tropical Belt Coal fiasco"(42), to take just two examples of Heyst's work, also associate him with the "genius". As Schopenhauer noted, "To be useless and unprofitable is one of the characteristics of the work of 'genius'; it is their patent of nobility. All other human works exist only for the maintenance or relief of our existence."(WWR II 388). When Heyst attempts the latter type of works, his efforts disastrously backfire, because "For practical life genius is about as useful as an astronomers telescope is in a theatre."(WWR II 146). Schomberg's works, on the other hand, from his "tables d'hote" to his concerts, can all be said to exist "for the maintenance or relief" of his customers and, of course, the profit of their purveyor.

As we would expect though when viewing Heyst and Schomberg through the novel's extended metaphor, apparent differences are belied by essential affinities.[306] The narrative links both men through their attraction to Lena and this attraction reveals the common driving force behind their apparently diverse personalities. As Schopenhauer noted,

> Sexual love is the ultimate goal of almost all human effort, it has an unfathomable influence on the most important affairs, interrupts every hour the most serious occupations, and sometimes perplexes for a while the most serious minds. (WWR II 533)

It will be remembered that although Heyst "had made up his mind to withdraw from the world in hermit fashion, yet he was irrationally moved by [a] sense of loneliness which had come to him in his hour of renunciation."(68) When he first sees Lena at Schomberg's hotel, he doesn't observe her philosophically or as an object of aesthetic contemplation but "anxiously, as no man ever looks at another man"(71). Also, for the first time since the heyday of the TBCC, Heyst acts "unchecked by any sort of self consciousness"(72) and speaks with "a tone of conviction"(81). The "blessed, warm mental fog"(87) has obviously returned to his mind since deliberate action has again become possible for him and his confident communications to Lena ("that horrible female has done something to you. She has pinched you, hasn't she? I am sure she pinched you just now" p73) are in direct contravention of his father's advise to "Look on - make no sound"(150). But, as Heyst Senior had

---

306 As Sharon Kaehele and Howard German have noted, "The observation about the chemical likeness between coal and diamonds hints at an unsuspecting similarity lying beneath vastly different appearances."(p56) Hence, Heyst's and Schomberg's martial appearances and the fact that thery are both victimized by Jones and co.

written, "the consolation of love" is the "most subtle" of all "the stratagems of life"(184) and here we see it overcoming Heyst's "profound mistrust of life"(87).

His sexual passions having been engaged, Heyst's "serious mind" becomes "perplexed", just as in Schopenhauer's description, and he loses his "mental self-possession"(12). His reason thereby resumes its natural function of "justify[ing] the obscure desires that move our conduct"(80) and ceases to be "a clear mirror of the world": "Formerly, in solitude and in silence, he had been used to think clearly and sometimes even profoundly, seeing life outside the flattering optical delusion, of an ever expected happiness. But now he was troubled; a light veil seemed to hang before his mental vision; the awakening of a tenderness indistinct and confused as yet, towards an unknown woman."(80) Conrad 's use of language serves to reflect Heyst's gradual movement away from the clarity of knowledge to the confusion of willing: "solitude", "silence", "clearly", "profoundly" - "delusion", "troubled", "veil", "indistinct", "confused", "unknown". It is worth quoting Schopenhauer on the loss of will-less contemplation at this point because his thoughts correspond very closely to Conrad's portrayal of Heyst at Schomberg's hotel:

> at the moment when, torn from the will, we have given ourselves up to pure, will-less knowing, we have stepped into a different world [...] but who has the strength to remain in it for long? As soon as any relation to our will, to our person, even to those objects of pure contemplation, again enters our consciousness [...] we fall back into knowledge governed by the principle of sufficient reason [...] we are again abandoned to all our woe. (WWR I 197)

The "veil" reference in this passage is also distinctly Schopenhauerian evoking "Maya, the veil of deception", which "covers the eyes of mortals and causes them to see a world which one cannot say either that it is or it is not; for it is like a dream"(WWR I 7). Heyst Senior claimed that "the desire [of love] is the bed of dreams"(184) and here we see the infatuated Heyst beginning to view life more like a dream ("flattering optical delusion") and less philosophically.

His subsequent attachment to Lena shows that, like "all the past victims of the Great Joke"(68), Heyst too has "sexual love" as his "ultimate goal". The narrative suggests that the courtly pretext[307] of offering assistance to a lady in distress, with which Heyst approaches Lena, is no more than a romantic sublimation of the same impulse which moves Schomberg to corner her in the corridors of his hotel.[308] When Lena confesses to him that she has been "worried and pestered by fellows like this before"(81) - meaning before Schomberg's advances - Heyst betrays his subconscious motivation and smarts at the thought that his own actions may be interpreted in the same light:[309] "Heyst had removed his arms from her suddenly and had recoiled a little. 'Is it my fault?', asks Lena thinking Heyst has been repelled by her admissions, "'I didn't even look at them. I tell you straight. Never! Have I looked at you? Tell me. It was you that began it.' In truth, Heyst had shrunk from the idea of competition with fellows unknown, with Schomberg the hotel-keeper."(82) It is apparent that the difference between Heyst and the other "fellows" who have approached Lena unbidden in the past lies more in Heyst's mind than in reality. But, as Schopenhauer argued, "the intellect is the secondary phenomenon, the organism the primary"(WWR I 201) and, ironically, Heyst himself will echo this idea when he says to Lena "I don't think. Something in me thinks - something foreign to my nature."(282)

The differences between Heyst and Schomberg are also present in Lena's mind ("You aren't like the others"p83 she tells him) and render Heyst all the more attractive as a result: "any man who did not resemble Schomberg appeared for that very reason attractive"(77), remarks the narrator. Heyst's diamond-like polish is set off, as it were, by Schomberg's coarseness. Schomberg's advances to Lena are made in "quiet corners and empty passages" where light does not penetrate, and he communicates his affections in "deep mysterious murmurs from behind, which notwithstanding their clear import, sounded horribly insane somehow. The contrast of Heyst's quiet, polished manner gave her special delight and filled her with admiration."(77) Heyst originally approaches Lena confidently and in public but he then proceeds to "steal"(78) her away from society to the solitude of Samburan; as with Schomberg's sexual advances which are shrouded in mystery, these subsequent actions of Heyst's betray a bad conscience concerning his relations with Lena. It is as

307 C. B. Cox notes that Heyst's "decision to rescue Lena is quixotic, but it reveals a darker side to his nature."(p131) *Joseph Conrad: The Modern Imagination*.

308 Robert F. Haugh sees it the other way round: "[Schomberg's] proposals to Lena [...] were grotesque, odd notes on a theme inverted from Heyst's noble purposes with her."(p108)

309 Helen F. Reiselbach notes that "although there is a strong component of sexual desire in Heyst's attraction to Lena, he shrinks from recognition."(p119)

though she were indeed some 'stolen treasure' the possession of which compromises him morally,[310] prompting him to hide her from the world: "you are not for them to look at - to talk about"(260), Heyst tells her. Before his final confrontation with the desperadoes Heyst directs Lena to dress in black and hide in the forest, saying "I defy anybody to find you out before daylight"(299) but she disobeys him and waits for Ricardo who tells her: "It's you who are my treasure. It's I who have found you out where a gentleman had buried you to rot for his accursed pleasure!"(317) And the metaphor of Lena as stolen property is further supported by Schomberg's confused exclamations: "My cash-box! My - he - look here, captain Davidson! [Heyst] ran off with a girl? what do I care for the girl? The girl is nothing to me."(52) But of course, Schomberg "doth protest too much".

The narrative suggests a baser interpretation still for the elopement. Schomberg is said to "prowl around" Lena, "mute, hungry, portentous"(77) like some carnivorous animal stalking its prey - a view of Lena which has been anticipated by the narrator's sarcastic comment to Davidson: "You say that [Heyst's] mad. Schomberg tells us that he must be starving on his island: so he may yet end by eating her."(50) The image which emerges from all this is not very flattering for Heyst; it is as though, having beaten Schomberg to the kill, he carries his victim off to his 'lair' to enjoy her at greater leisure. In fact, this view of Samburan accords well with Davidson's description of it as a wild and frightening place, not fit for human habitation:

> The loneliness, the ruins of the spot, [...] That black jetty, sticking out of the jungle into the empty sea; these roof-ridges of deserted houses peeping dismally above the long grass! Ough! The gigantic and funeral blackboard sign of the Tropical Belt Coal Company, still emerging from a wild growth of bushes like an inscription stuck above a grave (48).

But, as we know, Heyst is not left in peace with his prize on Samburan - "we are after the fruits of your labours", Jones will explain to him, "It's the way of the world - gorge and disgorge!"(307)

---

[310] R. J. Andreach presents an alternative but equally valid interpretation of Heyst's actions: "Because of his mistrust of life, Heyst will not admit he needs Lena. He will acknowledge her only privately; you acknowledge her publicly would be to admit an incompleteness in himself,"(p98) *The Slain and Resurrected God.*

Although Heyst and Schomberg create the opposite impression on Lena, she has a very similar effect on them both and on men in general, it seems: "I don't know what comes to them"(81), she says about the fellows who pester her without any provocation on her part. Indeed, *Victory* views sexual passion as a kind of madness which leads men to reveal the inherent irrationality and unpredictability of their will. Davidson, who has never actually seen Lena, interprets Heyst's elopement as an act of unmitigated folly: "It needed a lunatic like Heyst", he claims, "Brooding alone on Samburan has upset his brain. He never stopped to consider or he couldn't have done it. No sane man [...] It's madness."(50) And his first interview with Heyst following the elopement will confirm these suspicions while suggesting the probable cause of Heyst's 'malady': "He had never heard anybody speak like this before; certainly not Heyst, whose conversation was concise, polite, with a faint ring of playfulness in the cultivated tones of his voice. 'He's gone mad' Davidson thought to himself [...] Then he remembered [...] that Heyst now had a girl there. This bizarre discourse was probably the effect of the girl."(56-7) But Davidson has heard somebody else talk madly and act irrationally on account of Lena - that "disappointed lover"(142), Schomberg: "All of a sudden, in the same hoarse sinister tone, he proceeded to call Heyst many names, of which 'pig-dog' was not the worst, with such vehemence that he actually choked himself. [...] He had seized Davidson by a button of his coat, detaining him in the doorway, and exactly in the line of Mrs Schomberg's stony gaze."(51-2) Similarly, when Ricardo first sets eyes on Lena, the little "self-restraint" he is master of comes to an abrupt end: "The instinct for the feral spring could no longer be denied. Ravish or kill - it was all one to him, as long as by the act he liberated the suffering soul of savagery repressed for so long."(237) And Jones' response to Lena's presence on Samburan, notwithstanding his "exaggerated dislike of women"(218), ironically follows the same pattern: he loses his "iron self-possession"(306) and begins to "feel very savage"(310). It dawns on him that the "treasure" which Ricardo has been 'sniffing out' has been Lena all along: "'On the track! On the scent!' he cried, forgetting himself to the point of executing a dance of rage in the middle of the floor."(311) Jones has also become madly abusive in his rage recalling Schomberg's reaction to Heyst's deceitfulness: "it won't be you that I'll shoot", he tells Heyst. "It's the other woman-lover - the prevaricating, sly, low-class, amorous cuss! And he shaved - shaved under my very nose. I'll shoot him!' 'He's gone mad,' thought Heyst"(310).

Besides depriving men of their reason, Lena also has the power to unman her various suitors in a way which paradoxically unites the whole sex. Masculinity is defined in the novel as "that seductive strength allied to an absurd delicate shrinking from the recognition of the naked necessity of facts"(250) so one could say that Lena is merely bringing to the surface traits which are present within men but not immediately apparent - their common denominator, as it were. Both Schomberg and Heyst use Lena as an excuse for their lack of courage in facing the desperadoes - Schomberg because he doesn't possess her and Heyst because he does: "Ah, if he [Schomberg] only had the girl with him he would have been masterful and resolute and fearless - fight twenty desperadoes"(99); and Heyst's excuse runs: "only two months ago I would not have cared. I would have defied their scoundrelism [...] But now I have you! You stole into my life, and - "(263), the sentence appropriately peters out at this point. But Lena's disarming influence is most strongly and literally felt by Ricardo who confesses to her "I went tired this morning, since I came in here and started talking to you - as tired as if I had been pouring my life-blood here on these planks for you to dabble your white feet in."(317) Despite his ruthless reputation and much vaunted readiness to "kill with extreme ease - a growl and a spring"(234), Ricardo is easily turned into a fawning pussy-cat by Lena "clasping her ankle, [he] pressed his lips time after time to the instep, muttering gasping words that were like sobs, making little noises that resembled the sounds of grief and distress."(320) The image which Ricardo evokes of the power relationship between himself and Lena is a striking example of the "strength" allied to a "delicate shrinking" which was said to typify the male psychology: "What you want", he announces to her, "is a man, a master that will let you put the heel of your shoe on his neck"(317).

The idea of male superiority, like the 'superiority' of diamonds over coal, is thus radically undermined by *Victory*.[311] Lena feels that she can never satisfy Heyst, "as if her passion were of a hopelessly lower quality, unable to appease some exalted and delicate desire of his superior soul."(268) Yet it is she who proves "heroically equal to every demand of the risky and uncertain future"(16). By disarming Ricardo of his knife, she plays an active part in the fight against the desperadoes in contrast to the

[311] Paul Kirchner claims that "the theme of the novel emerges as the conflict between masculinity and femininity", adding that Conrad "seems bent on vindicating the feminine principle as opposed to the masculine."(p166) *Joseph Conrad: The Psychologist as Artist.*

morally squeamish[312] Heyst who is content to keep up gentlemanly appearances when his and Lena's lives are at stake. This echoes the way Mrs Schomberg is forced to search the desperadoes' luggage for weapons because her husband is too cowardly[313] to do it himself: Schomberg's "part, ten days after his guests arrival had been to lounge in manly, careless attitudes on the veranda - keeping watch - while Mrs Schomberg [...] was 'going through' the luggage of these strange clients. Her terrible William had insisted on it."(97) Here we see a subversion of Victorian sexual stereotypes pertaining to ornamental women and functional men. Although Heyst tries to keep Lena out of the conflict, his obvious reluctance to compromise himself morally by actively opposing their enemies leaves Lena with no option but to get involved herself[314] and she rises to the occasion: "all her energy was concentrated on the struggle that she had wanted to take upon herself, in a great exaltation of love and self-sacrifice, which is a woman's sublime faculty"(257).

Like Mrs Schomberg when "engaged with the task of defending her position in life"(58), Lena proves "more resourceful than you would give her credit for"(57), but only from a male point of view. The way she repulses Ricardo's assault shows that she has never really needed Heyst's protection[315] despite offering herself to him "in a desire of safety"(89): "She defended herself [...] from the force of instinct which is the source of every great display of energy"(239). It is Lena's will or "instinct" which protects her in this instance but only because it is supported by the "saving illusion" of Heyst's love and her Christian upbringing which allows her to redeem her unworthiness through an act of self-sacrifice: "She resisted [...] because of the faith that had been born in her - the faith

---

312 Daniel R. Schwarz writes: "The narrator is proposing that the salvation of the race lies in women because contemporary life shows that men have forfeited the right to moral leadership and because it is women more than men who have retained the necessary passion and energy."(p72) I would put the emphasis more on what women seem to represent in Conrad's fiction - the life-force, instinct, saving illusion - than on women themselves.

313 "Men are always cowards", wrote Conrad, "I think only women have true courage."(p191) *Collected Letters, Vol. I* ,to Marguerite Poradowska, 6 or 13/12/94.

314 Helen F. Reiselbach observes: "As in the preceding novels, Conrad asserts that it is women who are capable of dealing with unpleasant realities, which men's finer sensibilities prefer to ignore."(p130)

315 Thomas Moser has noted a decline in Conrad's portrayal of "the woman" in *Victory*: "No longer is the woman a vigorous character like Jewel ready to judge her beloved a "false", like Mrs Gould, capable of making a judgement against herself. Now the woman is defenceless, existing to be rescued."(p107) This argument would hold except that Lena *does* accuse her lover of not really loving her (p185); she *does* make a judgement herself ("You took me up from pity. I threw myself at you" p285, she says to Heyst); and she *does* defend herself perfectly adequately against Ricardo while it is Heyst who needs rescuing from the desperadoes.

in the man of her destiny, and perhaps in the Heaven which had sent him so wonderfully to cross her path."(239) Heyst, on the other hand, a man of universal scorn and unbelief"(169), has persistently rejected all illusions and so finds that he cannot call upon the same source of energy as Lena when threatened by the evil that is Jones:[316] "His very will seemed dead of weariness. He moved automatically, his head low, like a prisoner captured by the evil power of a masquerading skeleton."(312)

The same instinct of survival which abandons Baron Heyst to "all the mental degradations to which a man's intelligence is exposed"(15) has the effect of elevating[317] the low-born Lena to a status more in keeping with her tragic outcome. At the climax of the novel Ricardo, Heyst and Jones are all assembled around her like courtiers or supplicants while she sits "as if enthroned,[318] with her hands on the arms of the chair."(313) In Lena we see the will sharpened in adversity and sublimated[319] through illusion so that it is she rather than Heyst who comes to be associated with light; one could say concerning Lena's development in the novel that the dullness of coal under pressure has become the brilliance of the diamond: "She no longer wondered at that bitter riddle [the reason of her existence], since her heart found its solution in a *blinding* hot *glow* of passionate pride. She passed by Heyst as if she had indeed been *blinded* by some secret *lurid* and consuming *glare* into which she was about to enter"(295) (my italics). During the final confrontation between the lovers and the desperadoes all the light seems to be emanating from her as she is seated in the veranda: "the eight candle-flames[320] [...] flung around her an intolerable brilliance which hurt Heyst's eyes, seemed to sear his very brain with the radiation of infernal heat."(314) Like the night which accentuates the light

---

316 As Donald A. Dike observes, "Heyst, unlike Lena, is ill-equipped to resist violation."(p105)

317 "In the course of the novel", writes Paul L. Wiley, "it is [Heyst] who shrinks, whereas Lena grows steadily to near heroic size."(p152) *Conrad's Measure of Man.*

318 Helen F. Reiselbach has also observed that "Lena seems to become larger as the narrative progresses, until at the end she is seen as a sort of enormous idol, sitting on Heyst's veranda."(p124)

319 The difference between this sublimation and the sublimated sexual desire which makes Heyst shine at Schomberg's hotel is that Lena doesn't wake up from her dream into reality as Heyst does: "I have allowed myself to be tempted into action. It seemed innocent enough, but all action is bound to be harmful"(57). As Donald A. Dike points out, Heyst "tries to climb out into the air as inexperienced people do."(p104)

320 John A. Palmer points out that "Lights and candles have previously been associated with 'life' in the novel" but adds that "The novel's symbolic play is too little analyzed to permit easy judgement."(p191) *Joseph Conrad's Fiction.* The present study addresses itself to this "symbolic play". (see previous note)

surrounding the bungalow, Lena's black costume only sets off her radiant face still more.

The "heat" radiating from Lena strikes Heyst as "infernal" because he has been seduced by Jones into viewing the life-force as something base and degrading: "Mud souls obscene and cunning", says Jones while watching Ricardo and Lena, "Mud bodies, too - the mud of the gutter!"(314)[321] But it is not the instinctive Lena or even her "soul mate" Ricardo, "the man of violence and death" (315) who we are meant to look down upon - it is Jones, the Enemy of life, with his pathological abhorrence of everything natural and the weak-willed Heyst in "spectral fellowship"(314)[322] with him who, by not resisting evil, serves to perpetuate it.[323] Heyst can be said to be instrumental in Lena's death[324] because he has had more than one opportunity to overpower Jones before they reach the bungalow and has done nothing: "If I want to kill him, this is my time,' thought Heyst; but he did not move."(310) He realises that instead of Lena betraying him, as Jones has suggested, he has betrayed Lena and "a great shame descended upon Heyst - the shame of guilt, absurd and maddening."(314) But he has by then been engulfed by the evil of Jones who "drew him still farther back into the darkness of the veranda" while Ricardo, previously "the embodied evil of the world", is shrouded in divine light through his association with Lena.

The life-force which Lena so brilliantly reflects prior to her death is not extinguished by the darkness that Jones represents; his "little black bullet-hole" only serves to highlight her "dazzling and as it were sacred whiteness"(323) while all her former attractiveness remains intact: "there was hardly a trace of blood to mar the charm, the fascination, of that mortal flesh."(323) The language of the scene suggests that Lena finally achieves a transcendence and that her will is not really destroyed upon

---

321 Sharon Kaehele and Howard German claim that in this scene Jones "functions almost as an allegorical figure personifying Heyst's contempt" and this exclamation "is only a more extreme expression of Heyst's thoughts."(p60)

322 C. La Bossiere points out, "Heyst comes to learn that the denial of life leaves him not innocent, but of the very party of Satan-Jones"(p87). *Joseph Conrad and the Science of Unknowing.*

323 As Conrad points out, "abnegation carried to an extreme [...] becomes not just a fault but a crime; and to return good for evil is not profoundly immoral but also dangerous in that it whets the appetite for evil in the maleVol.ent and arouses (perhaps unconsciously) that dormant tendency towards hypocrisy in the - let us call them - benevolent."(p107) *Collected Letters, Vol. I,* (p107) to Marguerite Poradowska, 5/3/91. This idea is echoed by Ricardo's repeated claims that Heyst is a "Blamed 'ypocrit"(243).

324 R. J. Andreach suggests that this is less accidental than it may appear: "Doubting Lena, [Heyst] allows Jones, or the Jones part of his psyche, to fire the gun at Ricardo, or the Ricardo part of his psyche, killing [Lena]."(p106)

her death but shines undimmed, desiring life still: "The flush of rapture flooding her whole being broke out in a smile of innocent, girlish happiness; and with that divine radiance[325] on her lips she breathed her last, triumphant, seeking for his glance in the shades of death."(324) Lena's sunset with its "shades of death" is simultaneously a dawn ("flush", "flooding", "broke out", "radiance"). Schopenhauer himself frequently employs the metaphor of the setting sun to convey the indestructibility of the will: "Death (the repetition of the comparison must be excused) is like the setting sun, which is only apparently engulfed by the night, but actually, itself the source of all light burns without intermission, brings new days to new worlds and is always rising and always setting."(WWR I 360)

But to what extent is Lena's self-sacrifice "a triumphant end"(16) as Conrad stresses in the Author's Note? The narrative seems to imply that, like all action, Lena's capture of the "sting of death in the service of love"(323) is only a "barbed hook, baited with the illusion[326] of progress"(149). "Oh, my beloved,' she cried weakly, "I've saved you!"(324), "all my own at last!(322) but Heyst "dared not touch her", as though still infected by his father's scepticism (or Jones' disgust with the physical). Even as Lena lies dying, her spirit "clung to her triumph convinced of the reality of her *Victory* over death"(324) and there is bitter irony in her words "I knew you would come back in time! You are safe now"(322): she has ostensibly 'saved' Heyst so that he may commit suicide by throwing himself in the flames of her funeral pyre.[327] But this final act of "self-assertion", like Heyst's previous ones, is far more affirmative than it appears for it shows a willingness to change[328] something through direct

---

[325] Lena is associated with Apollo, the god of light and illusion, as this term suggests.

[326] "That this is an illusion", writes Henry J. Laskowsky, "is demonstrated by the irony of her belief on her death-bed 'in the reality of her victory over death' [...] but that it is a necessary illusion is borne out by the efficacy of allowing her to die triumphantly happy."(280) And this view is echoed by Sharon Kaehele and Howard German who claim "Conrad views illusions with an ambivalence, even though several statements in the novel show that he regards them as a necessary element in life (e.g. "every age is fed on illusions."(p65)

[327] Helen F. Reiselbach claims that Lena's "self-immolation merely frees [Heyst] for death (the death which he seems to have been seeking all along)" p132. The whole question centres around one's conception of death. From a biological point of view, death is not only a part of life but an indispensable part; Heyst, as "man of the last hour"(289), represents a life-form that has reached its peak, and cannot evolve any further. Both as a species and as an individual there is nowhere else for him to go, as it were.

[328] Henry J. Laskowsky observes that "This is the penultimate metamorphosis of Heyst, who, unable to cope with the unnatural physics of the financial world or the world of human relationships, commits himself to the natural physics of combustion."(p284)

intervention. As Schopenhauer claimed, "The suicide wills life and is dissatisfied merely with the conditions in which it has come to him. Therefore he gives up by no means the will-to-live, but merely life, since he destroys the individual phenomenon."(WWR I 318) Also fire, which originally associated Heyst with a volcano and had suggested a common underlying 'will', has successfully converted his illusory 'representation' into 'thing-in-itself'. Like coal and diamonds being reduced to their constituent element, Heyst's and Lena's substances are finally and irreversibly fused in the blaze: "He is - ashes, your excellency," says Davidson as an epitaph, "he and the girl together [...] fire purifies everything."(327) It no longer matters who was 'coal' and who 'diamonds' because both are carbon now.

Seen in this light, Lena's *Victory* is less pyrrhic than it would appear at first glance. Heyst kills himself not as an act of Buddhistic will-negation but in protest at the meaninglessness of his existence deprived of Lena's love. It is she, after all, who "gave him a greater sense of his own reality than he had ever known in all his life."(170) Viewed from a Schopenhauerian perspective it is only the individual 'phenomenon' of Heyst that perishes; his 'will', like Lena's, is indestructible and in the act of suicide shows that it desires life still[329]- only under different circumstances. Thus, shortly before his death he exclaims: "Ah, Davidson, woe to the man whose heart has not learnt while young to hope, to love - and to put its trust in life!"(326) At Heyst's age it is too late to start believing in "hope" and "love" and "trust" but Lena has taught him through her death that life is insupportable without such illusions.[330]

The truth according to Heyst Senior cannot be lived, because, as Nietzsche pointed out, "knowledge kills action, action requires the veil of illusion"(BT 53).[331] The novel suggests that one has to surrender to the impulses of the heart in Quixotic[332] fashion, regardless of the objective

---

329 Jocelyn Baines arrives at the opposite conclusion , calling Heyst's suicide "the conclusive act of renunciation of life [...] an act of total despair"(p239) *Joseph Conrad: A Critical Biography*. But, as with Heyst's "inertia" at the beginning of the novel, there can be no final exegesis, only a plethora of interpretations.

330 As Sharon Kaehele and Howard German point out, Conrad presents illusion in the novel "as a possible antidote for Heystian scepticism"(p65).

331 As Leon F. Seltzer concludes, "truth is chilling and stultifies all effort; vague insubstantial belief (as long as it is not recognised as such) is reassuring and provokes worthwhile endeavours."(p96) *The Vision of Melville and Conrad*.

332 Tony Tanner also likens Heyst to Don Quixote because he "desired naively to escape with his body from the intolerable reality of things"(p114). One fundamental difference, however, between these two heros is that Don Quixote escapes through action, whereas Heyst is for the

merits of doing so, for, as Conrad claimed "reason is feeble and short-lived and will is ever-lasting and strong. One must serve the stronger master, [...] one must keep the world going without worrying about eternal Error, for it is full of truth whose triumph we must assist",[333] and this is what Lena instinctively does. Thus, although *Victory* rejects Schopenhauer's prescription of ascetic detachment and will-mortification as the path to salvation, it nevertheless incorporates his fundamental ontology - particularly as regards 'will' and 'representation'. Conrad's personal attitude to life and art, as *Victory* expresses it, is finally more Nietzschean:[334]

> Affirmation of life even in its strangest and sternest problems, the will to life rejoicing in its own inexhaustibility through the *sacrifice* of its higher types [...] *Not* so as to get rid of pity and terror [...] but, beyond pity and terror, to *realize in oneself* the eternal joy of becoming(Z 5).

The artist's "joy of becoming" may not be apparent in Heyst, the man who has tried to live in Schopenhauerian detachment, but it is paradoxically in Lena at the point of her death: "The flush of rapture flooding [Lena's] whole being broke out in a smile of innocent, girlish happiness."(324) And since Heyst follows her, even unto "the shades of death", what more, indeed, could Conrad "have done for her rehabilitation and her happiness?"[335]

---

most part "inert". As Conrad wrote to Edward Garnett "to move is vital - it's salvation"(p392), *Collected Letters, Vol. I,* 8/10/97.

333 *Collected Letters, Vol. I,* to Marguerite Poradowska, 3/7/95.

334 As Edward W. Said points out, in his essay "Conrad and Nietzsche", Nietzsche felt that Schopenhauer "had devise a cowardly retreat from life by preaching stoic withdrawal. Nietzsche's repeated statements of this criticism are echoed by Conrad's treatment of Heyst in *Victory,* from *Joseph Conrad: A Commemoration,* Papers from the 1974 International Conference, p65.

335 Author's Note, p16.

Bibliography

Works by Joseph Conrad:

Unless otherwise specified, *The Collected Works by Joseph Conrad* (London: J. M. Dent & Sons, 1948)

Heart of Darkness, Penguin Twentieth Century Classics, edited with an introduction by Paul O' Prey, (London: Penguin Books, 1989)

Lord Jim, Penguin Twentieth Century Classics, edited by Cedric Watts and Robert Hampson, with an introduction by Cedric Watts, (Middlesex: Penguin Books, 1987)

The Nigger of the 'Narcissus', The World's Classics, edited with an introduction by Jacques Berthoud (Oxford: Oxford University Press, 1989)

The Secret Agent, Penguin Twentieth Century Classics (Middlesex: Penguin Books, 1987)

Under Western Eyes, Penguin Twentieth Century Classics, with an introduction and notes by Boris Ford, (Middlesex: Penguin Books, 1985)

Victory, Penguin Modern Classics, (London: Penguin Books, 1985)

Letters by Joseph Conrad:

Karl, Frederick R. and Davies, Laurence, (eds.) *The Collected Letters of Joseph Conrad, Vols I (1861-97) & II (1898-1902),* (Cambridge: Cambridge University Press, 1983 and 1986)

Watts, Cedric, T. (ed.) *Joseph Conrad 's Letters to R. B. Cunninghame Graham* (Cambridge: Cambridge University Press, 1969)

Works by Friedrich Nietzsche:

Beyond Good and Evil, translated by R. J. Hollingdale (Harmondsworth: Penguin Books, 1973)

The Birth of Tragedy and The Geneology of Morals, translated by Francis Golffing (New York: Doubleday Anchor Books, 1956)

The Gay Science, translated by Walter Kaufmann (New York: Random House, 1974)

A Nietzsche Reader, selected and translated by R. J. Hollingdale (Middlesex: Penguin Books, 1977)

Thus Spoke Zarathustra, translated by R.J. Hollingdale (Harmondsworth: Penguin Books, 1961)

Twilight of the Idols, translated by Walter Kaufmann (New York: Random House, 1974)

Untimely Meditations, translated by R. J. Hollingdale, introduced by J. P. Stern (Cambridge: Cambridge University Press, 1992)

Works by Arthur Schopenhauer:

Selected Essays, with an introduction by Ernest Belfort Max, (London: George Bell & Sons, 1891)

The World as Will and Representation, Vol. I & II, translated by E. F. J. Payne (New York: Dover Books, 1969)

All other works:

Andreach, Robert J., *The Slain and Resurrected God: Conrad, Ford and the Christian Myth* (New York: New York University Press, 1970)

Ambrosini, Richard, *Conrad's Fiction As Critical Discourse* (Cambridge: Cambridge University Press, 1991)

Baines, Jocelyn, *Joseph Conrad: A Critical Biography* (London: Weidenfeld and Nicolson, 1960)

Batchelor, John, *Lord Jim*, Unwin Critical Edition (London: Allen & Unwin, 1988)

Bergonzi, Bernard, *The Early H. G. Wells* (Manchester: Manchester University Press, 1961)

Berthoud, Jacques, *Joseph Conrad: The Major Phase* (Cambridge: Cambridge University Press, 1978)

Bonney, W. W., *Thorns and Arabesques: Contexts for Conrad's Fiction* (Baltimore & London: Johns Hopkins Press, 1980)

Brooks, Peter, *Reading for the Plot* (Oxford: Clarendon, 1974)

Bruss, Paul S., "Marlow's Interview with Stein: The Implications of the Metaphor", *Studies in the Novel*, Vol. V, no.4 (1973) pp491-503.

Butte, George, "What Silenus Knew: Conrad 's Uneasy Debt To Nietzsche", *Comparative Literature*, 41 (1989) pp155-169.

Carabine, Keith, *The Life and the Art: A study of Conrad's Under Western Eyes* (Amsterdam: Rodopi, 1996)

Comfort, Alex, *Darwin and the Naked Lady* (London: Routledge & Kegan Paul, 1961)

Cox, C. B., *Joseph Conrad: The Modern Imagination* (London: Dent, 1974)

Daiches, David, *The Novel and the Modern World* (Chicago: University of Chicago Press, 1960)

Daleski, H. M., *Joseph Conrad: The Way of Dispossession* (London: Faber, 1977)

Davidson, Arnold E., "The Abdication of *Lord Jim*", *Conradiana*, Vol. XIII, no. 1 (1981) pp19-34.

Dike, Donald A., "The Tempest of Axel Heyst", *Nineteenth Century Fiction*, 17 (September, 1962) pp95-113.

Dowden, Wilfred S., *Joseph Conrad: The Imaged Style* (Vanderblit University Press, 1970)

Eliot, T. S. *Selected Essays* (London: Faber, 1966)

Epstein, Henry S., "*Lord Jim* as a Tragic Action", *Studies in the Novel*, Vol. V, no. 2 (1973) pp229-47.

Fleishman, Avrom, *Conrad 's Politics* (Baltimore, Md: Johns Hopkins University Press, 1967)

Freud, S., *On Creativity and the Unconscious: Papers on the Psychology of Art, Literature, Love, Religion*, trans. Joan Riviere (New York: Harper, 1958)

Frazer, Robert, (ed.) *J. G. Frazer and the Literary Imagination* (London: Macmillan, 1990)

Galsworthy, John, *Reminiscences of Conrad* (privately published: Freelands, 1930)

Garnett, Edward, *Friday Nights*, The Travellers Library Series (London: Jonathan Cape, 1929)

Geddes, G., *Conrad's Later Novels* (Montreal: McGill-Queens University Press, 1980)

Gibbons, T. H., *Literary Criticism and the Intellectual Milieu* (Doctoral dissertation, University of Cambridge, 1965)

Gibson, Andrew & Hampson, Robert (eds.) *Conrad and Theory* (Amsterdam: Rodopi, 1998)

Gillon, Adam, *The Eternal Solitary* (New York: Bookman Associates, 1960)

Glassman, Peter J., *Language and Being: Joseph Conrad and The Literature of Personality* (New York: Columbia University Press, 1976)

Glickberg, Charles I., *Modern Literature and the Death of God* (The Hague: Martinus Nijhoff, 1966)

Gose, Elliot B. Jnr., "Pure Exercises of Imagination: Archetypal Symbolism in *Lord Jim*, PMLA (March, 1964) pp137-47.

Guerard, A. J. *Conrad the Novelist* (Cambidge, Mass.: Harvard University Press, 1958)

Gurko, Leo, *Joseph Conrad: Giant in Exile* (London: Macmillan, 1962)

Hall, Linda M., *The Theme of the Outcast* (London: Doctoral Dissertation, 1974)

Hamburger, Michael, *From Prophecy to Exorcism: The Premises of Modern German Literature* (London: Longman's, 1965)

Hampson, R. G., "Frazer and Conrad", *The Modern Language Review*, Vol. 85, part 1, pp184-185.

Hampson, R. G., *Joseph Conrad: Betrayal and Identity* (Basingstoke: Macmillan, 1992)

Haugh, Robert F., *Joseph Conrad: Discovery in Design* (University of Oklohoma Press, 1957)

Hawthorn, Jeremy, *Joseph Conrad: Language and Fictional Self-Consciousness* (London: Edward Arnold, 1979)

Hawthorn, Jeremy, *Joseph Conrad: Narrative Technique and Ideological Commitment* (London: Edward Arnold, 1998)

Hay, Eloise Knapp, *The Political Novels of Joseph Conrad* (Chicago: University of Chicago Press, 1963)

Henricksen, Bruce, *Nomadic Voices: Conrad & the Subject of Narrative* (Urban & Chicago: University of Illinois Press, 1992)

Hewitt, Douglas, *Conrad: A Reassessment* (London: Bowes and Bowes, 1975)

Kaehele, Sharon, and German, Howard, "Conrad's *Victory*: A Reassessment", *Modern Fiction Studies*, 10 (Spring, 1964) pp55-72.

Karl, Frederick R., *A Reader's Guide to Joseph Conrad* (New York: The Noonday Press, 1960)

Kirchner, Paul, *Joseph Conrad: The Psychologist as Artist* (Edingburgh: Oliver & Boyd, 1968)

La Bossiere, Camille R., *Joseph Conrad and the Science of Unknowing* (Frederikton: York Press, 1979)

Laskowsky Henry J., "Esse est Percepi: Epistomology and Narrative Method in *Victory*", *Conradiana*, Vol. IX, no.3 (1977) pp275-286.

Lester, John, *Conrad and Religion* (Hong Kong: Macmillan, 1988)

Lester, John, *Journey Through Despair 1880-1914: Transformation in British Literary Culture* (Princeton, 1968)

Mann, Thomas, *The Living Thoughts of Schopenhauer* (London: Cassel & Co., 1946)

Miller, J. Hillis, *Fiction and Repitition* (Oxford: Blackwell, 1982)

Morf, Gustav, *The Polish Heritage of Joseph Conrad* (London: Sampson, Low, Marston, 1930)

Moser, Thomas, *Joseph Conrad: Achievement and Decline* Cambridge, Mass.: Harvard Univesity Press, 1957)

Mudrick, Marvin, (ed.) *Joseph Conrad: A Collection of Critical Essays* (New Jersey: Prentice Hall, 1966)

Najder, Zdzislaw, *Conrad in Perspective: Essays on Art & Fidelity* (Cambridge: Cambridge University Press, 1998)

Nuttal, A. D., *A Common Sky* (London: Chatto & Windus, 1974)

Palmer, John A., *Joseph Conrad's Fiction: A Study in Literary Growth* (Ithaca, NY: Cornell University Press, 1968)

Purdy, Dwight H., *Joseph Conrad's Bible* (Norman, Okla.: University of Oklahoma Press, 1984)

Raval, Suresh, *The Art of Failure: Conrad's Fiction* (London: Allen and Unwin, 1986)

Reilly, Jim, *Shadowtime: History and Representation in Hardy, Conrad and George Eliot* (London: Rutledge, 1993)

Reiselabach, Helen F., *Conrad's Rebels*, Studies in Modern Literature, no. 42, UMI Reasearch Press (1980)

Roberts, Andrew Michael (ed.) *Conrad and Gender* (Amsterdam: Rodopi, 1993)

Rosenfield, Claire, *Paradise of Snakes* (Chicago: University of Chicago Press, 1967)

Ross, Daniel W., "*Lord Jim* and the Saving Illusion", *Conradiana,* Vol. XX, No. 1, (1988) pp45-69.

Roussel, Royal, *The Metaphysics of Darkness* (Baltimore, Md.: Johns Hopkins University Press, 1971)

Schwarz, D. R., *Almayer's Folly to Under Western Eyes* (London: Macmillan, 1980)

Schwarz, D. R., "The Journey to Patusan: The Education of *Lord Jim* and Marlow in Conrad's *Lord Jim*", *Studies in the Novel,* Vol. 4 (1972) pp442-58.

Secor, Robert, "The Rhetoric of Shifting Perspectives: Conrad's *Victory*", *The Pennsylvania State University Studies,* no. 32 (University Park, 1971)

Seltzer, Leon, *The Vision of Melville and Conrad* (Athens: Ohio University Press, 1970)

Stevenson, Richard C., "Stein's Prescription for "How to Be" and the Problem of Assessing *Lord Jim* 's Career", *Conradiana,* Vol. II, no. 3, (1975) pp233-43.

Stewart, J. I. M., *Joseph Conrad* (London: Longman, 1968)

Tanner, J. E., "The Chronology and Enigmatic Ending of *Lord Jim*", *Nineteenth Century Fiction*, vol XXI (March, 1967) pp369-80.

Tanner, Tony, "Butterflies and Beetles - Conrad 's Two Truths", *Chicago Review* XVI (Winter/ Spring, 1969) pp123-40.

Tanner, Tony, "Gentlemen and Gossip: Aspects of Evolution and Language in Conrad 's *Victory*", *L'Epoque Conradienne* (May, 1981) pp1-56.

Tanner, Tony, "Joseph Conrad and the Last Gentleman", *Critical Quarterly*, Vol. 28, nos. 1 & 2 (Spring/ Summer, 1986) pp109-42.

Tanner, Tony, "Nightmare and Complacency: Razumov and the Western Eye", *The Critical Quarterly*, IV (1962) pp197-214.

Vulcan, Daphne Erdinast, *Joseph Conrad and the Modern Temper* (Oxford: Clarendon Press, 1991)

Watt, Ian, *Conrad in the Nineteenth Century* (London: Chatto and Windus, 1980)

Watt, Ian, (ed.) *The Secret Agent Casebook* (London: Macmillan, 1973)

Watts, Cedric, *The Deceptive Text: An Introduction to Covert Plots* (Brighton: Harvester Press, 1984)

Watts, Cedric, *A Preface to Conrad* (London: Longman, 1982)

White, Andrea, *Joseph Conrad and the Adventure Tradition* (Cambridge: Cambridge University Press, 1993)

Whitehead, Lee M., "The Active Voice and the Passive Eye: Heart of Darkness and Neitszche's *The Birth of Tragedy*", *Conradiana*, no. 7, (1975) pp121-35.

Wiley , Paul L., *Conrad's Measure of Man* (Madison, Wis: University of Wisconsin Press, 1954)

Winner, Anthony, *Culture and Irony: Studies in Joseph Conrad's Major Novels* (Charlottesville: The University Press of Virginia, 1988)

Yeats, W. B., *Autobiographies* (London: Macmillan, 1961)

Index

E

F

H

I

K

L

M

N

O

P

U

V

W

ANGLO-AMERIKANISCHE STUDIEN - ANGLO-AMERICAN STUDIES

Herausgegeben von
Rüdiger Ahrens (Würzburg) und Kevin Cope (Baton Rouge)

Band 1 Hedwig Kiesel: Martin Luther - ein Held John Osbornes. *Luther* - Kontext und historischer Hintergrund. 1986.

Band 2 Monika Hoffarth: Martin Luther King und die amerikanische Rassenfrage. Stereotypenkorrektur und humanitäre Erziehung durch literarische Rezeption. 1990.

Band 3 Peter Erlebach/Thomas Michael Stein (eds.): Graham Greene in Perspective. A Critical Symposium. 1992.

Band 4 Kevin L. Cope (Ed.): Compendious Conversations. The Method of Dialogue in the Early Enlightenment. 1992.

Band 5 Zaixin Zhang: Voices of the Self in Daniel Defoe's Fiction. An Alternative Marxist Approach. 1993.

Band 6 Berthold Schoene: The Making of Orcadia. Narrative Identity in the Prose Work of George Mackay Brown. 1995.

Band 7 Wolfgang Gehring: Schülernahe Lebensbereiche in Englischbüchern für die 7. Jahrgangsstufe. Ein Beitrag zur landeskundlichen Lehrwerkkritik. 1996.

Band 8 Klaus Stierstorfer: John Oxenford (1812-1877) as Farceur and Critic of Comedy. 1996.

Band 9 Beth Swan: Fictions of Law. An Investigation of the Law in Eighteenth-Century English Fiction. 1997.

Band 10 Catharina Boerckel: Weibliche Entwicklungsprozesse bei Jane Austen, Elizabeth Gaskell und George Eliot. 1997.

Band 11 Rosamaria Loretelli / Roberto De Romanis (Eds.): Narrating Transgression. Representations of the Criminal in Early Modern England. 1998.

Band 12 Nic Panagopoulos: The Fiction of Joseph Conrad. The Influence of Schopenhauer and Nietzsche. 1998.

Peter Lang · Europäischer Verlag der Wissenschaften

Hermann Fink / Liane Fijas (Eds.)

America and Her Influence upon the Language and Culture of Post-socialist Countries

Frankfurt/M., Berlin, Bern, New York, Paris, Wien, 1998. VIII, 93 pp.
Freiberger Beiträge zum Einfluß der angloamerikanischen Sprache und Kultur auf Europa.
Herausgegeben von Hermann Fink und Liane Fijas. Bd. 5
ISBN 3-631-33193-2 · pb. DM 45.–*
US-ISBN 0-8204-3577-5

After numerous predominantly quantitative and linguistic systems oriented investigations of the Anglo-American influence upon the German and other West European languages, this volume seeks to throw a little light onto the respective conditions of so-called post-socialist societies. By means of authentic opinions and experiences of some linguists living in these countries, it aims less at the quantitative impact of the Americanism there than at its possible economic, social, political, and cultural implications.

Contents: Socio- and psycholinguistic as well as cultural analysis of the impact of the United States upon countries of the former East European Socialism

Frankfurt/M · Berlin · Bern · New York · Paris · Wien
Distribution: Verlag Peter Lang AG
Jupiterstr. 15, CH-3000 Bern 15
Fax (004131) 9402131
*incl. value-added tax
Prices are subject to change without notice.